Hi Linda,
Congratulations on your graduation. This is one great stone rolled away from your past to move into your future. May your after-graduation days and years be filled with God's special love, peace and joy, now and always in Jesus' name.
I love you, Tom and Caleb.
  In Christ
    Foye Adedokun.
      Adedokun 12/10/04

Attributes Of A Working Faith

by

Foye Adedokun

authorHOUSE

1663 LIBERTY DRIVE, SUITE 200
BLOOMINGTON, INDIANA 47403
(800) 839-8640
www.authorhouse.com

© 2004 Foye Adedokun.
All Rights Reserved.

No part of this book may be reproduced, stored in a retrieval system, or transmitted by any means without the written permission of the author.

First published by AuthorHouse 07/31/04

ISBN: 1-4184-2155-3 (e)
ISBN: 1-4184-2156-1 (sc)

Printed in the United States of America
Bloomington, Indiana

This book is printed on acid-free paper.

All Scripture references are taken from the King James Version of the Holy Bible.

All Emphases In Scripture Passages Mine.

DEDICATION.

This book is gratefully dedicated to the Glory of God,
The Mighty and Faithful.
And to my husband, Tade Adedokun.
Our trying periods have been worth it all.
God at last is taking all the glory.

<u>Appreciation</u>

- ♥ My gratitude goes first to my Lord and Savior Jesus Christ, Immortal, Invisible, The Only Wise God.
Many Were The Troubles And Trials We Faced,
Many Were The Afflictions And Confusions We Experienced.
But Because Of Your Unfailing Love And Grace,
Lord, We Were Able To Sail Through The Race.
And Even When The Devil Would Have Us Fear,
Thank You Lord For Being So Near.

- ♥ I thank my dear mother, my sisters and my only brother; all back home in Nigeria. In everything, you remained prayerfully faithful. You have been very supportive and loving. Thank you for those words of encouragement. Though many a time I read and received them with tears, but they were always as soothing balm to my aching spots. I specially thank my oldest sister and her husband for being there when I needed financial help to get through this time of my life. May the Lord reward you richly. I consider myself fortunate to have you as my people.

- ♥ To my husband, I say thank you very much for your support. Though it's been one tough journey together, but we have not trusted God in vain. He proved Himself faithful.

- ♥ To my boys, Toyin and Tayo, and my girl Tobi, I say you're special. Thank you for the understanding you showed in your own different ways. When I seemed too busy to attend to you,

you put up with me. Upon every remembrance of you, I will continue to thank the Lord.

- ♥ To the Adedapos, thank you for the various helps you rendered. Your gifts and words of encouragement are not forgotten. They helped to uphold us when we seemed to be going down the hill.

- ♥ To Jacob Ifabiyi, I'm deeply grateful. A friend in time of need you have been to my family. You were never tired of us. You are a friend indeed.

- ♥ To the Togunde family, I thank God for you. You mean a lot to me. Intercessors and givers are not easy to find. But you have chosen to make it a ministry.

- ♥ Pastor Sam Farina (my father in the Lord), Sandra Gist, and Cynthia Mason, all in Columbus, OH; accept my sincere appreciation for allowing me to mention your names in this book. I owe a lot to all of you.

- ♥ And to you the reader of this book, you're the most important person. For without you, it will not be a success.
  The LORD Bless Thee, And Keep Thee:
  The LORD Make His Face Shine Upon Thee,
  And Be Gracious Unto Thee:
  The LORD Lift Up His Countenance Upon Thee,
  And Give Thee Peace (Numbers 6:24-26).
  I LOVE YOU ALL.

Even so faith, if it hath not works,

is dead, being alone.

James 2:17

INTRODUCTION

I love children and I had always wanted at least four, if not six. When I had my second child in 1989, I didn't intend for him to be the last. But by the time we were planning to have another one, I had an ectopic pregnancy, followed by miscarriages, followed by two molar pregnancies. After the second molar, I went for an ultrasound scan and received the greatest shock of my life–my womb would no longer carry a baby because I would never see my period again. You can easily imagine how I felt. But instead of staying crushed, I saw it as a battle of faith between Satan and me and I made up my mind he wasn't going to win.

The Bible describes faith as "the substance of things hoped for, the evidence of things not seen" (Hebrews 11:1). The exercise of faith in any life situation is one of perceiving as possible something that is otherwise realistically impossible. Commanding a mountain to move is the most unrealistic and impossible thing anyone can do. But faith says if you command it to move from one spot to another, it will move (Mark 11:23).

As a substance, faith makes real to the eyes what could have otherwise been discarded as an ordinary shadow. 'Things hoped for' are our desires. Faith makes real to the Spirit that lives within us, those desires that are not real to the senses and should have been written off as mere wishful thinking.

An evidence is something that makes another thing evident. Things not seen are things not visible to the eyes. As an evidence of things not seen, faith makes visible beyond any reasonable doubt, to our spiritual eyes –the eyes of faith–things that are invisible to our physical eyes–the eyes of flesh.

When that doctor told me in 1993 that I would never see my period again, he wasn't medically wrong, he just wasn't spiritually right; for I knew the Lord that I believed. I knew that by God's unfailing power, I would still have another child. The devil cannot dictate to me what I do with my life. That I would stop when led to do so was a decision I would not allow Satan to make for me. Sure the period was no longer coming, but I saw my baby through an eye of faith. She received her name long before she was born. After thirty-eight months, that which was pronounced dead received life and on March 22, 1997, we had a beautiful baby girl.

Has it ever occurred to you how much your faith can achieve for you if put to work? Do you even know that God deposited His faith into you the moment you surrendered the control of your life over to Him? The Bible confirms, "God hath dealt to every man the measure of faith"(Romans 12:3).

But what are those things your faith can accomplish for you? How do you see your faith and how does God see you and the faith He has given you? God's Word has a lot to say about this great aspect of our spiritual journey. The Bible says, "What doth it profit, my brethren, though a man say he hath faith, and have not works? can faith save him? <u>Even so faith, if it hath not works, is dead,</u> being alone. Yea, a man may say, Thou hast faith, and I have works: <u>shew me thy faith without thy works and I will shew thee my faith by my works. Ye see then how that by works a man is justified, and not by faith only</u>" (James 2:14, 17-18, 24).

Works! What exactly did brother James mean by "works"? I thought it meant going to work, clock in and clock out, get enough hours each day, so you're able to meet your needs. That's not bad. Our God will not have us indolent. We don't serve a lazy God. But the passage means more than secular works. It's actually talking about our spiritual works, how we can use our deeds to establish our faith, and prove to those who don't know the Lord what it means to have faith in Him.

There are different definitions of faith in the different versions of the Bible. They all say the same thing, only from different views. Two things however remain constant in all the definitions. One, there's a purpose for which faith is being exercised and two, there's the person exercising the faith, who will be the recipient of the miracle. One cannot be without the other. Stones don't need faith because they don't expect from God. They're inanimate objects. It's we human beings that exercise faith. Without us, there will be no need for faith.

When we observe the different roles of faith in the Bible, they all had to do with a desire for the better. A person has a current situation with which he's not pleased. There's a longing for something better. The better seems so impossible and requires an exercise of something greater than ordinary. That is faith. It's faith that gives us an assurance that what we hope for is going to happen. The phrase *assurance* makes the whole knowledge about faith come out so powerful.

We have to realize that having faith in difficult situations of life can be very challenging. At times, it's easier not to exercise than it is to exercise faith. But when we realize that the problem, trial or tribulation for which we're exercising the faith will surely come to pass, this keeps us going. It energizes our Spirit system.

When you run out of fuel in your vehicle, you don't exercise any doubts when refueling. Once you put enough gas, there's only one thing to do. Turn the ignition and go. When you buy medications, you don't ask for the breakdown of the components. A body in pain has no time for questions. All you want is a relief. If care is not taken, you will end up breaking down by the time you hear all the stuff that goes into your system. The medical terms are so complex you will hardly understand. But as long as it works, who cares? And even when you take it, you don't crack your brain, trying to figure out how a medication that goes into the stomach, finds its way to your head and stops the migraine. Everything goes through the mouth. Yet they find their ways when they get inside. That in itself requires faith. The trust is always there that once you take it, it will work. If we can have this much faith in something man made, we should have much more faith in the Maker of man.

In this book—ATTRIBUTES OF A WORKING FAITH—I used all letters of the alphabet (save X) to identify eighty-eight works of faith: what your faith should be, should have, should do and should never do, all based on the Word of God, the Bible. It's not intended to tell you what your faith is at present; but rather to let you know what God expects of your faith. When I say, "Faith never Doubts," does that mean you and I never doubt? No. It only shows there's a *crack* on the wall of our faith that needs fixing. No one is perfect. But we all can do better than good.

As you read through the pages, receive a new strength. Though I don't know what in your life you've been battling with. It seems like an insurmountable odd and you've given up all hope. Let me remind you that many of us are going through a lot of struggles in life. This book is born out of a struggling period in my own family. It's been like rolling a mountain each day just to survive. But God has taught us and is teaching us, that only our faith in Him can see us through. He has never for one day failed. When He seemed so far away, He assured us through His provision that He was closer than we thought.

I would have loved to say you would never have any problems, so long you're in the faith, but that would make me a liar. There's no one free from the fiery darts of the enemy. For as long as we're still here, the battle continues. The more faith you have, the more fight you get. Let the succeeding pages minister to you. And by the unfailing grace of the unfailing God, you shall never remain the same in Jesus' name.

You will notice there are many Scripture passages included. That is to make for your convenience, even when you don't have your Bible within easy reach. And I have tried as much as possible to include all references.

I LOVE YOU WITH THE LOVE OF JESUS.

A

1. FAITH ACTS   2

2. FAITH ASKS   7

1
FAITH ACTS

THIS CARD CANNOT BE USED UNTIL ACTIVATED.

To activate your card please call toll free….

When I received my bankcard, there was a little sticker at the back with the above message. I'm sure most of us are familiar with it.

As I think on the subject of faith, I see a similarity between this statement and our faith. The Bible confirms that each one has been given a measure of faith. But I'm convinced that not everyone's faith has been activated. Or let me put it this way; not everyone who claims to have faith has actually called the faith bank to activate his or her faith. It's there in your life all right. But it's as good as an inactivated bankcard. You have it, but you can't use it because you have decided to hold on to it and refuse to put it to action.

The same thing with faith. We cannot have faith for the fun of having it. We must put it into action. How do we put faith into action? I like to start with Peter's walking on water.

> And straightway Jesus constrained his disciples to get into a ship, and to go before him unto the other side, while he sent the multitudes away. … And when the disciples saw him walking on the sea, they were troubled, saying, It is a spirit; and they cried out for fear . … And Peter answered him and said, Lord, if it be thou, bid me come unto thee on the water. And he said, Come. And when Peter was come down out of the ship, he walked on the water, to go to Jesus. But when he saw the wind boisterous, he was afraid; and beginning to sink, he cried, saying, Lord, save me. And immediately Jesus stretched forth

his hand, and caught him, and said unto him, O thou of little faith, wherefore didst thou doubt? (Matthew 14:22-31).

Definitely Peter was outstanding amongst the disciples. He was a disciple with an amazing courage. He had been with Jesus for quite sometime now. So he knew the Jesus he saw. But when Jesus asked him to come, if he had only sat inside the boat and had not acted upon the commandment of the Lord, if he had not attempted the seemingly impossible from human perspective, we would not be reading about him today. Though a little faith, yet he put it into action.

Do you think there were no distractions around? You bet there were. The sight of the water was enough to scare him. The other disciples could have tried to discourage him from walking, but he walked anyway. Challenges must never hinder us from putting our faith into action. Those challenges were there for the great men and women of God we read about in the Bible. They were there for Jesus. They were there for the disciples and will continue to be for as long as the Lord tarries. They must not stop us from putting our faith to action.

Just as Peter for a moment lost his focus of Jesus, we too will have moments when we seem to loose the focus of our faith. Instead of the Savior we see the sea. Our faith evades us and unwanted doubts bombard us. Then we feel like we're about to sink. Seems like we have missed it. We suddenly begin to give in to fear. The good news is still the same: Jesus is very close by. He's right there in front of you. Just cry out 'Lord, help me,' and He will always be there to reach out and grab you.

The woman with the issue of blood put her faith into action. She knew Jesus was a miracle worker. She had not only heard it, she had seen it. But she needed a miracle for herself. No matter how many miracles take place around us, we all long for a personal experience. The blind wants to see the lame walk; the deaf wants to hear the dumb speak; the leper wants to be clean so he can have lunch with him who was once a lunatic; the man with the withered hand wants his hands restored, so he can carry the baby of the barren. Jesus had more than a coat of many colors; He had a crowd of many concerns. We are human beings with diverse needs.

So was the case with this woman. She longed for a personal experience. Before she came to Jesus, she had gone to physicians. Talk of being tough, this woman was. Woman, can you imagine yourself bleeding for twelve months non-stop, or even twelve days incessantly? Now I would be honest with you. I don't want this problem in my life. Ordinary five days put me off. How did she go for twelve years?

Read her story.

And a certain woman, which had an issue of blood twelve years, And had suffered many things of many physicians, and had spent all that she had, and was nothing bettered, but rather grew worse, When she had heard of Jesus, came in the press behind, and touched his garment. For she said, If I may touch but his clothes, I shall be whole. And straightway the fountain of her blood was dried up; and she felt in her body that she was healed of that plague. And Jesus, immediately knowing in himself that virtue had gone out of him, turned him about in the press, and said, Who touched my clothes? ... But the woman fearing and trembling, knowing what was done in her, came and fell down before him, and told him all the truth. And he said unto her, Daughter, thy faith hath made thee whole; go in peace, and be whole of thy plague (Mark 5:25-34).

She had spent all her livelihood on physicians. I bet by now she must be smelling foul. People didn't need to see her before they knew she was coming. Her odor gave her away. She did all she could but nothing worked. Doctors fed off her, physicians were enriched through her. Her bleeding was their blessing. Then came her day of breakthrough, the day she heard about Jesus. All of a sudden it occurred to her, He was going to be the solution to her situation. And nothing would change that. She got desperate for a miracle but she knew she had to act. She had no problem with faith, but that faith had to be backed up by her action. Did it really matter what people would say when they saw her going through the crowd to disturb them with her odor? That to her was no issue compared to the issue she had. In spite of the crowd, she found her way through and touched His garment. Bingo! She got her miracle. The cure she had sought for twelve years she got in less than twelve seconds, just a fragment of a time. Even Jesus felt power go out of His body and asked, "Who touched Me?" That was a touch from a woman who put her faith into action.

We also put our faith into action when we operate on God's principle and function in accordance with His ordinance. He said, "And I will rebuke the devourer for your sakes, and he shall not destroy the fruits of your ground; neither shall your vine cast her fruit before the time in the field, saith the LORD of hosts. And all nations shall call you blessed: for ye shall be a delightsome land, saith the LORD of hosts" (Malachi 3:11, 12). That is His promise for us. But we have to remember there's a condition for Him to do that in our lives. Something comes before the promise: "Bring ye all the tithes into the storehouse, that there may be meat in mine house, and prove me now herewith, saith the LORD of hosts, if I will not open you the windows of heaven, and pour you out a blessing, that there shall not be room enough to receive it" (v.10).

Before He can rebuke the devourer, we must put our faith into action by bringing our tithes into the storehouse. Not the store where we do grocery shopping. It is the house of God, the church where you fellowship with other believers. The reason many believers are not blessed is because they withhold that which belongs to God and yet, they expect Him to "rebuke the devourer." No He won't. We have to first do our part and then expect Him to do His part.

I don't doubt your faith. But if you don't put it into action, it's only as good as a brand new vehicle permanently parked in your garage. As long as you don't use it, it's not serving you any good. Not putting your faith to action does not please God and if care is not taken, He will take it from you and give it to the one that is ready to make the best use of it.

Your faith is not given to you to brag about it or make a yard sale out of it. You are to use it to and for the glory of God Almighty and unless that is done, you're not fulfilling the purpose for which God has bestowed it upon you. So receive the challenge, *ACT*.

2
FAITH ASKS

The Bible says, "Ask, and it shall be given you" (Matthew 7:7).

How do we ask? We ask in prayer. When our children have needs [though some of them turn out to be ordinary selfish wants], they need to ask, so we can be aware of their needs or desires.

There's one thing I notice each time they ask, they do so with confidence. Why? Because they're asking mom or dad and they believe the last thing we will do is disappoint them. Unfortunately many times we have disappointed them because we're humans with limited resources. We fall short of their expectations. But when we fail to meet one desire, next time they still come with the same confidence. That is because they trust us and believe in us. They know we won't give them bone for bread. And yet, we're far short of God's standard when it comes to giving.

As human beings, though we fail to meet the needs of our children, God can and never will fail to meet our needs. Jesus said, "If a son shall ask bread of any of you that is a father, will he give him a stone? or if he ask a fish, will he for a fish give him a serpent? Or if he shall ask an egg, will he offer him a scorpion? If ye then, being evil, know how to give good gifts unto your children: how much more shall your heavenly Father give the Holy Spirit to them that ask him?" (Luke 11:11-13).

Our Father God is much more willing to give than any earthly father, more willing to hear our petitions than we are willing to ask. All He's asking is that when we ask, we do so with confident faith and according to His will, and we shall have the petitions that we desired of Him (1 John 5:14-15). Apostle James advised us to ask without doubting, for he who doubts is a double minded man (James 1:5-6). God does not want us to come to His presence doubting. That's like asking Him to do what we know He does not have the ability to do, and that can never be the case, for there's no impossibility in Him.

I know my children think we can always meet their needs anytime they ask. That's obviously wrong. But I will feel bad if they don't ask because of doubt. My son did that once. He needed money for something in school. He didn't ask because he thought he wouldn't get it. That hurt. Unfortunately, it wasn't something bad. But he by doubting missed his chance of receiving. Much as we realize they can't have everything they ask because we love to guide what they get; at the same time, they should at least ask. We know what to give and what not to give.

The same principle applies to our faith. It's not everything we ask from God we can get. But He knows what to give and what not to give.

> Be not ye therefore like unto them: for your Father knoweth what things ye have need of, before ye ask him (Matthew 6:8).

Daddy already knows what we need before we ask. But He wants us to ask anyway, not doubting. He loves to hear our voices. We never bore Him with our asking.

In 1 Samuel, we read about Hannah, the mother of Samuel. When she got married to Elkanah, she was barren. Year after year, the whole family, Elkanah, Hannah, Peninnah and her children went up to Shiloh to sacrifice to the Lord of hosts. Elkanah would give portions to Peninnah, her sons and her daughters. To Hannah, Elkanah gave a double portion. But that was not what she wanted. Hannah wanted a child she could carry in her arms, and kiss, and hug and just love, and love and love. Year after year, no child, and no joy. Her own yearly sacrifice was never short of tears. All she could remember was her barrenness.

But one particular year, Hannah petitioned the throne of heaven and asked a child of the God she loved.

> So Hannah rose up after they had eaten in Shiloh, and after they had drunk. Now Eli the priest sat upon a seat by a post of the temple of the LORD. And she was in bitterness of soul, and prayed unto the LORD, and wept sore. And she vowed a vow, and said, O LORD of hosts, if thou wilt ... give unto thine handmaid a man child, then I will give him unto the LORD all the days of his life, and there shall no razor come upon his head. Wherefore it came to pass, when the time was come about after Hannah had conceived, that she bare a son, and called his name Samuel, saying, Because <u>I have asked him of the LORD</u> (1 Samuel 1: 9-11, 20).

Hannah was desperate for a child, so desperate that even the prophet Eli thought she was drunk when she was praying. What did she ask for? A male child. And because she asked in faith, what did she get? A male child. Hallelujah. Hannah the barren became Hannah the bearer. And guess what, she got more than she asked.

> And the LORD visited Hannah, so that she conceived and bare three sons and two daughters. And the child Samuel grew before the LORD (2:21).

When we ask, we get. Discouragements are definitely going to show up. People will pass the most unexpected comments. They will call us crazy and nickname us insane. For a moment, our faith may be shaken. That's okay. The outcome will justify the asking. By the time we get our miracle, they who called us crazy will congratulate us. And then we shall have the greatest opportunity to testify of the power of God.

As you're reading this book, take a step and ask in faith for that child you have long awaited, that home of your dream, that health that has evaded your body for a long time. Ask in faith from the God of all provision and He will give you the desire of your heart.

B

3. FAITH BEARS FRUIT — 12

4. FAITH BELIEVES — 15

5. FAITH BLESSES — 18

6. FAITH is BOLD (BRAVE) — 20

3
<u>FAITH BEARS FRUIT</u>

I stayed in the dormitory all through my high school year. Right behind the dorm was a tree and for the five years plus that I spent in that school, not a single fruit grew on it. It was as barren and dry as the sand by the shore. To be barren is to be unproductive.

When we come to Jesus, we're like a newly wed. As time goes by, we're expected to give birth to spiritual children by winning other souls to the kingdom. When I got married, I had a desire to have children. Today I have three children in the flesh. I already signed off my old last name. I changed from one last name to another. And so the children go by that name.

Before we get saved, there's an old name we go by. We have a different identity. But the moment we give our lives to Jesus, we change our identity. We go from world to Lord, from Satan to Savior, from flesh to faith. And just as we have children in the flesh who go by our new name, we're also expected to produce children in the faith who will go from their old identity with Satan and take up the same new identity that we now have, which is Savior.

When we receive Jesus as our Lord and Savior, we are the good soil into which the seed (God's Word) falls. But when the soil receives the seed, it doesn't just keep it to itself. There are different hearts on which the Word of God falls. But there's only one heart on which the Word germinates and that's the good heart that hears the Word, believes, and comes to the faith. It refuses to let the wicked one snatch away what has been sown and rejects the cares of this world by not allowing the deceitfulness of riches to choke the Word out of its heart. It stands firmly rooted through tribulations and persecutions. It is the good soil. But it has not received the Word for fun. It must produce and bear other fruits, bring forth seeds of like nature that will in turn produce other fruits; thus the law of spiritual multiplication occurs. If it only receives the Word without bearing fruit, it's disqualified and hewn down.

We are to also bear fruits of the Spirit unto righteousness. Our faith must be evident in our actions. When people see an orange tree, it's the fruit that gives it away, not the body of the tree. People don't see an apple tree and call it a mango tree. As people of faith, there must be obvious changes in our lives. There must be fruits of noticeable and worthy repentance. When people still see us the way they saw us before we got converted, something is definitely wrong. If all we do is make a show of the faith, we're like the good for nothing fig tree. We draw people's attention to us. By the time they get to the real us, we're not the same and they get disappointed and discouraged.

Jesus didn't curse the fig tree because it was a fig tree; He cursed it because it had no fruits on it. It was flashy for deceit. People saw it and thought it was alive and fruitful. But it was dead and fruitless. Once we profess our faith, we also bear fruits. We can't be so Christ-like in professing and yet so fig-tree in producing. That will make us hypocrites, who only profess but don't produce. There must be something to show forth for what we claim to be. We have a brand new identity in Christ, so also must be our attitude.

> I am the true vine, and my Father is the husbandman. Every branch in me that beareth not fruit he taketh away: and every branch that beareth fruit, he purgeth it, that it may bring forth more fruit. I am the vine, ye are the branches: He that abideth in me, and I in him, the same bringeth forth much fruit: for without me ye can do nothing. If a man abide not in me, he is cast forth as a branch, and is withered; and men gather them, and cast them into the fire, and they are burned (John 15:1-2, 5-6).

No matter how much we profess to be in the faith, God knows those who are His. Let's be fruitful, so we won't be cast out.

4
__FAITH BELIEVES__

To believe is to take as true or real, to have confidence in a statement or promise of another person. Several times, people have told me stories and I believed without questioning. Most of the time, I believe them because they're children of God. If I can believe a man, how much more should I believe my God, the Creator of man? A faith that believes also begets.

In Matthew, two blind men got their healing because they had a faith that believed in their Jehovah-Raphe, the Lord that heals.

And when Jesus departed thence, two blind men followed him, crying, and saying, Thou son of David, have mercy on us. And when he was come into the house, the blind men came to him: and Jesus saith unto them, Believe ye that I am able to do this? They said unto him, Yea, Lord. Then touched he their eyes, saying, According to your faith be it unto you. And their eyes were opened; and Jesus straitly charged them, saying, See that no man know it (Matthew 9:27-30).

There were three reasons they cried after Him. One, they were blind; two, they wanted their eyes opened; three, and most important, they believed Jesus could heal them. And because they believed, they received.

In Mark, we read the story of Jairus, a synagogue ruler.

And when Jesus was passed over again by ship unto the other side, much people gathered unto him: and he was nigh unto the sea. And, behold, there cometh one of the rulers of the synagogue, Jairus by name; and when he saw him, he fell at his feet, And besought him greatly, saying, My little daughter lieth at the point of death: I pray thee, come and lay thy hands on her, that she may be healed; and she shall live. And Jesus went with him; and much people followed him, and thronged him. While he yet spake, there came from the ruler of the synagogue's house certain which said, Thy daughter is dead: why troublest thou the Master any further? As soon as Jesus heard the word that was spoken, he saith unto the ruler of the synagogue, Be not afraid, only believe (Mark 5:21-24, 35-36).

When this ruler came to Jesus, the daughter was not dead. She was only sick. But while in His presence, he got the news that his daughter had died. There will be times in our journey of faith that things will appear worse than it was before we came to Christ. Before you accepted Jesus, you had a thriving business. People knew you. Your family loved you. Your name was their fame. Suddenly, your life started going down the hill after your faith. That leaves you wondering if the leap is really worth the taking. The devil reminds you of Dr. Y and Mrs. Z, who after accepting Christ were diagnosed with cancer. And not long after that, they died. That's his trick to get you back and burned in hell. He will never tell you of their blissful eternity with the Lord, which they could have lost had they not accepted Him. He only shows one side of the coin. Don't be deceived. Nobody that comes to the Lord will leave worse than before. He will turn your sadness into songs, and your tragedies into triumphs, if only you believe. The Bible says, "But without faith it is impossible to please him: for he that cometh to God <u>must believe</u> that he is…" (Hebrews 11:6).

Jesus saw the faith of this ruler, but He still asked him to *believe, only believe*. The Bible says, "Therefore I say unto you, What things soever ye desire, when ye pray, <u>believe</u> that ye receive them, and ye shall have them" (Mark 11:22-24). We will not only receive when we believe, we will also be blessed. When flesh is telling us, "receiving is believing," our faith says, "believing is receiving." Flesh says, "when I see, I will believe;" faith says, "when I believe, I will see." Let's put behind us the doubting Thomas syndrome, who did not believe until he saw. Jesus said, "blessed are they that have not seen, and yet have believed" (John 20:29).

Aren't you glad you have never set your physical eyes on the Lord and yet believe that He was, He is and He forever will be? You are blessed.

5
FAITH BLESSES

The giving of blessings is mostly in form of prayer on another person. The day God created Adam and Eve, before giving them their names, He first blessed them (Genesis 5:2). That confirms how important the act of blessing is to God. The Bible says, "By faith Isaac blessed Jacob and Esau concerning things to come [see Gen. 27:1-40.] By faith Jacob, when he was a dying, blessed both the sons of Joseph; and worshipped, leaning upon the top of his staff"[see Gen. 48:1-end] (Hebrews 11:20-21).

These were real pronouncements of blessings, which anybody can do. The young can bless the old and the old can bless the young as we saw in the above. The sick can bless the healthy, the poor can bless the rich. Jesus specifically asked us to do the difficult, to bless our enemies and pray for them that spitefully use us.

> But I say unto you, Love your enemies, bless them that curse you, do good to them that hate you, and pray for them which despitefully use you, and persecute you (Matthew 5:44).
>
> Bless them which persecute you: bless, and curse not (Romans 12:14).

How easy is this for you? Hard, isn't it? Well, Jesus is not asking for our opinion. We're to bless those who curse us, period!

As people of faith, our tongues are anointed. The wise man Solomon said, "Death and life are in the power of the tongue" (Pro. 18:21). Whatever we pronounce with this tongue, whether life or death, blessing or cursing, shall come to pass. The Bible calls it a fire (James 3:6). That's why we need to watch what we say to others. Our tongue must be on fire for blessing, not cursing. The same tongue we use to call upon the name of Jesus must not be used to ascribe greatness to Satan, for that is exactly what we do when we curse.

Apostle James said we must not curse with the same tongue that we use to bless. That will be contradictory.

But the tongue can no man tame; it is an unruly evil, full of deadly poison. Therewith bless we God, even the Father; and therewith curse we men, which are made after the similitude of God. Out of the same mouth proceedeth blessing and cursing. My brethren, these things ought not so to be. Doth a fountain send forth at the same place sweet water and bitter? Can the fig tree, my brethren, bearolive berries? either a vine, figs? so can no fountain both yield salt water and fresh (James 3:8-12).

God wants us to bless others whether they bless or curse us. It doesn't matter what they do to us. All we can do is bless.

6
__FAITH is BOLD (BRAVE)__

Be brave; act brave; he's bold; be bold. We have all heard these phrases in our everyday activities. The first thing that comes up in the mind is danger or some weird situation that requires taking a drastic step to achieve an end. As believers, we constantly face situations that require us taking brave steps to prove God's faithfulness to others. The Bible says, "The righteous are bold as a lion" (Proverbs 28:1).

I've never gotten any close to a lion. The closest I have been is to look from a distance at the zoo. And though I realize the lion is within a fenced yard, I still look round to make sure there's no way it can jump out. You know why? That lion is not scared of me. He's the king of the jungle. A lion will jump at any meat that comes its way. No wonder the Bible compares the boldness of the believer to that of a lion.

In Daniel, we have the account of the three Hebrew men, Shadrach, Meshach, and Abed-Nego (originally Hananiah, Mishael and Azariah.) These were men of God who refused to allow an ordinary earthly king to stand between them and their heavenly King. But their story is better read than imagined or experienced. (Read Daniel 3.)

After asking the humiliating question in v.15, this self-exulted king made them know what would befall them should they answer 'yes.' I believe he did that to frighten them and suck the faith out of them. Unfortunately, he was dealing with men who were as radical for their God as he was for his gold.

But see the bold faith of these fellow spiritual comrades.

Shadrach, Meshach, and Abednego, answered and said to the king, O

Faith Is Bold (Brave)

Nebuchadnezzar, we are not careful to answer thee in this matter. If it be so, our God whom we serve is able to deliver us from the burning fiery furnace, and he will deliver us out of thine hand, O king. But if not, be it known unto thee, O king, that we will not serve thy gods, nor worship the golden image which thou hast set up (vv.16-18).

Hallelujah!! You know, I just can't figure out how these men could so well hold their peace in the midst of tension. The secret? They knew that faith does not eliminate tension; but in the midst of tension, faith will give peace. Not that they loved to be thrown into the furnace. Who does? Just stick your finger into your burner when it's on and see how it feels. Then you will appreciate their faith. They were ready to go inside the fire if the need be. That's a brave faith that is ready and prepared to make heaven at all cost, even if it means passing through the fire. That's the faith God honors and rewards and so He did for the Hebrew children. He made the heat kill the throwers and left the thrown unburned. Behold the power of our God, Himself a Consuming Fire.

Children of God who are brave in their faith will outlive their enemies, because if they're thrown into the fire, the fourth man will show up and instead of being consumed by the fire, they will be comforted by the Father.

How bold is your faith, brother? How bold is your faith, sister? And I also ask myself, how bold is my faith, writer? If the Hebrew men could take their stand in time of trouble and persecution, take my word for it, you and I can. Whether God delivered them or not had nothing to do with their decision. They were for God and nothing would make them change their minds. They knew the God they believed. The same king who spoke against that God now spoke in His favor (vv. 28-30). Oh Glory! I call this 'promotion born out of persecution.' That enemy that continues to frustrate you is going to repent and proclaim Jesus as Lord. All you need do is bravely take your stand for your faith in God. The fourth man will get you out of the fire of life unburned, unharmed, and unscorched. Just remember His Word that says, "when thou walkest through the fire, thou shalt not be burned; neither shall the flame kindle upon thee" (Isaiah 43:2).

As a young shepherd boy, there was no way David could have confronted Goliath without a brave faith. The Bible describes Goliath as a champion, whose height was six cubits and a span. He had a helmet of brass upon his head, and he was armed with a coat of mail (1 Samuel 17:4-7). I looked up the meaning of 'a coat of mail.' It's a flexible body armor made of small, overlapping metal rings, loops of chain, or scales. It also means a defensive armor. Now, I don't know about you; but I don't think I need this much to fight a big bull, talkless of a little boy. Talk of a man ready for war, Goliath was. But apostle Paul said, " If God be for us, who can be against us?" (Romans 8:31).

Nobody, not even his brothers, ever thought that an ordinary shepherd boy would be bold enough to confront a man of Goliath's size. Though the Bible does not clearly give David's height, but he was obviously smaller in size, shape and stature. And though the youngest of eight of his father's sons, David was the Lord's choice. But how did he overcome Goliath? The truth is when we have faith in God and make Him the giant of our life, every Goliath will become a dwarf. We serve a God who looks on the heart, and not our height.

The Bible says, "But the people that do know their God shall be strong, and do exploits" (Daniel 11:32). David knew the battle was the Lord's and He would fight the battle for Himself. Though smaller in size and stature, he was stronger in soul and Spirit. Definitely David had distractions from people around. His brother, Eliab rebuked him; Saul persuaded him not to try it. They saw Goliath with an eye of flesh. David knew better. He saw him through an eye of faith. Don't let anyone deceive you that victory is easy to come by. He who cannot be violent in faith cannot be victorious in fight. You have to fight every discouragement and remember that the Lord who saved you then will save you now. David said, "The LORD that delivered me out of the paw of the lion, and out of the paw of the bear, he will deliver me out of the hand of this Philistine" (1 Samuel 17:37).

These are not the words of an ordinary man. It takes knowing God and having a brave faith in Him to utter these words. David took his staff (God the father), five smooth stones (Jesus), and his sling (the Holy Spirit) in his hand. That's all we need to fight an enemy that comes to us in the power of his flesh and the spirit of his pride.

> And David put his hand in his bag, and took thence a stone, and slang it, and smote the Philistine in his forehead, that the stone sunk into his forehead; and he fell upon his face to the earth (1 Samuel 17:49).

To Goliath's faithful followers, that he was dead was sad. But that his head was chopped off with his very own sword was pathetic. It was shameful. It was a defeat of their ego. Well, the enemy of your life may not appreciate the power of God in your life until he sees it manifested. When the gunman comes to you with his gun, you can boldly stand and tell him according to God's Word: "No weapon formed against me shall prosper" (Isaiah 54:17). That is because you have allowed your faith in the saving power of your God to override your fear in the slaying power of his gun.

Back home in Nigeria, a member of our fellowship, Full Gospel Business Men's Fellowship, gave a testimony of how God delivered him from armed robbers. Traveling alone back to his destination, he got stuck on the freeway till about 1a.m. because he had a problem with one of his tires. As he prayed and asked God to send help from above, some armed robbers showed up.

How would you feel at that moment if you were in his shoes? Seeing them from a distance, he knew he was in for something. So he asked God for wisdom and peace. With the gun pointed at him, he decided to use that opportunity to preach to the gunman. As the gunman repeatedly warned him to draw back, he drew closer to him and with each step told him about the love of Jesus. The other robbers joined to see what was going on. I mean think of a single man, helpless and unarmed in the midst of heartless and armed fellows. He knew it could be the end of his life; but let the end meet him telling them about Jesus. Our God is a faithful God. The words cut into their hearts and he was able to lead one of them to Christ. And they who were supposed to harm him helped him.

At that particular moment, this man faced the Goliaths of his life. But it does not take a gun to overcome a giant; all you need is God. He's more than able. I have no idea who the Goliath is in your life. But one thing I know; when you boldly assert your faith in God and bravely stand for Him, He will turn your situation around and make you the champion over your enemy. If you lack it, pray for it.

When Peter and John were arrested after the healing of the lame man at the temple gate, they were ordered not to preach in the name of Jesus. But they did not allow that to hinder them from continuing. Instead, they prayed for boldness (Acts 4:18-31).

If the apostles of Jesus could pray for boldness, who am I not to ask God to impart His boldness into my life that I may be able to stand, and

Faith Is Bold (Brave)

having done all to stand? Be brave. Though it may not come easy, ask God and He will give you.

C

7. FAITH CARES	27
8. FAITH is CHASTE	35
9. FAITH COMFORTS	38
10. FAITH COMMANDS	41
11. FAITH is COMPASSIONATE	44
13. FAITH is CONFIDENT	47
13. FAITH has CONSCIENCE	51
14. FAITH is CONTENT	55
15. FAITH is COURAGEOUS	60

7
FAITH CARES

By care, I'm not inferring the kind of faith that thinks of nothing other than the things of the world. I'm talking of the faith that cares about the welfare of the other person, whether Christians or non-Christians.

When we profess to be in the faith, caring for other people is part of our calling. It was because God cared about us that He sent His son to come and die for our sins. And because Jesus cared, He accepted to come and die for us. And even up till this moment, He still cares. We're dear to Him and He thinks of us every moment. If then we claim to be His children, aren't we supposed to be like Him in caring for others? God wants us to care for one another.

People in your neighborhood know you go to church every Sunday morning and evening, and every Wednesday evening for Bible study. But when was the last time you asked your neighbor how he or she is faring? Do you have an idea what the problem is with him (her)? When did we become Cain who asked God, "Am I my brother's keeper?" You want an honest answer? Yes, you are.

Do you even know may be he's (she's) been waiting for you just to say hello, how are you doing? Is there something I can do to help? That in itself can make a difference. It may have been years that he (she) heard anyone say to him (her), 'I love you.' You want to know how it feels when no one cares about you? Ask David. He had been through it.

I cried unto the LORD with my voice; with my voice unto the LORD did I make my supplication. I poured out my complaint before him; I shewed before him my trouble. When my spirit was overwhelmed within me, then thou knewest my path. In the way wherein I walked have they privily* laid a snare for me. I looked on my right hand, and beheld, but there was no man that would know me: refuge failed me; no man cared for my soul (Psalm 142:1-4).

David had no one who cared about his soul. There was no one to whom he could point as a friend in need, a friend indeed. He went through it all alone. When we have people who go with us in our period of trial, people who care about what we're passing through, the burden feels lighter. Knowing that somebody is out there who feels the pain with you makes you feel loved. Many of us are slack concerning this.

When my husband lost his job, a sister called me, someone that I thought was close to me. I was disappointed by the comments she passed, telling me there must be something wrong with our faith, because 'her God' will not do that kind of evil. Oh well, that's okay. But we thank God for our dear sisters in the Lord who upheld us morally and spiritually. Cynthia Mason and Sandra Gist, we will never forget you. You cared when we were hurting. Your labor of love will forever be remembered.

My pastor said it's time we stopped asking, 'What Will Jesus Do?'–and start to 'Do What Jesus Did.' It's time we determined to be like Christ to those hurting around us. You don't know how that woman ended up a struggling single mother. All you know is that she's not living with her husband. And as far as you care, it's because she's not virtuous like you. But God's Word says of the virtuous woman, "She stretcheth out her hand to the poor; yea, she reacheth forth her hands to the needy; She openeth her mouth with wisdom; and in her tongue is the law of kindness" (Proverbs 31:20, 26).

The last time you saw that girl on your street, she was pregnant. And to make her case worse, she doesn't know the baby's father. Where do you stand as a Christian? What was your comment when you saw her? Deep within you, you condemned her. Do you have an idea how she ended up on the street? Of course there are wayward children who don't take to the good upbringing of their parents. But not all want to end up that way. Some are there for reasons they can't explain.

What should be our attitude? Definitely she needs somebody who cares and understands. Somebody who can tell her there's still hope at the cross. Somebody who can explain to her so she can understand. A faith that cares doesn't condemn.

When the woman caught in adultery was brought to Jesus, remember what Jesus said to her?

> When Jesus had lifted up himself, and saw none but the woman, he said unto her, Woman, where are those thine accusers? hath no man condemned thee? She said, No man, Lord. And Jesus said unto her, Neither do I condemn thee: go, and sin no more (John 8:10-11).

If we don't know the genesis of a situation, let's not quickly jump to a judgmental conclusion. Even if we know, it's still not enough reason not to care if we truly have the faith of God dwelling in us. If God had taken our sins into consideration, He would not send His only Son to come and die for us. The Bible says, "If thou, LORD, shouldest mark iniquities, O Lord, who shall stand?" (Psalm 130:3). If God were to mark iniquities, the truth is no one qualifies to be called His child.

We care so much about ourselves and forget those who are less privileged. We're so busy going about our daily activities and forget there are people who are wheel chair bound and cannot get out of their homes. We're so caught up with our short nails and forget those who have no fingers. We care so much about our short feet and forget people without legs.

Attributes Of A Working Faith

There are people who care so much about the color of their eyes and not once remember the blind. Some women care so much about their short hair and not once remember there are those with long hair, who are lying forever silent in their graves; some to eternal damnation to whom no second chance is made available. Remember how worried you are because you belong to the group of us that are short in stature? Take a time to think of how envious the migid is of you. What are we doing with our faith? All we care about is me, me, me. No wonder we end up mean, mean, mean.

What made the difference between the paralytic brought to Jesus by four friends and the Bethesda paralytic? Care, nothing but care.

> And again he entered into Capernaum after some days; and it was noised that he was in the house. ... And they come unto him, bringing one sick of the palsy, which was borne of four. And when they could not come nigh unto him for the press, they uncovered the roof where he was: and when they had broken it up, they let down the bed where in the sick of the palsy lay. When Jesus saw their faith, he said unto the sick of the palsy, Son, thy sins be forgiven thee (Mark 2:1-5).

Consider the caring faith of these friends in need. They were not concerned about how their friend became paralyzed. All they wanted was his healing. Imagine the trouble they went through to get him to Jesus. Were you that caring for that sister you saw in the store, struggling to get something from the shelf because of her handicap? What did you do to help? You were so occupied with your list of perishables and never noticed the precious soul beside you. Some men care so much that they're having only girls. I suggest you pay a visit to the barren. May be that will make you more appreciative of the gifts God has given you.

Now compare this man's case with that of the paralytic at the pool of

Bethesda.

> After this there was a feast of the Jews; and Jesus went up to Jerusalem. Now there is at Jerusalem by the sheep market a pool, which is called in the Hebrew tongue Bethesda, having five porches …. And a certain man was there, which had an infirmity thirty and eight years. When Jesus saw him lie, and knew that he had been now a long time in that case, he saith unto him, Wilt thou be made whole? The impotent man answered him, Sir, I have no man, when the water is troubled, to put me into the pool: but while I am coming, another steppeth down before me. Jesus saith unto him, Rise, take up thy bed, and walk. And immediately the man was made whole, and took up his bed, and walked: and on the same day was the sabbath. The Jews therefore said unto him that was cured, It is the sabbath day: it is not lawful for thee to carry thy bed (John 5:1-10).

I'm so touched that right now, as I'm typing, tears are running down my eyes. I was barren for thirty-eight months and I know how it feels to be bound. But to think that this man had been in that position for thirty-eight years breaks my heart. He had been paralyzed longer than Jesus had been born. For thirty-eight years, nobody cared. Were there no believers then? I strongly believe there were people of faith around him. They recognized his handicap. Most likely they gave him alms. But nobody cared to help him get inside the water. He missed the race of life for thirty-eight years. If he were married, he didn't know what it meant to have fun with his children. It would even be worse if he became paralyzed after he had raced with them, played basketball with them, got in the pool with them, the same pool he now helplessly wanted to enter but could not due to his handicap. It's bad and hard to lack it; but it's worse to have it and loose it. Lock yourself up in a wheel chair for thirty-eight hours and see how it feels to be bound. See how it feels to be without help for thirty-eight years. He was not sure what harm would come upon him the next moment. May be someone would put the gun to his chest. People were alive. People passed by him every moment. But nobody cared.

And what happened after his healing? The Jews noticed and became indignant at him carrying his bed on a Sabbath. They did not notice his restored feet. A man who had been paralyzed for thirty-eight years, who received his healing after a long, long time of pain and impotency. And all they cared about was the bed. They were a bunch of insensitive fanatics, who were functionally alive but 'faithically' dead.

Should people of faith make a difference in the lives of those around them? Absolutely. What made the Good Samaritan different from the priest and the Levite that passed by the man who fell among thieves while on his way to Jericho? Care. He cared more about the man's need than his nativity.

There are preachers and pastors who don't care about their flock. They're carried away with their religious activities. The care for the soul is secondary to that of the sanctuary. The building is sparkling with beauty; but the body of Christ is struggling with boredom. The sheep feel unnoticed and unimportant. Of course they hear the good message every Sunday morning and every Wednesday evening. But how about those inner struggles that are eating deep into them?

Mr. Preacher, you have a massive congregation in a gigantic Cathedral. But how many of your members do you know? Does Jesus see you the way you see yourself? If Jesus were to show up in your service, what would He call you, a shepherd or an hireling?

> I am the good shepherd: the good shepherd giveth his life for the sheep. But he that is an hireling, and not the shepherd, whose own

the sheep are not, seeth the wolf coming, and leaveth the sheep, and fleeth: and the wolf catcheth them, and scattereth the sheep. The hireling fleeth, <u>because he is an hireling, and careth not for the sheep</u> (John 10:11-13).

How much of the needs of your members do you care to know? If the government of this world would not excuse our ignorance of the law, God is not going to overlook our ignorance of the things of the Spirit.

Feed the flock of God which is among you, taking the oversight thereof, not by constraint, but willingly; not for filthy lucre, but of a ready mind; Neither as being lords over God's heritage, but being examples to the flock. And when the chief Shepherd shall appear, ye shall receive a crown of glory that fadeth not away (1 Peter 5:2-4).

Remember the man with a hundred sheep, who went in search of the missing one, leaving the ninety-nine behind? How could he leave ninety-nine to perish, because of one stray sheep that walked away from the master's care? How absurd to allow ninety-nine to suffer just because of one careless sheep? Those are the questions of the spiritually ignorant. One amongst ninety-nine may appear insignificant to you and I, but not to God the good Shepherd, who loves his flock and to whom every sheep is precious and important. Our Savior said, "joy shall be in heaven over one sinner that repenteth, more than over ninety and nine just persons, which need no repentance" (Luke 15:7).

And how about us to whom the pastors minister the word? Do we care about them? Do we care to know what they go through? Pastors are not gods, they're human beings like us. They have their life hassles. You know the hard thing about theirs? When we have problems, we go to them. When they have problems, to whom do they go? Do we care how they fare after they fast? God's Word commands us to care for them.

> Do ye not know that they which minister about holy things live of the things of the temple? and they which wait at the altar are partakers with the altar? Even so hath the Lord ordained that they which preach the gospel should live of the gospel (1 Corinthians 9:13-14).

This is not saying they should make the church their property; but that we to whom they minister spiritually should in turn minister to them physically.

> But I rejoiced in the Lord greatly, that now at the last your care of me hath flourished again; wherein ye were also careful, but ye lacked opportunity. Not that I speak in respect of want: for I have learned, in whatsoever state I am, therewith to be content. I know both how to be abased, and I know how to abound: every where and in all things I am instructed both to be full and to be hungry, both to abound and to suffer need (Philippians 4:10-12).

Was Paul acting a beggar? No. He was only emphasizing what the Lord expected of those believers. He ministered to their spiritual needs. They in turn were to minister to his physical needs. We're to care both in giving and praying. If truly we're of Christ and profess to have faith in Him, then let's be like Him, for Christ cares. Our little cares of today will add up for our crown of tomorrow when the great rewarder comes to take His own to be with Him forever.

* Secretly

8
FAITH is CHASTE

Chastity has more to do with women of faith. But as we shall later see, men are also commanded to be chaste. Apostle Peter, in his description of a chaste woman, referred to Sarah who called her husband Lord.

Likewise, ye wives, be in subjection to your own husbands; that, if any obey not the word, they also may without the word be won by the conversation of the wives; While they behold your chaste conversation coupled with fear. ... For after this manner in the old ime the holy women also, who trusted in God, adorned themselves, being in subjection unto their own husbands: Even as Sara obeyed Abraham, calling him lord: whose daughters ye are, as long as ye do well, and are not afraid with any amazement (1 Peter 3:1-6).

Yes, women of faith are to be chaste both in appearance and behavior. We're to show forth the glory of Him who called us to salvation. When it comes to the adornment of the body, women are naturally more conscious. (Sorry men. You are too. Huh!) We, unfortunately, sometimes focus more on our beauty than we do on our belief. There's nothing wrong with outward adornment. But if all we care about is how we look and forget the ordinances of our God regarding our conduct, then we need to retrace our steps.

Peter believed that an unbelieving husband would be won to the Lord much easier by our conduct than our costume and cosmetics. And to our God, the inner beauty is what matters. Not that His children should be shabby and dirty looking in appearance; but that we should not leave the substance to chase the shadow. Some things are more important than others.

In Paul's letter to Titus, he wrote, "The aged women likewise, that they be in behaviour as becometh holiness, not false accusers, not given to much wine, teachers of good things; That they may teach the young women to be sober, to love their husbands, to love their children, To be discreet, chaste, keepers at home, good, obedient to their own husbands, that the Word of God be not blasphemed" (Titus 2:3-5).

The issue of chastity is so important that Paul felt the need for the older women to pass it on to the younger ones. However, he also penned some words for men concerning their chastity. Theirs involve their stomach and sex. (They need them things more than we do.)

> Meats for the belly, and the belly for meats: but God shall destroy both it and them. Now the body is not for fornication, but for the Lord; and the Lord for the body. …. **But he that is joined unto the Lord is one spirit.** Flee fornication. Every sin that a man doeth is without the body; but he that committeth fornication sinneth against his own body. What? know ye not that your body is the temple of the Holy Ghost which is in you, which ye have of God, and ye are not your own? For ye are bought with a price: therefore glorify God in your body, and in your spirit, which are God's (1 Corinthians 6:13-20).

However, let's not make the mistake that these words are for men only. They also apply to us as women. Adultery and fornication are works of the flesh. God wants us, men and women alike to keep ourselves pure in a world of moral decadence.

> Now concerning the things whereof ye wrote unto me: It is good for a man not to touch a woman. Nevertheless, to avoid fornication, let every man have his own wife, and let every woman have her own husband (1 Corinthians 7:1-2).

Marriage is sacred and children of God should be particular about the chastity of their relationship. As people watch us, they also watch our actions. How would you feel after you have preached or witnessed to people, they found out you were having immoral relationship with a brother or sister? It not only dents your faith, it destroys your testimony. And if you're not careful, you may end up a castaway after you have won others to the faith.

That was why Paul said that the single should marry if they cannot hold their passion. He was not saying it for the sole purpose of bearing children, but for the main reason of not defiling the Holy name of our God. Not all men have the same strong heart like Joseph (Jacob's son) who refused to stain his chastity while he had every opportunity to do so with Potiphar's wife. And not all men can be like Joseph (Mary's husband) who decided not to have any affair with his betrothed until after the birth of our Savior. There's absolutely no need pretending to be what you know you are not.

Chastity also applies to our day-to-day relationship with others, including our conversation.

> But fornication, and all uncleanness, or covetousness, let it not be once named among you, as becometh saints; Neither filthiness, <u>nor foolish talking, nor jesting,</u> which are not convenient: but rather giving of thanks. ... For ye were sometimes darkness, but now are ye light in the Lord (Ephesians 5:3-11).

God wants us to be chaste in everything, so we can bring glory to His name. As we strive to remain chaste with our faith, He will give us the grace to carry on. We cannot do it in our own strength. But with Him as our guide, the end would be glorious.

9
<u>FAITH COMFORTS</u>

Overnight, I wanted to get something downstairs for my girl. I turned the hallway light on, but it didn't come on. It occurred to me that I used that light less than an hour ago. I thought to myself, the bulb must be out. Then I noticed light downstairs. My son was in the parlor. He helped me turn on the hallway light from downstairs, because it's a two-way switch. Then I began to wonder what happened? As I went back to bed, I kept thinking what lesson was God teaching me.

God said to me, "you are about to write on comfort. The comfort you can offer to anyone this moment, don't delay till later. For just as the light was and then was no more, so also it is with people. You see them one moment. The next time you hear about them, they're in another state or even another country. But they will never forget your words of comfort. If by chance they die, you will be eternally grateful that you did not withhold the comfort you could give. And if it's the other way round, then they will always remember your words of comfort."

We have the greatest Comforter in the person of the Holy Spirit. He comforts us in every situation. But God still wants us to comfort one another in our trials and hard times.

> Blessed be God, even the Father of our Lord Jesus Christ, the Father of mercies, and the God of all comfort; Who comforteth us in all our tribulation, that we may be able to comfort them which are in any trouble, by the comfort wherewith we ourselves are comforted of God (2 Corinthians 1:3-4).

God will never cease to be our comfort. The question is, are we ready

Faith Comforts

to comfort others? I'm not talking fake or pretentious comfort, the kind that Joseph's brothers offered their father Jacob after selling their brother (Genesis 37:31-35). That was a pseudo comfort. What was the basis of their comfort? They sold their brother and then comforted their father. That was hitting and rubbing and is not the kind of comfort I'm talking about, and definitely not the kind God would have us show to others.

Jesus said, "blessed are they that mourn: for they shall be comforted" (Matthew 5:4). While they receive comfort from the source of all comfort, the Holy Spirit Himself, we on the other hand are supposed to stand with them.

Job had a problem. Instead of people who could uphold him, all he got were some miserable comforters who condemned him. It would have been better if they had not shown up.

> Then Job answered and said, I have heard many such things: miserable comforters are ye all (Job 16:1-2).

Not that Job had no one to talk to him during his affliction. But he had no one who comforted. Those who came were not giving the type of comfort deserving for anyone in Job's condition. Many Christians are guilty of this. When someone is going through a hard time, we tend to appear holier than him or her. These friendly foes claimed to be comforting Job. But they were actually adding to his problem. For seven days and seven nights, they were silent. By the time they finally 'demuted' (pardon my English), it was a rain of criticisms and condemnations. The Bible says, "To him that is afflicted pity should be shewed from his friend" (Job 6:14).

In a time of inexplicable affliction, Job received no pity from friends. I've been in a situation when all I needed was comfort and all I received was condemnation. It was really demoralizing. For a moment, I saw God as unfair and unfaithful to His promises for us. But I thank God for the Holy Spirit that stepped in immediately. He brought the picture of the Red Sea to my mind. He reminded me that human beings may condemn us when they see us stuck at the Red Sea. But by the time God is done taking us through the dry land to the other side, they will marvel and wonder.

When we visit the bereaved, asking how and why may not be appropriate for that moment. Let's comfort them by reminding them that soon they will be reunited with their loved one, if such dies in the Lord. If otherwise, we might as well just visit and pray with them. The judgment is not ours to make. A hurting soul does not have enough strength to take criticism. When we visit the sick, they need to know that Jesus is the greatest Healer. Asking how they contacted the disease will not do any good. They're hurting already and if we can't relief them of it, we should not add to it.

What kind of faith do you have, the type that comforts or the type that condemns? Remember that one of these days, it may be your turn to receive comfort from those you have comforted. Be to people what you would have them be to you. And people of God, let us daily examine our actions to those around us, believers and unbelievers. God wants us to comfort and not condemn.

10
FAITH COMMANDS

There are several instances of commanding faith in the Bible. But I like to start with our Lord Jesus Himself. I know you may be wondering what in the world that means. That Jesus had faith? Yes, Jesus had faith.

Looking unto Jesus the author and finisher of our faith (Hebrews 12:2).

Jesus is the Alfa and Omega of our faith; He's the beginning and the end of our faith. If the Bible calls Him the author of our faith, then only He can be our best example to emulate, since it originated from Him.

Even Jesus referred to His faith in Revelation.

I know thy works, and where thou dwellest, even where Satan's seat is: and thou holdest fast my name, and hast not denied my faith, even in those days wherein Antipas was my faithful martyr, who was slain among you, where Satan dwelleth (Revelation 2:13).

Here is the patience of the saints: here are they that keep the commandments of God, and the faith of Jesus (Rev. 14:12).

Jesus had faith and He used it to command evil spirits out of many and to heal sicknesses and diseases.

When he was come down from the mountain, great multitudes followed him. And, behold, there came a leper and worshipped him, saying, Lord, if thou wilt, thou canst make me clean. And Jesus put forth his hand, and touched him, saying, I will; be thou clean. And immediately his leprosy was cleansed (Matthew 8:1-3).

The leprosy had no choice. When the Lord speaks, leprosy has to obey. Having said that, let's now see the commanding faith of believers in the Bible.

Attributes Of A Working Faith

In Acts, Paul commanded an evil spirit out of a girl that had had the spirit of divination for a long time. The Bible records she used it to bring much profit to her masters by fortune telling. They would never want the spirit out of her since it was a source of money for them; lovers of gain than lovers of God. She followed Paul, Silas and Timothy for many days. But when a holy anger sprang up inside Paul, he commanded the spirit out of her life.

> And this did she many days. But Paul, being grieved, turned and said to the spirit, I <u>command</u> thee in the name of Jesus Christ to come out of her. And he came out the same hour (Acts 16:18).

Peter and John were going to the temple to pray and at the gate was a man born lame, collecting alms from people entering the temple. But then came a fateful day that would be his last to ask for alms because he was about to have an encounter with a commanding faith.

> And Peter, fastening his eyes upon him with John, said, Look on us. And he gave heed unto them, expecting to receive something of them. Then Peter said, Silver and gold have I none; but such as I have give I thee: In the name of Jesus Christ of Nazareth rise up and walk. And he took him by the right hand, and lifted him up: and immediately his feet and ankle bones received strength (Acts 3:4-7).

Left to Peter, whether the man wanted to walk or not was completely irrelevant. Just get up and walk; and at least save some money into people's pockets. And immediately, he leaped, he walked and hallelujah, he praised God.

In Joshua, after God had granted the Israelites victory over the Amorites, the man of God Joshua, attempted the impossible, such as had never been and may possibly never be in the history of man.

> Then spake Joshua to the LORD in the day when the LORD

delivered up the Amorites before the children of Israel, and he said in the sight of Israel, Sun, stand thou still upon Gibeon; and thou, Moon, in the valley of Ajalon. And the sun stood still, and the moon stayed, until the people had avenged themselves upon their enemies. Is not this written in the book of Jasher? So the sun stood still in the midst of heaven, and hasted not to go down about a whole day. And there was no day like that before it or after it, that the LORD hearkened unto the voice of a man: for the LORD fought for Israel (Joshua 10: 12-14).

Joshua commanded the sun and the moon to stand still. Did the sun obey? Did the moon stand still? Of course they had to. A man of faith had issued "a stay thou still decree" and they must obey. That was faith; the kind of faith that commands the work of the hands of God. No boundaries overstepped. God Himself says, "Ask me of things to come concerning my sons, and concerning the work of my hands command ye me" (Isaiah 45:11).

What is it you're struggling with that simply won't let go? You probably need to command before it can hear you speak. Yes, command and victory shall be yours in Jesus' name.

11
FAITH is COMPASSIONATE

The act of compassion is one of feeling or having a deep sympathy for someone else. You feel what that person is feeling, as if you're the one going through the problem. You put yourself in the person's position and try to imagine what you expect to be done for you and then you do the same for him or her.

This was practically demonstrated by our Lord. He always had compassion on the crowd that followed Him, either to hear the word or to be healed.

And Jesus went about all the cities and villages, teaching in their synagogues, and preaching the gospel of the kingdom, and healing every sickness and every disease among the people. But when he saw the multitudes, <u>he was moved with compassion on them,</u> because they fainted, and were scattered abroad, as sheep having no shepherd (Matthew 9:35-36).

And Jesus went forth, and saw a great multitude, and <u>was moved with compassion toward them</u>, and he healed their sick (Mat. 14:14). Then Jesus called his disciples unto him, and said, <u>I have compassion on the multitude</u>, because they continue with me now three days, and have nothing to eat: and I will not send them away fasting, lest they faint in the way (Matthew. 15:32).

Jesus taught us to be compassionate. He was never weary of the people. His compassion far exceeded His crowd. As people of faith, we have no reason to shut our doors of compassion to people in need. You may assume this was Jesus and you are not. Well consider this parable that Jesus used to emphasize the importance of compassion.

> And, behold, a certain lawyer stood up, and tempted him, saying, Master, what shall I do to inherit eternal life?... And who is my neighbour? And Jesus answering said, A certain man went down from Jerusalem to Jericho, and fell among thieves, which stripped him of his raiment, and wounded him, and departed, leaving him half dead. And by chance there came down a certain priest that way: and when he saw him, he passed by on the other side. And likewise a Levite, when he was at the place, came and looked on him, and passed by on the other side. But a certain Samaritan, as he journeyed, came where he was: and when he saw him, <u>he had compassion on him</u>, And went to him, and bound up his wounds, pouring in oil and wine, and set him on his own beast, and brought him to an inn, and took care of him. .... Which now of these three, thinkest thou, was neighbour unto him that fell among the thieves? And he said, He that shewed mercy on him. Then said Jesus unto him, Go, and do thou likewise (Luke 10:25-37).

This was an unconditional compassion, the kind that made God send His only Son to come and die for our sins. A Samaritan and a Jew were like words and opposite. He was least expected to have compassion on this man. The so-called priest and Levite, who were closer to the man in race and religion, did nothing to help. They were 'incompassionately' religious.

We cannot claim to be in the faith and be lacking in compassion. Our religious services are unacceptable when people come and all they see is a 'DO NOT DISTURB' hanger on our doors of compassion. It doesn't have to be visible before they notice. And if people don't notice, God does. You cannot hide from the One who knows you in and out.

Finally, be ye all of one mind, having compassion one of another, love as brethren, be pitiful, be courteous (1 Peter 3:8).

Compassion is a must if we so wish for faith without fault. It has nothing to do with color, gender, race or culture. We must show compassion so we can receive compassion.

12
FAITH is CONFIDENT

Lack of confidence comes from fear. If I lack the confidence to drive a vehicle, it's likely to be a result of my fear of other road users. How do I get in the midst of the fast moving traffic and go at the same speed? The moment fear sets in, I'm bound to loose my confidence to ever operate a vehicle. But when the confidence is there, I know I can do it without any fear. The Bible says, "And this is the confidence that we have in him, that, if we ask any thing according to his will, he heareth us" (1 John 5:14). Before we get results, we see our miracles coming. We believe and then we receive.

We must have confidence in our faith in God and not allow fear to snatch it from us. "Cast not away therefore your confidence, which hath great recompense of reward" (Hebrews 10:35).

Confident faith has rewards and one of them is victory over peril. When Paul and some other prisoners were in the boat on their way to Rome, a tempest arose. There was a great panic on board as hopes of survival got dim. In the midst of the turmoil was a man of confident faith, one who knew his God. He spoke the words of faith in the midst of fear (Acts 27:21-25).

Elijah had a confident faith and he believed whatever he said would surely come to pass. He prayed there would be no rain in the land of Israel and the rain ceased until he reversed his prayer after a period of three years and six months. When he stood against the four hundred and fifty prophets of Baal and four hundred prophets of Asherah, he acted based on his confidence in God. He was all by himself, one against eight hundred, fifty. The secret? One with God is a majority. When you have a confident faith in God, it won't matter how many are against you.

> Then said Elijah unto the people, I, even I only, remain a prophet of the LORD; but Baal's prophets are four hundred and fifty men. … And call ye on the name of your gods, and I will call on the name of the LORD: and the God that answereth by fire, let him be God. And all the people answered and said, It is well spoken (1 Kings 18: 22-24).

They had no choice. A man of God just spoke. When you confidently speak the words of faith, demons have no choice but to listen and obey. You're not the one speaking. It's the Spirit of God that lives inside you.

> And it came to pass at noon, that Elijah mocked them, and said, Cry aloud: for he is a god; either he is talking, or he is pursuing, or he is in a journey, or peradventure he sleepeth, and must be awaked. And they cried aloud, and cut themselves after their manner with knives and lancets, till the blood gushed out upon them (18:27, 28).

They prophesied until the time of the offering of the evening sacrifice and shed their blood for their god, but there was no voice. No one answered, no one paid attention. I just wish there was a video recording of the scene. It would definitely put some laughter into my mouth. In spite of all the cutting and crying, no one answered!! Too bad.

I don't claim to know it all, for no one does. But one thing I know–that god is no god, for whom the worshippers shed blood, either their own blood or the blood of other innocent people. There's neither peace in bloodshed nor bloodshed in peace. A religion that sheds the blood of other people for the course of their belief is completely out of order and so are the worshippers. The blood had been shed once for all.

And to you bloodthirsty demons parading as servants of god, here's a word for you.

Faith Is Confident

But thou, O God, shalt bring them down into the pit of destruction: bloody and deceitful men shall not live out half their days (Psalm 55:23).

If you shed innocent blood for the course of your blind gospel, you shall die premature. And unless you repent and turn to the living God, you shall forever burn in hell, in the pit of destruction.

Now let's see the real God in action; the God who never sleeps nor slumbers. The Omnipresent, Omniscient, Omnipotent God. He hears when we call, He answers when we ask. He's only a prayer away from His own. He's the ever-present, ever-abiding King of kings and Lord of lords; the God that never fails, the God that never disappoints His people; the One who was, who is and forever will be.

And it came to pass at the time of the offering of the evening sacrifice, that Elijah the prophet came near, and said, LORD God of Abraham, Isaac, and of Israel, let it be known this day that thou art God in Israel, … Hear me, O LORD, hear me, that this people may know that thou art the LORD God, and that thou hast turned their heart back again (1 Kings 18:36-37).

If I were to say the same prayer, using the same words, it should not last more than a minute. But the result? A lifetime. When we confidently put our faith in God, wonders will happen.

Then the fire of the LORD fell, and consumed the burnt sacrifice, and the wood, and the stones, and the dust, and licked up the water that was in the trench. And when all the people saw it, they fell on their faces: and they said, The LORD, he is the God; the LORD, he is the God (18:38-39).

The Consuming Fire Himself came down with power, such as was never seen before, to glorify His name, so much so that the people confessed the Lord indeed is God. Hallelujah!!! God will *never* put you to shame. He says, "I am the LORD: that is my name: and my glory will I not give to another, neither my praise to graven images" (Isaiah 42:8).

God did not give His glory to Baal because it was a carved image. He did not give it to the carved image of Nebuchadnezzar; He did not give it to the carved image of king Darius. Our God is a jealous God and His glory He will not share with any other god.

Whoever will not give you peace because you mention the name of God, that person is a carved image. He's a graven object and worthy of no honor. Maintain your confidence in God and He will deal with him or her. One of these days, he's going to bow at the mention of the name of Jesus. He's going to acknowledge that your God indeed is Lord.

13
FAITH has CONSCIENCE

Cain, Abel's blood brother, was the first born of Adam and Eve. He and his brother offered sacrifices unto God. The sacrifice of Abel was acceptable to God because it was righteous; but that of Cain was rejected, because it was not righteous. Cain got angry and killed his brother. But then we should ask, why would he kill his brother over something as trivial as sacrifice? And even after the murder, how come he was not disturbed in the spirit? There's only one answer I can give to that; he had no conscience.

How best can we describe conscience? It is an awareness to do something right, not to get human approval or praise, not because anyone is watching, but because it's the right thing to do. Conscience plays a great role in the life of man. These are the days when children say bye to mom and never get the chance to come back home and say hi. Their lives are cut short by those who lack conscience, those to whom killing is fun. Nothing pricks them in the heart. They do it without any feelings for the victim of their evil act or the loved ones he or she will be leaving behind. The reason for their action is not a hard one to figure out. Satan controls them. And any heart controlled by Satan is a heart void of conscience.

People of faith are to be people of conscience in two ways. The first one is what apostle Paul described in 1 Corinthians.

But meat commendeth us not to God: for neither, if we eat, are we the better; neither, if we eat not, are we the worse. But take heed lest by any means this liberty of yours become a stumblingblock to them that are weak. For if any man see thee which hast knowledge sit at meat in the idol's temple, shall not the conscience of him which is weak be emboldened* to eat those things which are offered to idols; And through thy knowledge shall the weak brother perish, for whom Christ died? But when ye sin so against the brethren, and wound their weak conscience, ye sin against Christ. Wherefore, if meat make my brother to offend, I will eat no flesh while the world standeth, lest I make my brother to offend (7:8-13).

Just as we're different in strength, so are we in spirit. Some of us are stronger in spirit than others. In the above passage, apostle Paul was correcting the erroneous idea that some Christians developed over eating or not eating of meat. That a man eats meat does not in any manner make him holy; and that he abstains from eating does not make him sinful. And vice-versa. In the judgment of God, meat has no place. However, we must be cautious not to make nonsense of our spiritual liberty. If eating meat will make another brother stumble, especially one who is weaker in the faith, then the stronger in faith should abstain from eating. Why? Not because God forbids eating meat, but because when we make another person fall, we render the death of Christ for that soul of no value.

And we have to remember that any harm done to that soul is done to the Lord, who shed His blood and gave His precious life as ransom for the purpose of saving that soul from hell. The stronger in faith should be careful to avoid what will offend the weaker, or lay a stumbling block in their way. This does not have to do with meat per se. It applies to every area of our spirit being. Only a soul void of conscience will care less what effect his actions have on another life.

Does it mean we can please everybody? Absolutely not. There are people who will always find something wrong in other people. But as much as it lies within our power to do, we're to avoid anything that will offend another soul. We too should be able to say like brother Paul, "If meat make my brother to offend, I will eat no flesh while the world standeth, lest I make my brother to offend." Otherwise, we make a shipwreck of the faith (1 Timothy 1:19) and fail to hold the mystery of it in pure conscience (1 Timothy 3:8).

The second perspective is the feeling of guilt when we sin. When we act contrary to the will of God and disobey His laws, conscience will convict us and lead us to repentance. That is the power of the Holy Spirit.

Peter was a man of faith. There's no other word I can use to describe his attempt to walk on water, except faith. But at a time he was supposed to stand with the Lord, Peter denied Him. But His conscience convicted him of the crime and he wept bitterly for his action.

God put Adam and Eve in the garden and gave them the grace to enjoy every fruit except one.

> And the LORD God commanded the man, saying, Of every tree of the garden thou mayest freely eat: But of the tree of the knowledge of good and evil, thou shalt not eat of it: for in the day that thou eatest thereof thou shalt surely die (Genesis 2:16, 17).

Adam and Eve disobeyed His order. They ate of the fruit and fell. But when God called to them in the cool of the day, the Bible records they did something.

> And they heard the voice of the LORD God walking in the garden in the cool of the day: and Adam and his wife hid themselves from the presence of the LORD God amongst the trees of the garden. And the LORD God called unto Adam, and said unto him, Where art thou? And he said, I heard thy voice in the garden, and I was afraid, because I was naked; and I hid myself (Genesis 3:8-10).

Why did they hide when they heard God's voice? Because their conscience convicted them of their sin of disobedience. As people of faith, we're not perfect. We're still subject to the flesh from time to time. But when we miss the mark and do contrary to God's expectation, we must immediately feel the impact and seek God's face for forgiveness. God is calling us to that higher level, where we live our lives conscience clear and void of offence towards Him and towards men. May the Lord interpret His word into our hearts in Jesus' name.

* Be made bold

14
FAITH is CONTENT

Human beings by nature are never satisfied with their present condition. In winter it's too cold; in spring it's too grassy; in summer it's too hot; in fall it's too dirty. No matter how religious, man perpetually desires a change for the better. Well, in a way, it's good if applied in the right direction. But God cannot have us professing to be in the faith and be greedy at the same time. Contentment is a sign of godliness.

> But godliness with contentment is great gain. For we brought nothing into this world, and it is certain we can carry nothing out. And having food and raiment let us be therewith content. But they that will be rich fall into temptation and a snare, and into many foolish and hurtful lusts, which drown men in destruction and perdition. For the love of money is the root of all evil: which while some coveted after, they have erred from the faith, and pierced themselves through with many sorrows (1 Timothy 6:6-10).

There is a reminder for us there. Since we brought nothing into this world, we should be content with what we have. That's not saying for us to be comfortable with poverty and accept it as our cross all in the name of Christ. But that we should not loose our place with God while chasing what does not belong to us. If we brought nothing into this world, it implies we met everything here. Before we are, they were. They had been here longer than we had been born. So what's the rush? People of the flesh can run after those things, but we know better and therefore should act better. The bad news is when we're dead, all the things we use our precious time and energy pursuing will reject us.

Therefore I hated life; because the work that is wrought under the sun is grievous unto me: for all is vanity and vexation of spirit. Yea, I hated all my labour which I had taken under the sun: because I should leave it unto the man that shall be after me. And who knoweth whether he shall be a wise man or a fool? yet shall he have rule over all my labour wherein I have laboured, and wherein I have shewed myself wise under the sun. This is also vanity. Therefore I went about to cause my heart to despair of all the labour which I took under the sun. For there is a man whose labour is in wisdom, and in knowledge, and in equity; yet to a man that hath not laboured therein shall he leave it for his portion. This also is vanity and a great evil. There is nothing better for a man, than that he should eat and drink, and that he should make his soul enjoy good in his labour. This also I saw, that it was from the hand of God (Ecclesiastes 2:17-21, 24).

No matter how much time we spend on them, once we die, they're no longer interested in us. They want new owners for which they can be useful. Is that worth loosing eternity for? I don't think so.

I learned of recent that dead people's suits don't have pockets. Why? Because there's nothing to put inside and they don't even need anything. If buried naked, they won't know. Let's remember that it was apostle Paul that penned the words we read in the passage in 1Timothy 6. He wasn't poor. He was learned. He knew what wealth was. But to him, nothing he had could be compared to the kingdom he wanted to have.

And apart from the evil it can do to our faith, greed causes lack of rest. If anyone deserves true rest, it is the child of God. "The sleep of a labouring man," the Bible says, "is sweet, whether he eat little or much: but the abundance of the rich will not suffer him to sleep" (Ecclesiastes 5:12). The term 'will not suffer' can be interpreted 'will not allow or permit.' Rich people who don't know God always want more and are never satisfied.

Flesh says, "I need more." Faith says, "I am content with such as I have. And if I need more, then my God shall supply all my need according to His riches in glory by Christ Jesus" (Philippians 4:19). Which of these do you want as somebody who claims to have faith in God?

Solomon was a wealthy king. Even Jesus referred to his earthly glory. Yet he knew the secret of contentment.

> Better is a dry morsel, and quietness therewith, than an house full of sacrifices with strife (Proverbs 17:1).

A dry morsel is not referring to lack or want. But just a little that is enough, is far more peaceful than much feasting in sorrow. There are so many that are feasting today but are doing so in sorrow. There's no joy in their lives. They have enough to buy an estate, but lack enough to give them peace. Contentment cannot be bought. It's priceless. Only faith in God gives true contentment. When we have it, it brings peace. Because once we surrender our lives to Jesus, we have invited the Prince of Peace to our hearts.

Of course there will be times that we have needs. But then the Word of God has promises for us.

> Let your conversation be without covetousness; and be content with such things as ye have: for he hath said, I will never leave thee, nor forsake thee (Hebrews 13:5).

If He promised never to leave us, nor forsake us, then there's no reason not to be content with what He has given us for now. Contentment cannot be done in the power of the flesh. It's the Spirit of God that makes content. A soul without Jesus will die of greed.

Judas was with Jesus for three years. He saw His compassion for others. He witnessed His miracles of healing and cleansing. But did he have Jesus in his life? No. He was never content. The Bible calls him a thief (John 12:4-6). That's because flesh only thinks of the here and now. Faith thinks of heaven, the hereafter. That's why apostle Paul said, "If ye then be risen with Christ, seek those things which are above, where Christ sitteth on the right hand of God. Set your affection on things above, not on things on the earth" (Colossians 3:2). There's nothing of worth in this world that is enough to make a child of God loose his faith in Jesus and loose his eternity with God.

Judas had every opportunity to make heaven. But covetousness took it from him. And how come people don't name their children Judas? Can you name your child Judas? Why? Because one Judas out of six was a devil. We forget the remaining five, one of them a blood brother to Jesus (Matt. 13:55). Covetousness born out of greed tarnished that name for life. When the Spirit of contentment evades a child of God, the spirit of evil will take over and push him (her) to his (her) destruction.

Unfortunately, there are people who are spiritually covetous. They're never satisfied with their roles in the church. They want to be everything and be in everything. Man of God, sister of faith, relax if you don't want to regret. God knows your ability. That's why he put you where you are. His Word says for you to walk as you're called.

> But as God hath distributed to every man, as the Lord hath called every one, so let him walk (1 Corinthians 7:17).

How has He called you? As an usher? Then stay there. Give room for others who also want to be used of God. You cannot do everything because you don't know everything. You are not omniscient. That attribute is for God only. The day you make yourself believe you know everything, you're already loosing the anointing God has bestowed upon your life. Be content with such

as you have or do. Don't make an Adam and Eve out of your faith. Don't eat the fruit that will chase you out of the garden of God's love. Be content.

15
<u>FAITH is COURAGEOUS</u>

Courage is facing and dealing with any situation recognized as dangerous, difficult or painful, instead of withdrawing from it. Reading the stories of children of God who in various situations displayed courageous faith, I always ask myself, 'if I had been in the same situations, would I have courageously taken my stand?' The answer is Yes! As long as their God is my God and I have the same faith they had.

It's one thing to have faithless courage; it's another thing altogether to have a courageous faith. When you exercise a faithless courage, the devil defeats you; but when you exercise a courageous faith, you defeat the devil. It won't matter what the circumstances are that surround you. You realize that though your courage is not an absence of fear, but your fear knows that if God be for you, no one can be against you (Romans 8:31).

The Bible says, "By faith Moses, when he was born, was hid three months of his parents, because they saw he was a proper child; and they were not afraid of the king's commandment" (Hebrews 11:23).

Moses was hidden for three months because king Pharaoh issued a decree that all male infants be put to death by the Hebrew midwives (Exodus 1:15-17). But the Lord used them to save and preserve the life of the babies amongst who was Moses, son of Amram and Jochebed (Exodus 6:20). His mother hid him for three months. Hide a baby for three months?

I'm a mother of three, 16yrs; 15yrs; and 7yrs. To hide them for three days would definitely run me crazy. But to hide a baby for three months seems to me unimaginable. Well, Jochebed did; not because she feared the king's command, but because she saw in her son the hand of the God she believed.

She had a courageous faith and God honored it.

Moses was rescued by the daughter of the king who would have killed him, and was raised in the palace of the Pharaoh who would have erased his future; all because of a mother's courageous faith.

Wait on the LORD: be of good courage, and he shall strengthen thine heart: wait, I say, on the LORD (Psalm 27:14).

Be of good courage, and he shall strengthen your heart, all ye that hope in the LORD (Psalm 31:24).

In as much as we don't hope in any other thing, our God will honor our courageous faith. He strengthens our heart the instant He knows we're ready to take a stand for Him. He did it for Jochebed not because of Moses; but because of Jochebed. He did it for the three Hebrew children.

The same God did it for Daniel (Daniel 6). How would you like to take an hour off work and spend it with the lions in the zoo? Daniel was in a situation where he could have denied the Lord for fear of lions. But he was a man of courageous faith. Though he realized he didn't have enough fist to fight the lions, he had enough faith to face them.

What started out as a promotion for Daniel turned into a problem because of those who hated his God. It's not a new thing to be persecuted because of your love for God. Pressure will arise because you always pray. As it was in the days of Daniel, so it is today. But one thing is sure. When enemies gather against us because of the Lord, they shall fall for our sake (Isaiah 54:15).

Though warned to cease praying, Daniel didn't stop calling on God. On the final analysis, the king commanded that Daniel be thrown into the lions' den.

Then the king commanded, and they brought Daniel, and cast him into the den of lions. Now the king spake and said unto Daniel, <u>Thy</u>

> **God whom thou servest continually, he will deliver thee** (Daniel 6: 16).

And then the Bible records, "Then the king went to his palace, and passed the night fasting: neither were instruments of musick[*] brought before him: and his sleep went from him" (6:18). The faithless Darius went home sad, starving and sleepless; while the faithful Daniel passed a peaceful night with the lions. And though the king sealed the stone to the lions' den, the King of Heaven sealed the mouths of the lions in the den. That's what happens when we exercise a courageous faith in the living God. He never puts His own to shame. He will fight the battle for us. He will do to our enemies exactly what they planned for us. Since Daniel's accusers had never been inside the lions' den, the king thought these enemies of God wouldn't be a bad company for the lions for a night. In fact, they would have more fun since their wives and children would go with them. Unfortunately, they never lived to tell of their den experiences.

> And the king commanded, and they brought those men which had accused Daniel, and they cast them into the den of lions, them, their children, and their wives; and the lions had the mastery of them, and brake all their bones in pieces or ever they came at the bottom of the den (6:24).

WOW! Those lions must be dead hungry. Remember the angel forced them to fast through the night by shutting their mouths. But then came food, enough for them to grab and grub.

[*] Music

D

16. FAITH DECLARES	64
17. FAITH DESIRES	67
18. FAITH is DILIGENT	72
19. FAITH DISCERNS	77

16
FAITH DECLARES

I love quiet people and have nothing against them as long as they're not too boring for me to relate to. I consider them blessed. But when a child of God carries his quietness to his faith and cannot declare his stand for Christ, I no longer see him as blessed but spiritually dead. At any moment in our life, people ought to know what we stand for. If people can no longer differentiate us from the world, then there's a problem.

Sure they see you go to church. You never fight, you never fornicate. Those are good qualities. But the truth is, there are unbelievers who are that morally good and do none of that stuff. People need to know to whom we belong. They need to hear us talk about our faith in Jesus. When they hear, they will be touched sooner or later.

The psalmist David said, "I will declare thy name unto my brethren: in the midst of the congregation will I praise thee" (Psalm 22:22). If we claim to have faith in Jesus, how can we keep quiet about His goodness and loving kindness? How can we be comfortable when others talk ungodly talks near us and all we do is laugh at their jokes? How can people come to us with unholy advices and rather than let them know where and for whom we stand, we gently walk away in an attempt to be at peace with all men? Your advisers of today will be your accusers of tomorrow. There's no way you can be for Jesus and be at peace with all men. Try hard as you may, some will never be at peace with you until they have a personal encounter with the Prince of Peace.

The apostles of old never kept their faith secret. They seized every opportunity they had to declare the gospel and the wonderful works of Jesus. They were jailed, beaten, stripped naked or sawn into two. Their flesh would have them quiet, but not their faith. Even in the face of death, these Jesus radicals kept on talking. They used every breath left in them to declare the Lord Jesus to a dying world.

> And the apostles and elders came together for to consider of this matter. And when there had been much disputing, Peter rose up, and said unto them, Men and brethren, ye know how that a good while ago God made choice among us, <u>that the Gentiles by my mouth hear the word of the gospel, and believe</u> (Acts 15:6, 7).

This was a Faith Declaration Rampage. God ordained Peter to declare the gospel to the Gentiles. If he had kept quiet, chances are you and I would not have had the privilege to be what we are today, sons and daughters of God. And if we choose not to declare our faith and tell others about Jesus, we shall be held accountable for the souls that pass us by and end up in hell. Don't be ashamed to be called Jesus' freak. That's the best name anyone can give you.

Apostle John was a close disciple to Jesus. He walked, talked, dined and wined with Jesus. He said, "That which was from the beginning, which we have heard, which we have seen with our eyes, which we have looked upon, and our hands have handled, of the word of life; …That which we have seen and heard <u>declare we unto you</u>, that ye also may have fellowship with us: and truly our fellowship is with the Father, and with his Son Jesus Christ. And these things write we unto you, that your joy may be full. This then is the message which we have heard of him, and declare unto you, that God is light, and in him is no darkness at all" (1 John 1:1-5).

We are to declare and just keep on declaring. Declare your salvation like the apostles did. Declare your healing like the two blind men did. After receiving their sight, Jesus warned them not to tell it to anyone. But the Bible records they left His presence and spread the news about Him in all that country (Matthew 9:27-31). Declare the glory of God like the heavens do. Never get tired of declaring so that at the end, you too may be able to say like the apostle Paul that you're innocent of the blood of all men, for you have not shunned to declare to them the whole counsel of God (Acts 20:27).

17
__FAITH DESIRES__

Desire is a longing of the heart. We desire something because we want it. Should Christians have desires? To that I answer yes. I don't see anything wrong with me having desires. But when the desire is not according to the will of God, or when I desire something that completely contradicts my faith, then it tends to sin.

The enemies of Jesus had a desire to see Him crucified. They desired that a robber be released in place of a Redeemer. To them Barabas should live and Jesus should die.

> But ye denied the Holy One and the Just, and desired a murderer to be granted unto you (Acts 3:14).

This was an evil desire and it's not the kind we want. Our desires must be based on the Word of God.

> The fear of the wicked, it shall come upon him: but the desire of the righteous shall be granted (Proverbs 10:24).

We are righteous when we stand and remain in His will. His delight is our delight. We love pleasing Him.

I love my children. I desire to see them become great in life both secularly and spiritually. I desire to see my God fearing daughters-in-law and son-in-law someday. I tell my children at least once a day that I love them because I desire for them to know that I do. But when they disobey and go against my wish, I get mad at them. I desire to see my children do my will. That's exactly how God wants us to be to Him.

> Delight thyself also in the LORD: and he shall give thee the desires of thine heart (Psalm 37:4).

To delight in the Lord is to make His will our will and obey Him in all things. We hate what He hates and love what He loves. We make His Word a lamp onto our feet and a light onto our paths (Psalm 119:105). We hide His Word in our hearts so we do not sin against Him (Psalm 119:11). We believe and trust Him all the way. As we do that, He grants our hearts' desires.

> The law of the LORD is perfect, converting the soul: the testimony of the LORD is sure, making wise the simple ... More to be desired are they than gold, yea, than much fine gold: sweeter also than honey and the honeycomb. Moreover by them is thy servant warned: and in keeping of them there is great reward (Psalm 19:7-11).

We all know how precious gold is. We place great value on it. I don't mind to have gold. David was however saying I should have a greater desire for things of the Lord than for gold. Gold can perish, wealth can be exhausted. But the Word of God is forever and ever. David knew the best thing to desire.

> One thing have I desired of the LORD, that will I seek after; that I may dwell in the house of the LORD all the days of my life, to behold the beauty of the LORD, and to enquire in his temple (Psalm 27:4).

This is the best desire anyone can and should have in life. The love of the Lord should consume us to that extent we forget to desire things of this world. There are people who desire to dwell in the house of gambling and pornography all the days of their life. Well I don't wish and don't pray to be like them. Whether I'm eating or exercising, drinking or driving, all I want is to think of my Lord and Him crucified. To continuously imagine what heaven will be like and know that one day I'll be in the multitude of people singing hallelujah forever and ever. Awesome!

Peter admonished us to desire the Word of God just the way a new born desires the pure milk, for that's the only way we can grow. He called on the Corinthian believers to desire spiritual gifts. That was not for them only, it is for us today as well. We must pursue spiritual gifts with all our hearts. They help us in times of weakness. When the foundation of a house is solid and firm, it will help it to stand in time of storm. It's the same thing with our soul. When we feed our souls with the correct stuff, they shall remain with us when all else fails, and will render the wrong stuff of no value to us.

The moment you begin to have a greater desire for things below and loose desire for things above, that's a signal that the temperature of your faith needs checking. Get your 'spiritometer' and see what your spiritual temperature reads, for you may already be going down in the Spirit.

Some preachers have lost their anointing long time ago. Sure they still preach and people's lives are changed, but they're no longer operating in the Spirit. They have strayed from the will of God. What do you think happened to Adam and Eve in the garden? Their desire changed from the Father to the fruit, from their God to the garden.

> And when the woman saw that the tree was good for food, and that it was pleasant to the eyes, and <u>a tree to be desired</u> to make one wise, she took of the fruit thereof, and did eat, and gave also unto her husband with her; and he did eat (Genesis 3:6).

It was their desire that led to their fall.

Judas never ceased to be Jesus' disciple. But as at the time he ate and drank with Jesus, he was no longer a faithful follower. He was no longer loyal. His desire had changed from following to forsaking, from serving Him to selling Him. Because of a covetous desire, He made the worth of a slave out of a Savior. Does that mean we don't desire anything here below? No. But such must not be at the expense of our faith.

Desire can also be applied to our expectations from God. Many people in the Bible desired one thing or the other and that desire drove them to the Lord, the only One who can satisfy our desires.

The woman with the issue of blood desired healing. It was her desire that made her touch the hem of Jesus' garment. Her desire was granted. She was made whole that instant.

Abraham desired a child. The Lord granted his desire and gave him Isaac.

Hannah desired a son. The Lord gave her prophet Samuel.

The woman of Canaan (Matthew 15:21-28) desired deliverance for her demon-possessed daughter. She refused to leave the presence of Jesus until she got what she desired.

Therefore I say unto you, what things soever ye desire, when ye pray, believe that ye receive them, and ye shall have them (Mark 11:24).

Desire serves as our spiritual propeller. It drives us to action and eventually leads to our receiving. Back in Columbus, Ohio, we attended a very vibrant church, the Christian Assembly. And I remember a story our pastor had told a few times about his vision for people from other nations. He had always desired that God give him the opportunity to minister to people from other parts of the world. At the same time, he had to stay and pastor the church that had been handed over to him. In a situation like this, what could a man of God do? Well, he put his faith in God and trusted that though he may not be able to go to nations, God, in His infinite wisdom, would bring nations to him. Years after the vision, when it seemed the dream would never come true, the faithful Jehovah started sending people from all races to Christian Assembly, of which we are a living proof. Though Pastor Sam Farina could not go preaching to nations; God granted his desire and gave him an opportunity to preach to people of different cultures and ethnic backgrounds, all under one roof.

There's nothing wrong with having desires, so long they glorify God and we don't allow them to take His love from our hearts. God saw my pastor's desire and gave him an opportunity to preach to nations by bringing nations to him. The Bible says, "Behold, thou shalt call a nation that thou knowest not, and nations that knew not thee shall run unto thee because of the LORD thy God, and for the Holy One of Israel; for he hath glorified thee" (Isaiah 55:5). Today, Christian Assembly is a Church of All Nations. (Hey, that won't be a bad name for the church. Just kidding.)

18
FAITH is DILIGENT

Diligence is having a faithful and committed approach to one's vocation, conviction or belief. It's the quality of a hardworking character. There's a determination to have a good result. He keeps his heart with all diligence because he knows that out of it are the issues of life (Proverbs 4:23). There's a craving from the heart, not the head, for a successful outcome. He does not interpret patience in adversity to mean complacency in poverty. He puts his body and soul into whatever he does because he hates to fail. He does it as if without it he can't survive. He loves being caught doing it because it earns him a good name. As believers, we're to apply the same principle to our faith.

Faith is not something we possess just for the sake of having it. It's not a table decoration for the display of its beauty. We must have a purposeful commitment towards it. We must use it to achieve a glorious end after our journey here is ended. Our service unto God must consume us to that extent people will nickname us for our spiritual efficiency.

When we go to College, we put in all our efforts and work with all diligence because we desire good grades. I've been through it. Talk of sleepless nights and foodless days. Why? I wanted to make good grades. It paid off for me. If I had such diligence towards a degree I had hardly used since then, how much more should I be diligent with my faith that will last eternity?

I have great respect for American firefighters. There's something about their job that goes beyond salary. They do it with all their heart. To them, to live is to save and to die is heroic. I only pray they all come to the knowledge of Christ; because I love to see them in heaven, where they can finally rest from all their labors, for then there will be no more fires to put out. If people can be this diligent with secular job, we of the faith should be much more with things of the Spirit.

When we set our hearts on success, there will be a moving force that pushes us towards achieving our goal. Jesus told the parable of the lost coin.

> Either what woman having ten pieces of silver, if she lose one piece, doth not light a candle, and sweep the house, and seek diligently till she find it? And when she hath found it, she calleth her friends and her neighbours together, saying, Rejoice with me; for I have found the piece which I had lost (Luke 15:8-9).

This woman searched for the lost coin as if without it, she would not be able to survive. I learnt a lot from my children when they were babies. At the crawling stage, there was that sense of curiosity in them. They wanted to grab every toy. When they spotted an attractive toy, they put in so much effort to get it by all means. They stretched, they cried, they rested and then continued. To them, the toy was worth the trouble. Isn't your faith worth putting all your life into it?

> But without faith it is impossible to please him: for he that cometh to God must believe that he is, and that he is a rewarder of them that diligently seek him (Hebrews 11:6).

We're to diligently seek the Lord. Diligently seeking Him is not the same thing as searching for a home to buy or a car to finance. Seeking Him does not come with promises of beds of roses here on earth. But it has an eternal value of walking the streets of gold in heaven, if we do not look back. It's a commitment worth making.

> Wherefore the rather, brethren, give diligence to make your calling and election sure: for if ye do these things, ye shall never

fall (2 Peter 1:10).

What will I do with this temporal world when an everlasting kingdom with my Lord is awaiting me? Though there will be persecutions from within and without, but the goal is worth the going.

When athletes compete in a race, there's a determination to finish the race at all costs. Not that they don't get tired, but they want to reach the finish line. They put their hearts into it. What have we got to loose? Nothing. Should it even matter if we loose all for the kingdom? What did Christ have left when He hung on the cross? Yet He was diligent all through. The Bible says, "And in the morning, rising up a great while before day, he went out, and departed into a solitary place, and there prayed. And Simon and they that were with him followed after him. And when they had found him, they said unto him, All men seek for thee. And he said unto them, Let us go into the next towns, that I may preach there also: for therefore came I forth" (Mark 1:35-38). His heart was in the preaching for which purpose He came.

What's the purpose of my faith if all I do is sleep and wake up and protect my treasured trash? What did Paul have left after his death? Nothing.

> But what things were gain to me, those I counted loss for Christ. Yea doubtless, and I count all things but loss for the excellency of the knowledge of Christ Jesus my Lord: for whom I have suffered the loss of all things, and do count them but dung*, that I may win Christ (Philippians 3:7-8).

For the sake of the kingdom, he and the other disciples lost everything, except their works of faith and the souls that had been saved through their diligent preaching.

When you depart this world, what will you leave behind? Your spiritual diligence or spiritual negligence? What are you passing on to your children, spiritual legacy or spiritual fallacy?

> And these words, which I command thee this day, shall be in thine heart: And thou shalt teach them diligently unto thy children, and shalt talk of them when thou sittest in thine house, and when thou walkest by the way, and when thou liest down, and when thou risest up (Deuteronomy 6:6-7).

How will your children remember your faith after you, as spiritually worked-out or as a spiritual wreck?

Ruth was a diligent character. When she followed her mother-in-law to a foreign land, she never thought the Savior of the world would come through her lineage. Her diligence did not begin in Judah. She had it right from the time they were in Moab. She was married for better and for worse. To her, the death of a husband was not enough reason to forsake a mother-in-law. She took 'till death do us part' a step further than ordered. It was that same diligent spirit she carried with her to Judah. When she went to work in the barley fields, the Bible records she did so from morning till evening, with a little rest (Ruth 2:7). Her heart, her hand and her head all worked together. The Lord rewarded her diligent faith and brought a respectable character into her life. She got married to wealthy Boaz, a relative of her dead father-in-law. They both gave birth to Obed. And through that lineage came the Lord Jesus (Matthew 1). What else could she have in return? Her diligence paid off. She had a reward both here and in eternity. Don't get jealous when you hear Jesus call her 'granny' in heaven. Remember she diligently worked for it. She chose not to be bitter inspite of her loss.

Pastors, how diligent are your members? You wonder how can you know? Well, it's not the number of offices we hold in the church that determines our commitment. Give the devil a chance, he will be more than happy to run all the offices his own way. But out of your one thousand plus members that show up Spirit-filled and hands lifting on Sunday, how many of them come to mid-week services? Or better still, how many would show up for Bible study on a cold winter night? Anybody can go to church on a bright Sunday morning. But the devil knows that the best time to discourage any committed believer is during the mid-week.

To leave the office and rush home, quickly get something ready for the night. Get the children ready, as the case is for some of us. Get on the busy road in the heavy rain and cold wind, and head to church for Bible study. Get back home by 9 p.m; rush something down the throat and get the children to bed, some of them already asleep in the car. By the time you eventually hit the bed, you have little or no strength left in you for the following day.

It takes a diligent heart to have a committed faith. Faith is not an issue of convenience, but a matter of commitment. God will not accept any excuses for our lack of diligence. Just as the apostles of old signed off their lives for the work, so does God expect of each believer. In fire, rain, snow, or sunshine, their love of the kingdom superceded them all. Nothing and absolutely nothing would hold them back. Not even their health as we see in Paul's case. You too can be diligent. Give your heart to the commitment. Remember, we shall never loose the reward of our faith, if we faint not.

*Waste

19
FAITH DISCERNS

Discernment is the spiritual ability to differentiate between spirits operating by the power of God and those that appear to be of God but are not. Many times I come in contact with people and right away, I feel repelled by their spirit. My spirit negates theirs. At such times, it's better to pray in the Spirit and ask for Holy wisdom.

Discernment is very scriptural and the Bible clearly warns us not to believe every spirit that professes to be of God.

> Beloved, believe not every spirit, but try the spirits whether they are of God: because many false prophets are gone out into the world. Hereby know ye the Spirit of God: Every spirit that confesseth that Jesus Christ is come in the flesh is of God: And every spirit that confesseth not that Jesus Christ is come in the flesh is not of God: and this is that spirit of antichrist, whereof ye have heard that it should come; and even now already is it in the world. Ye are of God, little children, and have overcome them: because greater is he that is in you, than he that is in the world.... Hereby know we the spirit of truth, and the spirit of error (1 John 4:1-6).

It's not always the case that we can know every spirit by mere feelings. That's why we need faith in God to lead and enable us to discern good and evil spirits. Not everyone has it, but anyone can ask for it. Just like speaking in tongues; not all speak in tongues, but anyone can pray for the gift.

> Now there are diversities of gifts, but the same Spirit. And there are differences of administrations, but the same Lord. And there are diversities of operations, but it is the same God which worketh all in

all ....To another prophecy; <u>to another discerning of spirits;</u> to another divers kinds of tongues; to another the interpretation of tongues: But all these worketh that one and the selfsame Spirit, dividing to every man severally as he will (1 Corinthians 12:4-11).

God has given these gifts–one of which is discernment–to us for the edification of His body. Discernment can be used in any situation and anywhere where spirits operate. As children of God and people of faith, ours is to be sensitive to His promptings in our hearts and remember that not all that come to us in the name of God are of God.

There are times it may not be this straight forward. Some may appear to be of God. We need to grow up to a stage that when such black appears white, we can still tell the difference and sense something wrong. The writer of Hebrews says, "Strong meat belongeth to them that are full of age, even those who by reason of use have their senses exercised to <u>discern</u> both good and evil" (Heb. 5:14).

I talked earlier about the encounter of Paul at Philippi with a girl who had the spirit of fortune telling and used it to bring her masters money (Acts 16:16-18). The girl called them servants of the Most High God. How sweet. But Paul, by the power of the Holy Spirit discerned that that which spoke in her was not of God but of the devil. In his letter to the Corinthians he said, "For what man knoweth the things of a man, save the spirit of man which is in him? even so the things of God knoweth no man, but the Spirit of God.... But the natural man receiveth not the things of the Spirit of God: for they are foolishness unto him: neither can he know them, because they are spiritually discerned" (1 Corinthians 2:11-14). If Paul were not in the faith, he would not have discerned the evil spirit in that girl. The term 'Most High God' was enough to fool him.

Spiritual discernment is a precious gift that all should seek to have. If you don't have it, pray for it. Remember God gives to all who ask in faith.

E

20. FAITH EDIFIES	81
21. FAITH ENCOURAGES	85
22. FAITH ENDURES	88
23. FAITH EXPECTS	91

20
FAITH EDIFIES

To edify is to build another person up, either morally or spiritually. The words we speak can have a great impact on a person's life. They either make or break; heal or kill; edify or petrify; build up or tear down.

As people of God, the words of our mouth should edify others, not destroy them in any way. Whether we're admonishing or just discussing, we need to be careful what words and expressions we use. What people hear us say go a long way to determine how they see us and think about us. I don't believe in first impresssion. It can always be wrong. But at the same time, there are some words I don't expect a true child of God to utter. True we're not to be selfishly separate, but we need to be wisely friendly. Foolish jestings or fables are not of the Spirit of God.

> As I besought thee to abide still at Ephesus, when I went into Macedonia, that thou mightest charge some that they teach no other doctrine, Neither give heed to fables and endless genealogies, which minister questions, rather than godly edifying which is in faith: so do (1 Timothy 1:3-4).

Some things are more important than others. When a preacher mounts the pulpit to discharge the Word of God, telling about old fables or jokes that contradict the true word will be totally out of order. People will end up confused than convinced.

What are some of the ways faith can edify.

a. Spiritual edification comes through the spoken word. Preachers don't mount the pulpit for show off. It is to discharge the undiluted Word of God. But in the process of preaching, people's needs are met–spiritual, physical, material and emotional. When people receive breakthroughs, they're lifted in the Spirit, thus edified. The words that come out will have a new, deeper and better meaning to them. If people come to church and go home the same, it signals lack of spiritual edification.

People need signs and wonders to enhance their beliefs. Not that they're doubtful of what God can do. But at the same time, it serves as an encouragement when they receive answers to prayers. A faithless mind cannot edify another faithless mind. It takes one with sight to lead the blind. When the blind leads the blind, they both fall into the ditch. A faithless preacher will only preach a powerless message. And a powerless message can never edify a weak soul.

The spoken word can also come through a friend. August 2000 was one of the most horrible times of our lives together as husband and wife. It was a tough period. Something happened that kept me shedding tears. But on Sunday August 6, 2000 as I relayed the incident to Sandra Gist, one of my sisters in the Lord, she didn't see any cause for alarm. She made just one statement: "If God has gone this far with you, He won't back out." She went straight into her car and took off.

I had never thought of God that way in my life. I know He's a faithful God. It just never occurred to me that He's not a God who backs out halfway. Whatever He starts, He finishes. That has been my anchor since then. It lifted my Spirit then, it still does up till now. Speak the word that others may be edified.

<u>b</u>. Prophecy is another channel of spiritual edification. When the Word of God comes out in form of prophecy, it's usually for the church as a body or for a person as an individual. But The Bible warns against prophesying in tongues without interpretation.

> Follow after charity, and desire spiritual gifts, but rather that ye may prophesy. For he that speaketh in an unknown tongue speaketh not unto men, but unto God: for no man understandeth him; howbeit in the spirit he speaketh mysteries. But he that prophesieth speaketh unto men to edification, and exhortation, and comfort. He that speaketh in an unknown tongue edifieth himself; but he that prophesieth edifieth the church. I would that ye all spake with tongues but rather that ye prophesied: for greater is he that prophesieth than he that speaketh with tongues, except he interpret, that the church may receive edifying (1 Corinthians 14:1-5).

Paul wasn't saying we couldn't speak in tongues. But for the purpose of edifying that brother or sister, he or she has got to understand what is being said. Tongues without interpretation will not edify someone who doesn't understand the language. But if there's an interpreter, then it edifies. That was why Paul said he who prophesies is greater than he who speaks in tongues without interpretation.

It will be necessary to mention that a fake and false prophecy is totally abhorred by the Lord Almighty. Saying, "Thus says the Lord," when the Lord has not said is a lie.

> I have not sent these prophets, yet they ran: I have not spoken to them, yet they prophesied. How long shall this be in the heart of the prophets that prophesy lies? yea, they are prophets of the deceit of their own heart (Jeremiah 23:21, 26).

If God has not sent you, do not say He has, for that makes you a liar.

c. The third channel of edification is through our interaction with others. As I said earlier, our conduct goes a long way to impact those around us, either for good or bad. Bad character doesn't edify. You don't win an unbeliever to the faith by stealing, fighting, fornicating or lying. It is good conduct and upright behavior that people are attracted to.

I know of people who never witnessed to me before I came to know the Lord. But I always knew there was something about their lives that was different from mine and I wished I could be like them. Today, I'm happy to belong to their fold. Imagine what the story would be if their lives had been the exact opposite of what I saw. Chances were I might never come to know the truth because their character would stand as a hindrance to my conviction and conversion.

The Bible says, "In all things shewing thyself a pattern of good works: in doctrine shewing uncorruptness, gravity, sincerity, Sound speech, that cannot be condemned; that he that is of the contrary part may be ashamed, having no evil thing to say of you" (Titus 2:7-8).

I have a prayer on the first page of my Bible. It reads:
"OH LORD, MY GOD, I PRAY THEE THIS DAY AND ALWAYS, THAT AS MANY AS GET TO KNOW ME WOULD DESIRE TO KNOW YOU. MAY MY LIFE NEVER BE A HINDRANCE TO THE HEAVEN OF ANOTHER. IN JESUS' NAME I PRAY. AMEN"

I hope that you make this your prayer too, so people who come across you may always be edified than petrified.

21
FAITH ENCOURAGES

We all have times in our lives when things don't work out the way we want and our faith seems too weak to carry us. Not that the faith is lost, but it feels like it's not there anymore. At such times, encouragement from others can go a long way to uphold. When one is weak, the faith of the strong should step in and say, I'm praying for you. That feels good to the ear and the soul. When you realize somebody is praying for you, you know you're not alone.

When David had problems with Saul, Jonathan (Saul's son) was an encouragement to him throughout. Saul had sought to kill David, to which Jonathan was greatly opposed. Jonathan had the Spirit of God and he knew his father's motive was wrong. He deliberately stood by David, against his father's wish

> And David abode in the wilderness in strong holds, and remained in a mountain in the wilderness of Ziph. And Saul sought him every day, but God delivered him not into his hand.... And Jonathan Saul's son arose, and went to David into the wood, and strengthened his hand in God. And he said unto him, Fear not: for the hand of Saul my father shall not find thee; and thou shalt be king over Israel, and I shall be next unto thee; and that also Saul my father knoweth. And they two made a covenant before the LORD: and David abode in the wood, and Jonathan went to his house (1 Samuel 23:14-18).

This was a tense period for David. If he had been left alone in this ordeal, it would have been harder on him.

When we encourage others, it does something in their lives. It soothes the hurting spot. As people of faith, it's our duty to be there for our brothers and sisters who are hurting. They need our encouragement. They need to hear us say, 'all will be well.' A mind void of faith cannot utter those words. You have to be able to encourage yourself before you can encourage others. It takes faith to know that there shall be peace after persecution.

Even when in the midst of others and there's a problem, let's take the initiative to encourage them. When Paul was on board the ship that was taking him to Rome, a tempest arose. He had earlier warned that they should not go on that journey. They did not listen. This did not make Paul loose his faith for encouragement in the midst of the sea. Though they had lost all hope for survival; yet Paul stood up in their midst to bring calmness to their disturbed minds (Acts 27:21-25).

There may be times we find ourselves where we never wanted or planned to be, due to the fault and the disobedience of others. Heaping blames may not be the wise thing to do, for you may be adding fuel to fire. Instead, first encourage yourself with the promises of God, and then encourage those who brought you into that situation. I believe Paul must have sought God's face in the midst of that trouble. That was why he was able to see and hear what they could not.

When disaster surfaces, what do you do? Do you panic or do you pray? Do you encourage or discourage? Do you strengthen the weak or weaken the strong?

> Strengthen ye the weak hands, and confirm the feeble knees. <u>Say to them that are of a fearful heart,</u> Be strong, fear not: behold, your God will come with vengeance, even God with a recompence; he will come and save you (Isaiah 35:3-4).

This was done in the practical sense when the Israelites fought with the Amalekites. For as long as Moses stood on top of the hill with his hands up and the rod in his hand, the victory continued. When his hands got weak, Aaron and Hur each held Moses' hands. The victory was accomplished because these two men strengthened the weak hands of Moses.

Christians, when others are weak in the spirit, let's receive the challenge to strengthen them with words of encouragement. We are to be spiritual Aarons and Hurs. When our fellow brother's spiritual hands are getting weak, we who are still strong in the Spirit should be ready to serve as their supports. Let's tell them it's okay to call when they need a hand, for at one time or the other, we will all need somebody to lean on. And together we shall be victorious in our spiritual battles.

22
FAITH ENDURES

To endure is to bear pain. Not that the pain is not felt; but for a greater vision ahead, the pain is rather tolerated than given up.

By faith Moses, when he was come to years, refused to be called the son of Pharaoh's daughter; Choosing rather to suffer affliction with the people of God, than to enjoy the pleasures of sin for a season; Esteeming the reproach of Christ greater riches than the treasures in Egypt: for he had respect unto the recompence of the reward. By faith he forsook Egypt, not fearing the wrath of the king: for he endured, as seeing him who is invisible (Hebrews 11:24-27).

Moses grew up in the palace of Pharaoh and was numbered amongst his children. He later realized that he was not an Egyptian. He was in fact the same tribe as the people that were being used as slaves. One would have thought that Moses would keep quiet and continue to enjoy the lavish pleasures of the palace. Oh no. He instead chose to identify with pain than pleasure.

After killing an Egyptian because of a Hebrew, Moses fled to Midian. From there God later called him to go and deliver the Israelites out of bondage in Egypt. That was a hard task for him. They pushed him to the extreme of his patience. They got him angry and hindered him from entering the Promised Land. But he endured all through.

How about Job? Job was a man of like nature with any man on earth today. One thing however stood out in his life that makes him different from any ordinary man–he was a man of many afflictions, who in it all never said anything against his God. Job had an enduring faith in God. He suffered the fire of affliction but came forth as gold.

> Behold, I go forward, but he is not there; and backward, but I cannot perceive him: On the left hand, where he doth work, but I cannot behold him: he hideth himself on the right hand, that I cannot see him: But he knoweth the way that I take: when he hath tried me, I shall come forth as gold (Job 23:8–10).

Yes, that is faith; the kind of faith that would rather focus on the Savior than the situation.

If you consider the succession of the terrible events in Job's life (Job 1:13-19), there was no time for him to get over one bad news before another one came. As one messenger left, another messenger came. What greater evil could befall a man in a day? His whole life was gone in a matter of hours or may be minutes. One would think he would say things against the God that had earlier boasted of him (Job 1:8). But instead Job said, "Naked came I out of my mother's womb, and naked shall I return thither: the LORD gave, and the LORD hath taken away; blessed be the name of the LORD. In all this Job sinned not, nor charged God foolishly" (Job 1:21-22). "Blessed be the name of the Lord" who did not prevent these evils?

An ordinary heart cannot say this. It will take an enduring faith to say these words in the face of terrible events in the life of an individual. Talk of a man who can have peace in the midst of tribulation, Job was. Though his problem did not end here, there's no record of him ever loosing faith in God or sinning with his lips, not once. He instead saw everything as adversity, nothing evil and definitely not enough to charge the Almighty. He even encouraged himself with words of faith.

> Oh that my words were now written! oh that they were printed in a book! That they were graven with an iron pen and lead in the rock

for ever! For I know that my redeemer liveth, and that he shall stand at the latter day upon the earth: And though after my skin worms destroy this body, yet in my flesh shall I see God: Whom I shall see for myself, and mine eyes shall behold, and not another; though my reins be consumed within me (Job 19:23-27).

Job held on to his faith. He endured as one that had hope for a better future and a better future he got.

Children of God, let us hold on to our faith in God. If we endure temptation; we shall be victorious at last. Apostle James said, "Blessed is the man that endureth temptation: for when he is tried, he shall receive the crown of life, which the Lord hath promised to them that love him" (James 1:12).

If truly we believe in Jesus, then we have to be like Him. We have to endure. There's nothing like 'thorns-free rose garden' salvation. Jesus said, "These things I have spoken unto you, that in me ye might have peace. In the world ye shall have tribulation: but be of good cheer; I have overcome the world" (John 16:33). To be of good cheer in the midst of tribulation is better read than realized. When we come face-to-face with trials and tribulations, will our faith still hold on? The only reason we can boast of our salvation is because Jesus endured the cross. My prayer is that the Lord will bestow upon each of us the grace to endure.

23
<u>FAITH EXPECTS</u>

Desire and expectation seem to be saying the same thing but actually are not the same. It's our desires that give birth to our expectations.

Hannah desired a child because she wanted to have her own. But when she prayed to the Lord at the altar, she had an expectation that God would grant her wish and open her barren womb to conception. My children have different desires, brand name shoes and clothes. These are their wants. But they have one expectation; that mom and dad would provide and meet those needs. We have control over their expectations, but we cannot control their desires. It's okay for them to have as many desires as they want. But they cannot force us to always live up to their expectations.

Is it a sin for a child of God to expect from Him? I say a big NO to that. It is absolutely right for believers, men and women of faith to expect from the Lord, the source of our provision. If we don't expect from God, from whom are we to expect? No passage in the Scripture goes against expecting from Daddy. We all have expected ends at one time or the other in our journey of faith. It's His delight when we expect from Him, for that tells Him we have accepted our insufficiency.

> For I know the thoughts that I think toward you, saith the Lord, thoughts of peace, and not of evil, to give you an expected end (Jeremiah 29:11).

In many miracles in the Bible, we read different accounts of people that came or sent to Jesus for different purposes, some because of barrenness, some for healing. Though their desires were different, their expectation was the same; that Jesus would put an end to whatever they were going through.

When Mary and Martha sent to Jesus, it was because they desired healing for their brother, Lazarus.

> Now a certain man was sick, named Lazarus, of Bethany, the town of Mary and her sister Martha. (It was that Mary which anointed the Lord with ointment, and wiped his feet with her hair, whose brother Lazarus was sick.) Therefore his sisters sent unto him, saying, Lord, behold, he whom thou lovest is sick (John 11:1-3).

But they expected that once Jesus heard the message, he would come and lay hand on their brother and he would be healed. That was their level of expectation. They knew Jesus very well and they had faith in Him. Our Lord has manifold ways of showing His power, to the glory of God the Father. One thing however is sure: when we come to Jesus expecting, we will get results. And though He may delay, He will not deny.

Jesus did not go right away. He waited till the fourth day by which time Lazarus was already stinking dead. However, the Lord would not put them to shame. In life or death, their expectation would be met.

As Mary and Martha mourned the death of their brother, the Lord over death showed up. Both sisters were disappointed. They thought it was all over for their brother. They thought their expectation had been shattered. They knew as much as you and I know. When the going is good, we shout for joy. When we don't receive immediate answer, we lose hope and find somebody to blame, most of the time God. We turn round and accuse the Giver of life. We feel spiritually let down. And instead of listening to the still small voice, we analyze the shortcomings of the Holy Spirit. Faith like a grain of mustard seed moving a mountain becomes completely senseless and unrealistic. And before we say forgive me Lord, we feel He might as well just forget it. That is our flesh at war with our faith.

Faith Expects

Dear reader, I don't know that for which you have put your expectation in the Lord Jesus. But one thing I know; though He may tarry, yet He will not fail. At the most appropriate and appointed time, God will show up to give life to the dead situations of your life. He who restored life to the dead body of Lazarus will visit every dead thing in your life. You just keep on expecting. He knows about it already.

Abraham expected a son from God. The child didn't come until twenty-five years after God had assured him he was going to have a son. If only Abraham were alive today, he would have told the story best. All we can do is read and explain. He never stopped expecting and he never lost faith. He held on to God's promise until he got his heart's desire. We too must not be discouraged.

Don't ever feel guilty for expecting from God. As long as your expectation is in line with His word, you're in order. Do what Mary and Martha did. They knew the right person to send to. They sent to the one whom death could not hold captive, for even in the grave, Jesus is Lord. He did not fail them. Their expectation was not dampened. Don't give up until you have been given. Be a Syrophenician in Spirit. Expect a miracle, expect healing, expect promotion; but more than any other thing, expect the Lord's return.

F

24. FAITH is FAITHFUL	95
25. FAITH FEARS GOD	99
26. FAITH FELLOWSHIPS	103
27. FAITH is FIRM	106
28. FAITH FORGIVES	109

24
FAITH is FAITHFUL

The dictionary defines faithfulness as a continued and steadfast adherence to a person or thing, to which one is bound by an oath, duty or obligation.

When we accept Jesus into our lives, a level of obligation is binding upon us. We have a duty to perform and that is to remain completely faithful to Him to the end, even if it means loosing our lives. Faithfulness to God is not an act of the head, but an attitude of the heart. We can never succeed if we try to do it in our own understanding, for that will only end in a fatal mess.

Faithfulness is a vocation for which you first pay, before you can be paid and it costs a lifetime to pay for it. Whether Christ returns soon or late has nothing to do it. We perform our faith duties as if He will return this very moment. Though no one is watching; we realize the Utmost watches over us, including our faithfulness and unfaithfulness. We cannot hide from Him.

Wherefore, holy brethren, partakers of the heavenly calling <u>consider the Apostle and High Priest of our profession, Christ Jesus; Who was faithful to him that appointed him,</u> as also Moses was faithful in all his house (Hebrews 3:1-2).

If Christ were faithful, what reasons have we to be unfaithful? If we claim to belong to Him, then we must act like Him in all things. Temptations are sure to come our way. That's not an excuse for us. The Bible says, He "was in all points tempted like as we are, yet without sin" (Hebrews 4:15).

In Matthew, the Bible gives a good example of what a faithful and wise servant is.

Who then is a faithful and wise servant, whom his lord hath made ruler over his household, to give them meat in due season? Blessed is that servant, whom his lord when he cometh shall find so doing. Verily I say unto you, That he shall make him ruler over all his goods. But and if that evil servant shall say in his heart, My lord delayeth his coming; And shall begin to smite his fellowservants, and to eat and drink with the drunken; The lord of that servant shall come in a day when he looketh not for him, and in an hour that he is not aware of, And shall cut him asunder, and appoint him his portion with the hypocrites: there shall be weeping and gnashing of teeth (Matthew 24:45-51).

God has made us rulers over His household. He has made us overseers and ministers of the gospel over those who don't know Him as Lord and Savior. We're to give them meat by preaching the word to them, telling them about the love of Jesus. We're to shine the light of the gospel to their dark world of fornication, evil practices and immorality. We're ministers of the word, a duty we are bound to perform. We must not be like the evil servant who expected his master's return and gave up after sometime. He who gives up the work of the Master will end up with the wrath of the Father.

Of the eleven disciples that outlived our Lord, only one of them died a natural death. The others were either sawn in two, beheaded or crucified head down. These things didn't come to them unawares. They knew they were in for impending dangers. But that was not enough to make them forsake their faithfulness to Christ and the preaching of the word. They preached till they were silenced. John, the only disciple that died a natural death, died an exile on the Island of Patmos.

Paul and Silas became Christ's disciples after His ascension. The moment they accepted Christ as their Lord, they signed off their lives for His work. If anyone had any reason to be unfaithful, Paul did. Jesus received thirty-nine stripes once, Paul received it five times. He was beaten with a rod, he was stoned, he was put in jail, he was shipwrecked. Uncountable sleepless nights, many days of forced fasting, several days of nakedness in the cold. But hear what brother Paul said: "Beside those things that are without, that which cometh upon me daily, the care of all the churches" (2 Cor. 11:28).

Take a moment and picture yourself going through all the things this faithful man of God went through. Then ask yourself a question, 'if I were in his shoes, would I still be found faithful to the calling?' This man was in real problem, a real torture to his flesh. Yet, he wasn't concerned about himself. Instead, he was deeply concerned for the church. In fact, he had a form of sickness that we're not clear about.

> And lest I should be exalted above measure through the abundance of the revelations, there was given to me a thorn in the flesh, the messenger of Satan to buffet me, lest I should be exalted above measure (2 Corinthians 12:7).

Lest he should be exalted in the midst of all these torments? Lest he should be exalted for being imprisoned? Lest he should be exalted for suffering for the gospel sake? Yes! Lest he should be exalted, because to him, suffering for Christ was an honor. Instead of seeing the thorn in the flesh as a humiliation, he saw it as a form of humility being forced upon him. Paul would not give up the Master's work for anything, not even for his dear life. The work was dearer to him than the world.

Such was Noah's faithfulness. In the midst of uncertainties, Noah remained faithful to the God who gave him instructions. When God asked him to build the ark, there was no sign of rain falling anytime soon. But he faithfully obeyed. Even in the construction of the ark, Noah was faithful to the last inch and cubits–three hundred cubits long, fifty cubits wide, thirty cubits high; lower, second and third decks, to be finished with a cubit above water. I wonder what kind of tape he used to get the measurements. But the Bible says, "Thus did Noah; according to all that God commanded him, so did he" (Genesis 6:22). No arguments, no thinking over. God said it, he believed it and that settled it. No wonder the Bible calls him a just and perfect man. The perfection has to do with his faithfulness, not his thoughtfulness, for no one is thoughtfully perfect.

How faithful are you, whether in big or little things? How faithful are you with your tithes and offering, commitments and vows? If God were to rate your faithfulness on a scale of 1-10, what would you get? Or better still, if you were to rate yourself, how faithful would you be? The same thing applies to me. How faithful am I in the things of God? Does God see my faithfulness the way I see it? Can the Lord depend on me when it comes to faithfulness?

Brethren, let's aspire to be counted faithful. Our difficult situations are only temporal (2 Corinthians 4:16-18). No matter how long we stay on earth, we shall stay much longer in eternity. When we press on and press forward, and overlook all distractions on the wayside, a crown of righteousness awaits us. May we be found faithful and worthy to receive it in Jesus' name. Amen.

25
FAITH FEARS GOD

Before we go into the details of the fear of God, let us consider fear in the physical realm. My little girl prefers that someone is awake to watch her anytime she needs to use the bathroom in the night. She hates to go all by herself. There's only one explanation I can give for her action. She's afraid and fears being alone in the middle of the night. Though the light is on, she still doesn't want to stay all by herself.

Naturally as human beings–faith or no faith–we all experience fear at one time or the other in our individual lives. Abraham, the father of faith is a typical example.

And Abraham journeyed from thence toward the south country, …and sojourned in Gerar. And Abraham said of Sarah his wife, She is my sister: and Abimelech king of Gerar sent, and took Sarah. But God came to Abimelech in a dream by night, and said to him, Behold, thou art but a dead man, for the woman which thou hast taken; for she is a man's wife. …Then Abimelech called Abraham and said unto him, What hast thou done unto us? and what have I offended thee, that thou hast brought on me and on my kingdom a great sin? … **And Abraham said, Because I thought, Surely the fear of God is not in this place; and they will slay me for my wife's sake** (Genesis 20:1-11).

Let's be honest, there's no one free from fear. While it will be wrong to justify Abraham's action for lying, we have to remember he was still as human as any of us living today. This was the same Abraham that God called to get out of his country and go to a land that He the Lord would show him. Though he did not know where he was going, he obeyed without questioning.

It was the same Abraham who by faith held on to God's promise of a child for twenty-five years. And it was still the same Abraham God asked to go and sacrifice his only son Isaac and without any hesitation obeyed.

In the above passage, the fear of what Abimelech would do to him shook his faith. Not that he lost his faith in God, but his faith gave in for fear of death. The fear of God is however different from this.

After the birth of Isaac, the long awaited promised child, God called Abraham and asked him to go and sacrifice him. He went on a three-day journey to go and offer his own son. Just as he was about to lay his hand on the boy, with the knife in his hand, he heard a voice.

> And they came to the place which God had told him of; and Abraham built an altar there, and laid the wood in order, and bound Isaac his son, and laid him on the altar upon the wood. And Abraham stretched forth his hand, and took the knife to slay his son. And the angel of the LORD called unto him out of heaven, and said, Abraham, Abraham: and he said, Here am I. And he said, Lay not thine hand upon the lad, neither do thou any thing unto him: <u>for now I know that thou fearest God,</u> seeing thou hast not withheld thy son, thine only son from me (Genesis 22:9-12).

This was not the same fear he had towards Abimelech. This was an awe of God's greatness and power. Though he didn't understand what God was doing, yet he obeyed Him because he feared Him, the One who gave him the son in the first place. He knew it would not take God more than a second to strike Isaac dead if he disobeyed. Not only that. He loved God to that extent he would not allow anything–not even Isaac–to stand between him and his awe of Him. To Abraham, it did not matter what men would say or think if they heard that he killed his beloved son.

Many times, the apostles were persecuted for their faith in God. They were badly beaten and thrown into jail. Their flesh cried for freedom from the torture of men, but their faith would not give up. These spiritual die-hards knew the Word of God. Jesus said, "And fear not them which kill the body, but are not able to kill the soul: but rather fear him which is able to destroy both soul and body in hell" (Matthew 10:28). When we refuse to give in to the fear of men, we're practically refusing to remain in their bondage. The fear of God not only brings wisdom, it also brings freedom. The fear of men puts men in bondage; the fear of God sets men free from bondage.

Men have no control over our eternity because they did not create us. They can torture our bodies, but they cannot take our eternity. They may attempt to make us deny the truth of the birth, death and resurrection of Jesus Christ. On the long run, the choice is ours to make.

There are people, who for fear of loosing their jobs, would not stand for truth and honesty in their places of work. Instead of being what they know and believe they should be, they join the majority to practice evil.

There are pastors who only preach what the congregation wants to hear, instead of what the congregation needs to hear. Why? Because they fear loosing their members, for that would amount to less contribution. These are fears of torment.

The fear of God is completely different. It is a respect of His Word, an honor of His name, an awe of His sovereignty; it's a fear of reverence, an acceptance of my inability and His ability, my inadequacy and His supremacy. It is complete obedience and total submission to His will, refusing to doubt Him even when I don't understand what He's doing. It is the fear that says though nobody is seeing me, I know God is watching me. I will not do anything that contradicts His law. It is the fear that chooses death over life in the face of persecution.

As I do that, He reveals His heart to me. His Word says, "The secret of the LORD is with them that fear him; and he will shew them his covenant" (Psalm 25:14). Things that an ordinary layman doesn't know and can never understand will be made clear to those who stand in awe of His law.

Don't get me wrong. I'm not in any way better than those who for fear of persecution from men have denied their faith. Unless one faces the real situation, it's easier to judge them weak. That's why we need to ask for the grace to finish the race. Only the grace of God can see us through. It's not an easy road to travel, for many are the dangers and afflictions on the way. But with God on our side and His fear in our hearts, we shall make it home in Jesus' name.

26
FAITH FELLOWSHIPS

I was in the house with my daughter when the phone rang. Hello! The voice from the other end sounded a bit crackly, but definitely it was a woman. She said she wanted to tell me the good news. At first I thought, 'did I know her'? By the time she introduced herself and where she was calling from, I realized I had never seen or met her in my life. But since she wanted to tell me the good news, I felt no other news could be better. She talked about the Bible and how Jesus died for the sins of the world. She was to call people and pass some 'information' to them. Sounding all religious and spiritual, I immediately concluded she was a Christian.

To pass an information to me. "What kind of information?" I asked. There we go, strike number one. She refused to tell me what the information was. It had to come in the mail. Well, now I had started asking for Holy Spirit direction. I could sense something wrong. I decided not to cut her off. Then I asked what church was she attending and the name of her pastor. Strike number two. She said she had no church. She didn't believe in church because she worshipped 'her' God inside her house. What? And she would preach salvation to me. I instead preached to her and used that opportunity to tell her about the importance of fellowshipping together with other believers. When she asked for my address, I gave her my church address. A few days later, my pastor handed me a letter with no return address. As he handed it over to me, the Spirit said I must not open it. I should just trash it. Then I related everything to my pastor, only to discover he had had a similar experience.

How in the world can a person claim to be a child of God and not believe in worshipping with other believers? To me that kind of faith is out of order. Jesus is our perfect example. While here on earth, He never had a one-man ministry. Right at the beginning of His ministry, the first thing He did was to select twelve men known as disciples. He was never alone throughout His entire ministry.

As Christians, the Bible strongly admonishes us not to forsake the assembling together with other brethren.

> And let us consider one another to provoke unto love and to good works: Not forsaking the assembling of ourselves together, as the manner of some is; but exhorting one another: and so much the more, as ye see the day approaching (Hebrews 10:24-25).

When the Word of God says we're not to forsake the assembling together of ourselves, I try to imagine how that can apply to a one-member congregation. I've never heard of a church that has only one member. Even two will be absurd. If we must preach Jesus to others, we must have enough things to show for it. Jesus gathered with people. He ate with people. The crowd followed Him everywhere He went. So how can we claim to be His followers in preaching but not in principle?

A lot of good things take place in fellowshipping with others. If one will chase a thousand, and two put ten thousand to flight (Deuteronomy 32:30), imagine what a congregation of three hundred will chase. When Christians are in fellowship, there's an agreement and a unity in the spirit. And where there's unity, great and miraculous events happen.

Before the descent of the Holy Spirit, the disciples had a testimony of agreement between them. The Holy Spirit didn't meet them divided. They were in fellowship. And even after that, they didn't cease being together.

> And they, continuing daily with one accord in the temple, and breaking bread from house to house, did eat their meat with gladness

and singleness of heart (Acts 2:46).

If they had been apart and divided, they would have missed that great event of Pentecost and would have missed the power of the Holy Spirit. They would have hindered the salvation and the healing of others and even the miracles that took place would not have happened. Many Evangelical teams visit my country and the Lord uses them in marvelous ways. But up till now, I've not heard of a one-man team. They always come in large numbers.

Fellowshipping together is vital to the body of Christ. It not only promotes its growth, it enhances its power. God honors the gathering together of His children.

> Again I say unto you, That if two of you shall agree on earth as touching any thing that they shall ask, it shall be done for them of my Father .... For where two or three are gathered together in my name, there am I in the midst of them (Mat. 18:19, 20).

I strongly believe that the Lord will answer if I call upon Him. He has promised He would. But I believe when others pray with me in unity of heart, I stand a better chance. That cannot happen unless I fellowship with them. Professing to be a Christian, a true follower of Jesus and not believe in worshipping with other children of God, please pardon me if I'm being judgmental; but I think it's un-Jesus like. (That's a new vocab.)

27
__FAITH is FIRM__

Yes, whoever will get results from God must be firm in his or her faith. To be firm in faith is to refuse to yield under pressure, to remain resolute and completely determined, even if it will end in death.

When God called Moses to go and bring the children of Israel out of bondage from Egypt, he knew he was going on a difficult mission. But he also realized it was a spiritual battle for which only God would take all the glory. One thing was sure; he had a firm faith that nothing could change.

After the ninth plague–three days of thick darkness–Pharaoh surrendered and was ready to let the people go on one condition.

And Pharaoh called unto Moses, and said, Go ye, serve the LORD; only let your flocks and your herds be stayed: let your little ones also go with you (Exodus 10:24).

For a people who had been in bondage for four hundred years, this should sound like a fair deal. But when it comes to a man with a firm faith, fair has no place in the deal.

And Moses said, Thou must give us also sacrifices and burnt offerings, that we may sacrifice unto the LORD our God. Our cattle also shall go with us; __there shall not an hoof be left behind;__ for thereof must we take to serve the LORD our God; and we know not with what we must serve the LORD, until we come thither (Exodus 10:25-26).

Not only would we take our stuff. You will give us your stuff to sacrifice to the Lord. And guess what? The children of Israel took more than their stuff.

And the children of Israel did according to the word of Moses; and they borrowed of the Egyptians jewels of silver, and jewels of gold, and raiment: And the LORD gave the people favour in the sight of the Egyptians, so that they lent unto them such things as they required. And they spoiled the Egyptians (Ex. 12:35-36).

The three Hebrew men, Shadrach, Meshach and Abed-Nego, under a terrible pressure, persecution, and evil pronouncements, refused to be moved. They would rather die for God than live for gold. They had a firm faith for which they were ready to lay down their lives.

Shadrach, Meshach, and Abednego, answered and said to the king, O Nebuchadnezzar, we are not careful to answer thee in this matter. If it be so, our God whom we serve is able to deliver us from the burning fiery furnace, and he will deliver us out of thine hand, O king. But if not, be it known unto thee, O king, that we will not serve thy gods, nor worship the golden image which thou hast set up (Daniel 3:16-18).

It will be amazing to see what was going on in heaven at that very moment. I bet God was so proud of these radical patriarchs of His. They were not scared of the furnace. The strength of their firm faith weakened the heat of the fiery furnace.

There's an old hymn that goes:

Firmly stand for God in the world's mad strife,
Tho' the bleak winds roar, and the waves beat high;
'Tis the rock alone giveth strength and life,
When the hosts of sin are nigh.
Chorus:
Let us stand on the rock!
Firmly stand on the rock:
On the rock of Christ alone:

Attributes Of A Working Faith

If the strife we endure,

We shall stand endure,

'Mid the throng who surround the throne. (Author unknown.)

The three Hebrew men had true bold hearts and a faith ever strong. They firmly stood for truth to the end. When there's need for us to frantically and firmly tell the truth, let's go ahead and do so.

28
FAITH FORGIVES

The subject of forgiveness is a difficult one. We all get offended at one point or the other but some offences carry greater weight than others. By offences, I'm not implying the person that bumps into you at the grocery store and rather than apologize, makes fun of you. Neither am I talking about the friend who fails to invite you to his or her birthday party. He or she has only saved you another gift to buy. Go and do something good with your money.

When I say offences, I mean those offences that can leave permanent damages in the hearts of the offended. In such cases, only the grace of God and faith in Him can bring healing to the aching heart. It's much easier for the offender to ask for forgiveness than it is for the offended to forgive. It's like a scar on the skin. No matter what you do, that scar will forever be a reminder of the injury sustained sometime ago. Though it hurts no more, the spot is still visible. A wound that takes a moment to have may take a lifetime to heal. And there are heart wounds that may never heal.

Children of God, let's be sensitive to the feelings of others. If you have the spirit of offence, pray that God will remove it from your life. Turning the other cheek is easier preached than practiced. To the one hitting it's a pleasure, but to the person being hit, it is pain. Provoking a person to anger or wrath is sinful.

> Let us therefore follow after the things which make for peace, and things wherewith one may edify another. ... It is good neither to eat flesh, nor to drink wine, nor any thing whereby thy brother stumbleth, or is offended, or is made weak (Romans 14:19-21).

Jesus said to his disciples, "It is impossible but that offences will come: but woe unto him, through whom they come" (Luke 17:1). We cannot but offend one another. But when you know what can get the other person offended and you don't care, it is evil. The Word of God declares a woe upon you. If you truly profess to be a child of God, then you need to pray that He imparts the sensitive spirit into your heart, so it will not be said you hindered the salvation of another soul. Be sensitive.

Having said that, let's now consider the forgiving attribute of faith.

Stephen, while being stoned to death, prayed for the forgiveness of his murderers. In this he was a type of Christ, our perfect example of forgiveness. Jesus forgave His murderers, which include you and I. And up till now He still forgives whosoever comes to Him in repentance. The ocean of His forgiveness never runs dry. He alone is qualified to preach forgiveness because He never offended.

Joseph–the 11th son of Jacob–was the brother of Benjamin. Rachel, his mother died while giving birth to Benjamin, which meant the two boys never knew much of their mother. But the Bible says, "Now Israel loved Joseph more than all his children, because he was the son of his old age: and he made him a coat of many colours" (Genesis 37:3).

I wonder how he got to be the child of his old age. Benjamin was younger. That only tells how much love his father had for him which led to his ordeal. The brothers got jealous and developed a spirit of hatred towards him. And to make it more complex, Joseph had a dream that got the brothers totally irritated at him (Genesis 37:5-11). To make sure the dream never came to pass, they sold him to slavery and lied to their father that a wild beast killed him. But God still had a plan for his life.

Then there passed by Midianites merchantmen; and they drew and lifted up Joseph out of the pit, and sold Joseph to the Ishmeelites for twenty pieces of silver: and they brought Joseph into Egypt.... And they took Joseph's coat, and killed a kid of the goats, and dipped the coat in the blood; And they sent the coat of many colours, and they brought it to their father; and said, This have we found: know now whether it be thy son's coat or no. And he knew it, and said, It is my son's coat; an evil beast hath devoured him; Joseph is without doubt rent in pieces (Gen. 37:28-35).

Though they fooled their father but they could not fool God. When they stripped Joseph of his tunic, they were only carrying out God's plan for his life. If Joseph had continued to wear that tunic, his success would forever remain tortured and tormented. It was a coat of many colors, a tunic of many troubles. It was a coat of hatred, a coat of envy, a tunic of jealousy, a tunic of resentment, dissension and death. Each time he wore that tunic, every symptom of anger rose up inside his brothers. To Joseph, the tunic was just a garment. To the brothers, it was a coat of contention borne out of favoritism. It reminded them that their father loved Joseph more than all of them. And since they could not continue to have him specially treated, something must be done about it. There had to come an end to him and his tunic.

Parents, be careful what you do with your children. Don't make one feel loved more or less than the other. Was Jacob wrong? Yes! But were Joseph's brothers right? No! Two wrongs will never make a right. You don't use wrong to correct wrong. God would rather have us overcome evil with good (Romans 12:21). Their reaction to their father's mistake was completely out of order.

However God was with Joseph every step of the way. When his brothers stripped him of his tunic and threw him into the pit, God used that <u>to preserve him from death</u>. When he ended up in the prison, God used that <u>to</u>

<u>prepare him for the greatness</u> that lied ahead. When he interpreted Pharaoh's dream in the palace, God used that <u>to promote him as the governor</u> over all Egypt. It was a dream that got him <u>forsaken</u> by his brothers; it was a dream that got him <u>familiar</u> with Pharaoh's officers; it was a dream that got him <u>favored</u> by the Pharaoh.

When Joseph was sold into slavery, he was seventeen years. By the time he became governor he was thirty years. Imagine yourself in his situation. How would you love to spend thirteen days behind bars for one offence, you had a dream? Joseph went through thirteen agonizing years because he had a dream. But because of his faith in God, though he did not forget what they did to him, he chose to forgive.

They because of their shortsightedness attempted to hinder the plan of God in Joseph's life, but they could not avert it. The book of Habakkuk says, "I will stand upon my watch, and set me upon the tower, and will watch to see what he will say unto me, and what I shall answer when I am reproved. And the LORD answered me, and said, Write the vision, and make it plain upon tables, that he may run that readeth it. For the vision is yet for an appointed time, but at the end it shall speak, and not lie: though it tarry, wait for it; because it will surely come, it will not tarry" (2:1-3).

Your vision may appear delayed, but it will not be denied. Joseph's dream was delayed but not denied. God never forgot him. His faith in God kept him all the thirteen years and when he finally revealed himself to his brothers, the same faith helped him to forgive them. It was not easy for him but he did it anyway. It must have been an emotional moment for them. How did the brothers feel when Joseph revealed himself to them? What could possibly be going through their minds? By now they thought Joseph was dead. No, he won't die. Remember they already sacrificed a goat's kid? (Gen.

37:31). The moment they dipped their brother's tunic in the blood of the kid, the price had been paid. The sacrifice had been offered. The kid had died Joseph's death.

For the brothers, it was a time of regret; but for Joseph it was a time for reconciliation. The past was gone and God was going to use him to save the lives of the men who sold him into the hands of men. And as far as he knew, they were only used to fulfill God's purpose in his life. The same Joseph, who was second to the last of his father's children, became second to the first in all the land of Egypt. He knew he would never have become a second in command to Pharaoh if he had not been sold to slavery.

The Bible says, "And we know that all things work together for good to them that love God, to them who are the called according to his purpose" (Romans 8:28). Whatever the enemy does to prevent you from realizing your dream cannot materialize. If that is God's plan for your life, the dream will surely come to pass. And when it seems like the devil is having the upper hand in your life, that's the time God is doing the greatest work. You will feed the mouth that starves you and he that abhors you will come and adore you. And when God is done elevating you to that position of authority and command, they that despise you will dread you for fear that you may want to revenge. When that happens, just go ahead and forgive. Remember, faith forgives.

G

29. FAITH GIVES   115

30. FAITH GROWS   120

29
__FAITH GIVES__

God has set the best example for us by giving us the greatest gift that can be given to the human race, His only begotten son.

For God so loved the world, that he gave his only begotten Son, that whosoever believeth in him should not perish, but have everlasting life (John 3:16).

For by grace are ye saved through faith; and that not of yourselves: it is the gift of God (Ephesians 2:8).

Our salvation is a gift from God. We did not deserve it. We did not merit it. But out of His abundant love, He gave it to us. No other gift can be greater than this. If then we profess to know Him and have faith in Him, we have to be like Him in giving. When we give to others, we shall never loose the reward. Jesus said to His disciples, "For whosoever shall give you a cup of water to drink in my name, because ye belong to Christ, verily I say unto you, he shall not lose his reward" (Mark 9:41).

Giving has to be part of our faith life if we don't want to come to the Lord and leave His presence sad. When the rich young ruler came to Jesus, he left His presence sad because he lacked a giving spirit.

And when he was gone forth into the way, there came one running, and kneeled to him, and asked him, Good Master, what shall I do that I may inherit eternal life? …. Then Jesus beholding him loved him, and said unto him, One thing thou lackest: go thy way, sell whatsoever thou hast, and give to the poor, and thou shalt have he treasure in heaven: and come, take up the cross, and follow me. And was sad at that saying, and went away grieved: for he had great possessions (Mark 10:17-22).

This was the only man that left the presence of the Lord sorrowful, not because he had no faith in Jesus, not because he didn't have enough to give; but because he lacked the heart that gives. He was blessed, but he refused to be a blessing to others. All he wanted was to inherit eternal life and keep his possessions to himself.

If we must follow Jesus, if truly we believe that He's the Son of God and we're joint heirs with Him, if we want others to see Jesus in our lives, if we really mean to inherit eternal life, then we must be willing and ready to give. Jesus gave Himself. So how can we profess to love Him without striving to be like Him?

When God blesses us His children, what exactly does He expect of us? Are we blessed to remain forever blessed or are we blessed to be blessings unto others? Not one verse in the Bible encourages hoarding of blessings. God wants to bless us as His children. It's His desire that we prosper. But He hates it when we refuse to be blessings unto others.

There are many less privileged people all around us. Blessing others does not mean praying for them only, for prayer will not feed a hungry sister. As we pray, we also give.

What doth it profit, my brethren, though a man say he hath faith, and have not works? can faith save him. If a brother or sister be naked, and destitute of daily food, And one of you say unto them, Depart in peace, be ye warmed and filled; notwithstanding ye give them not those things which are needful to the body; what doth it profit? Even so faith, if it hath not works, is dead, being alone (James 2:14-17).

Children of God are to seize every opportunity they have to do good and give to those in need. There are times we may have to give almost out of nothing; but when we do so, God will multiply the rest and we shall never lack. It takes a giving faith to make a getting faith.

When God sent the prophet Elijah to the widow of Zarephath, she had nothing. It was during a severe famine and the meal she had would be the last for her and her son. But because she shared with a man of God, because she gave out of the little she had, because she chose to be a blessing, she experienced a miracle. She gave little and got much. (See 1 Kings17:8-16.) A child of God can never give much for little. It'll always be the other way round.

Giving should be a pleasure thing for us to do, especially giving to men of God. And I think it takes some humility on the part of any man of God to ask for help. Sure there're fake ones, but we also have genuine ones. The judgment is not ours to make. If you feel too big to be asked for help, believe me you're too big to ask God for help. And if you hate to be asked for help, then don't ever ask God for help. Let Him help you only when He feels like. If we don't feel like giving, a golden silence will always be better than a grumbling statement.

Some of us can't give an ordinary smile to a hurting soul. We only smile to those we know or those who smile to us. And yet we expect the Lord to bestow His mercy upon us. Christ said we should clothe the poor, feed the hungry and visit those in prison, for then are we His true children. In fact, we're not doing ourselves any good by hoarding God's blessings.

> There is that scattereth, and yet increaseth; and there is that withholdeth more than is meet, but it tendeth to poverty (Proverbs 11:24).

If that widow had withheld her food from Elijah, no doubt she would have starved to death. I don't know what your situation is as you're reading this book and especially this topic. May be you're a single parent or a widow; and each day you wake up brings a fresh pain to your heart because you have no idea how you will survive that day.

The Lord is saying to you, "your bin of flour shall not be used up, your jar of oil shall not run dry." Take a step of faith, out of the little you have left, go in the name of the Lord and share with somebody who has nothing and see what God does with the rest. Give in faith and get in full. Always remember that giving has nothing to do with wealth. It's true the Bible specifically tells the rich to give and share (1 Timothy 6:17-18). But if giving has to do with wealth, God would not have sent Elijah to that widow, of all the people living in that land.

Remember the little boy in the crowd of five thousand, not counting women and children? (I wonder why. Hey! We're important too.) We serve a Lord who feeds us spiritually and physically. He cares about our Spirit and our stomach. He doesn't want us to go hungry in any form. He had compassion on the crowd. He knew there wasn't enough to feed such a large crowd. But guess what? A little boy had his sack lunch with him, five loaves and two fishes (John 6:1-14). How would you react if you heard that your son fed his class from the lunch you packed for him to school and came home with twelve full bags of remnants? Well, it happened. That boy's little became much because he blessed others with it. He gave to their needs.

When little is put into the hands of Jesus, it becomes much. Just as it has nothing to do with wealth, giving has nothing to do with age. This was a lad, not more than twelve years old. We need to learn to give and pass the lesson on to our children. I'm sure this boy went home rejoicing that Jesus used his lunch to feed five thousand. May be it even made the Headline News…'Five

Thousand Fed With Lad's Sack Lunch....' All of a sudden, his playmates would get jealous and wish they were the ones being talked about. Yes! That's what you get when you give and bless others. You become spiritually popular both on earth and in heaven. And you know what? Thousands of years later, people who were not born when you did it will still read the news. No wonder the Bible says it's better to give than to receive (Acts 20:35).

You were not there when this boy gave. But over two thousand years later, you're still reading about it. Permit me to say that you're doing yourself a great harm by refusing to give. The more you keep, the less you sleep and the faster your death. And why don't you give when you're still here and the recipient can appreciate your giving? You have no control over your soul. The Lord may demand it from you tonight. King Solomon knew this secret.

> There is an evil which I have seen under the sun, and it is common among men: A man to whom God hath given riches, wealth, and honour, so that he wanteth nothing for his soul of all that he desireth, yet God giveth him not power to eat thereof, but a stranger eateth it: this is vanity, and it is an evil disease (Ecclesiastes 6:1-2).

Give while the Almighty God can reward your giving. Don't wait till that time when people will loot your house and get rid of those vanities you refused to give in your lifetime. Give in faith and you shall receive in full. As God blesses you, be a blessing to others.

30
FAITH GROWS

When a baby is newly born, there are some things we would never expect from him/her. I don't expect my 7yr. old girl to behave the way she does now when she was only seven days old. Though God has embedded every learning power into her, they have to show up at different stages in her life. When she was a baby, she had special love for breast milk. That was normal.

As newborn babes, desire the sincere milk of the word, that ye may grow thereby (1 Peter 2:2).

When we give milk to our babies, it's for one purpose–that the baby may grow. If a plant is not watered, it soon withers. If a baby is not fed, he will die. But when he's fed and there's no growth, then there's a problem. That's exactly how we are to God. If at two years, my baby could not take more than milk, the doctor would have received some guests in his office.

If we claim to have faith in God and our faith never grows, we're not different from a pool of stagnant water. It has no life. All kinds of dirt will get inside it and there will be no resistance of any sort. Why? Because it has remained in the same spot–no flowing, no life. Children of God, who profess Jesus, must aspire for growth in their faith.

When my girl was 15 months, we started potty training. Now that she's in 1st grade, that's no longer an issue. She thinks and talks differently. This happens because she's growing. At the same time, my expectations of my teenage boys are way different. There are times they receive some discipline for misbehavior. Not because I love them less, but because I expect them to be more mature. The last thing God wants is chastise any of His children. But when the need be for Him to do so, He does not hesitate. It's an act of His love.

> And ye have forgotten the exhortation which speaketh unto you as unto children, My son, despise not thou the chastening of the Lord, nor faint when thou art rebuked of him: For whom the Lord loveth he chasteneth, and scourgeth every son whom he receiveth. If ye endure chastening, God dealeth with you as with sons; ... But if ye be without chastisement, whereof all are partakers, then are ye bastards, and not sons (Hebrews 12:5-8).

No matter how old we are, when we first come to Christ, we're babes. But God doesn't want us to remain babes forever. When He chastises us, it's because we have fallen short of His expectation of us. And the best way to correct us and call our attention to our fault is to give us some spiritual whipping. We are supposed to use it as an opportunity to grow out of our ignorance.

When I discipline my children, it hurts. But it hurts even more when there's no visible change. If they repeat the same mistake, I feel terrible. That's the same way God feels about me when I refuse to grow, when there are no visible changes inspite of His discipline.

The Moses that ran away from Pharaoh's palace was definitely not the same Moses that returned to that same palace forty years later. And more so, it was not the same Moses forty years after their deliverance from Egypt. Each hassle he encountered made him more spiritually grown. The more problems he endured, the more faith he developed.

A retarded faith is as good as dead. Some years ago when I came to Christ, there were certain things that I did and to me, were okay. I didn't consider them sinful. But you know what, God gave me the grace to grow. He knew the level of my knowledge. I know I've grown because now I see those same things as abominations. And I wonder how I got away with them. Like I said earlier, God saw me as a little babe and that was the best I knew to do then. If I try them now, He will deal with me accordingly. The Bible says, "And that servant, which knew his lord's will, and prepared not himself, neither did according to his will, shall be beaten with many stripes. But he that knew not, and did commit things worthy of stripes, shall be beaten with few stripes. For unto whomsoever much is given, of him shall be much required" (Luke 12: 47, 48).

The way the Holy Spirit speaks to my heart now was not the same way He did back then. I can't even remember if He spoke to me. The best I had were dreams. Not because He wasn't there; but because if He spoke to me, I would not hear. And if I heard, I would not understand. I wasn't grown. My faith could best be compared to that of a little child. But blessed be the name of God, I know there's difference.

> And he gave some, apostles; and some, prophets; and some, evangelists; and some, pastors and teachers; …. That we henceforth be no more children, tossed to and fro, and carried about with every wind of doctrine, by the sleight of men, and cunning craftiness, whereby they lie in wait to deceive; But speaking the truth in love, may grow up into him in all things, which is the head, even Christ (Ephesians 4:11-15).

Children of God must strive to grow into the likeness of Christ, not allowing instability to serve as a hindrance to the growth of our faith. For some it may be faster than others. But God requires that we all grow. We must not give room for carnality; it will not only deter the growth, it will destroy the faith. Fruit of the Spirit must prevail over the works of the flesh.

And I, brethren, could not speak unto you as unto spiritual, but as unto carnal, even as unto babes in Christ. I have fed you with milk, and not with meat: for hitherto ye were not able to bear it, neither yet now are ye able (1 Corinthians 3:1-2).

These were spiritual migids, totally retarded in faith. Carnality was a wall between them and Christ. No wonder they remained babes.

Just as we struggle for better things in life, we should apply the same principle to our faith. When faith grows, fears retard. The more you grow in faith, the less fearful you become of principalities and powers. When you get Born Again [B. A], don't be content. Aspire for Multiple Anointing [M. A]. As you receive it with thanksgiving, strive for the anointing to Pull Heavens Down [P.H.D].

Ten years ago, the devil could get away with many things in my life. By the power in the name of Jesus, if he tries that now, he will be in for a battle. And I know I've not come to the end of my growth. I will continue to grow till the appearing of my Lord and Savior.

In conclusion of this topic, I want to leave you with these words of apostle Paul, lest you allow your growth to slip out of your hand. "Ye therefore, beloved, seeing ye know these things before, beware lest ye also, being led away with the error of the wicked, fall from your own stedfastness. But grow in grace, and in the knowledge of our Lord and Saviour Jesus Christ. To him be glory both now and for ever" (2 Peter 3:17-18). Amen

H

31. FAITH HELPS	125
32. FAITH is HOLY	128
33. FAITH is HONEST	132
34. FAITH HOPES	136
35. FAITH is HOSPITABLE	140
36. FAITH is HUMBLE	142

31
__FAITH HELPS__

Most of the time when we render help to somebody, it's done to bring a relief. Though you're not the one feeling the pain, but you share in the pain by bringing a relief to the heart and body of the person helped.

The Bible is full of testimonies of those who helped the apostles in prayer. If they were not of the same mind with them, if they did not believe in the same God, that would have been difficult. When people of the world help, they usually expect something in return. But children of God, who claim to have faith in God, must help without expecting. The Bible admonishes us to help others in need.

> Let us therefore come boldly unto the throne of grace, that we may obtain mercy, and find grace to help in time of need (Hebrews 4:16).

Believers in Christ are supposed to be one body and when any part of that body hurts, all the other parts feel it. Professing to know Him and not helping others is anti-faith. People with various needs, corporate and individual are all around us and we can't afford to shut our eyes to them.

After Peter's sermon in Acts, the Bible records that many received the word and about three thousand souls were baptized. But it did not end there.

> And all that believed were together, and had all things common; And sold their possessions and goods, and parted them to all men, as every man had need (Acts 2:44-45).

These believers knew the importance of help in the body of Christ. They did not shut their eyes to the needs of those around them. They knew that though only Christ can heal, but Christians can help. They took it upon themselves to stand in the gap between their faith and the needs of others. This was a corporate action. There are other times the need may be personal.

Paul wrote to the Romans and testified about a helpful sister in the Lord.

> I commend unto you Phebe our sister, ...That ye receive her in the Lord, as becometh saints, and that ye assist her in whatsoever business she hath need of you: for she hath been a succourer*of many, and of myself also (Romans 16:1-2).

One good turn deserves another. Because that sister helped others in time of need, she also deserved to be helped. He who helps will in turn receive help, both from God and man. Paul didn't fail to mention the others too because he wanted to teach the Roman believers–and of course you and I–what it means to help.

Greet Priscilla and Aquila my helpers in Christ Jesus (Romans 16:3). What kind of help did they render?

> Who have for my life laid down their own necks: unto whom not only I give thanks, but also all the churches of the Gentiles (16:4).

I believe these people risked their lives for Paul's sake, just to help him in time of great danger.

It doesn't matter how little or how much. At times a little help may come so handy and the person helped will never forget. Don't wait till you can render a BIG help. You may never get the chance for one. Help when the need for you to do so arises and you have the resource, no matter how small. And don't base your help on color or culture. To render help has nothing to do with nationality or skin color. In Christ, there's no discrimination. Christ died for all.

> For by one Spirit are we all baptized into one body, whether we be Jews or Gentiles, whether we be bond or free; and have been all made

to drink into one Spirit (1 Corinthians 12:13).

When the Samaritan helped the man that fell among robbers, race was no hindrance. He made himself available. He didn't go and call somebody of the same race with the man. He did it out of pity. He had compassion on the man and helped him out of his ordeal. I am sure the man would never forget the Samaritan. Even Jesus did not.

I talked earlier about the paralytic that was brought to Jesus by his friends. The Bible doesn't say for how long the man had been paralyzed. We only know he was completely helpless. But thank God for friends who had faith and were ready to help. They were friends in need and friends indeed. They were not tired of helping. They didn't give up. They helped because they had faith that Jesus would heal their friend. And not only were his sins forgiven, his body was healed. He was healed in and out (Mk. 2:1-5).

In Ezra, when Zerubbabel and Jeshua were rebuilding the temple, the Bible records that prophets of God were there to help them. These were men of God who didn't function according to their hierarchy in the faith. They made themselves equal to the common men (Ezra 5).

Brethren the Lord is asking, "Do you have faith?" And He's also asking, "Do you help others either by prayer or by deed?" If you answer yes to the first but not sure of the second, you need to ask God to help you so you can help others. Pray that He imparts a helping spirit into your soul. One of these days, you may be the one in need of help. And the truth is, the help you render is the help you receive. When it seems like you need help and it's just not forthcoming, ponder and ask yourself, 'do I help others in need?'

*Helper

32
FAITH is HOLY

I had my second baby March 17, 1989. I usually didn't lactate until the third day after delivery. So I had no choice but to give artificial milk to my babies. But for an unknown reason, my little boy refused to take the milk. He survived on water for three days. By the third day, this baby pounced on the breast milk like he had never been fed since he came. All attempts to make him feed from bottle failed. Well for sometime I gave up.

Then it occurred to me to try something else. I expressed the breast milk into the bottle and gave it to him. Yours sincerely, my baby finished the whole thing. I then realized he had no problem with the bottle, but the artificial milk inside. That's exactly how we are when we allow unholy things to pollute our bodies.

To be holy is to be spiritually pure, untainted by evil or sin. When God called Moses to go and bring the Israelites out of Egypt, he was at mount Horeb, the mountain of God. As he drew closer, God asked him to remove his shoes, for the ground on which he stood was a holy ground (Exodus 3:5). The holiness factor there had to do with the shoes and not with Moses as a person. God would not have given him an assignment of that magnitude if he were unholy. He would not have spoken to him face to face if he were unholy (Exodus 33:11). He would not have called him and revealed to him where he was to die; and after his death, buried him if he were unholy (Deut. 33:48-52; 34:5-6). This rules out any notion of unholiness as regards Moses. But he had to remove his shoes because those shoes were not qualified to enter the holy ground. Moses was a holy servant of God in unholy shoes.

As people of faith, we must be ready to put off our unholy shoes before

Faith Is Holy

coming to His presence, so God can make the best use of us for the work of His kingdom. Many Christians are going about in unholy shoes. Not the shoes as eyes can see, but unholy practices that completely negate their profession of faith.

But ye, beloved, <u>building up yourselves on your most holy faith</u>, praying in the Holy Ghost (Jude 20).

To build ourselves up on our most holy faith entails removing every unholy shoe, for only then are we fit to come to His presence. Faith is holy and must not be tainted or tarnished with the things of the world, the lust of the eye, pride, adultery, fornication, envy, stealing etc. Unholiness amongst unbelievers is sad, but unholiness amongst believers is pathetic. A believer, who names the name of God, must do away with anything that contradicts his faith in that name. There must be visible changes in our lives, our conduct, our appearances and even our relationship with others, especially those who don't know the Lord and don't pretend to know Him. When they see changes, their hearts will be drawn to our God. But when there's no difference, how do we win them over to our side?

We live in an age where worldliness has crept into the church and into the body of believers. Men and women no longer realize they're the first epistles read by those outside the church. "Ye are our epistle written in our hearts, known and read of all men: Forasmuch as ye are manifestly declared to be the epistle of Christ ministered by us, written not with ink, but with the Spirit of the living God; not in tables of stone, but in fleshy tables of the heart" (2 Corinthians 3:2,3).

Christians who would rather porn than pray; children of God who prefer fornication to fellowship; believers who enjoy gambling than giving; God is not pleased with you.

> Be ye not unequally yoked together with unbelievers: for what fellowship hath righteousness with unrighteousness? and what communion hath light with darkness? And what concord hath Christ with Belial? or what part hath he that believeth with an infidel? And what agreement hath the temple of God with idols? for ye are the temple of the living God; as God hath said, I will dwell in them, and walk in them; and I will be their God, and they shall be my people (2 Corinthians 6:14-16).

If you want God to be your God, you got to be ready to be His child. You cannot yield your body to evil and expect the Holy Spirit to dwell therein. The Bible says, "Know ye not that ye are the temple of God, and that the Spirit of God dwelleth in you? If any man defile the temple of God, him shall God destroy; for the temple of God is holy, which temple ye are" (1 Corinthians 3: 16, 17). You have to keep this temple clean if you so desire to continue to have fellowship with Him.

God loves us as we are, but He will not have us polluted with unholy stuff. Otherwise, we're just like my baby's feeding bottle, wanted bottle filled with unwanted milk, holy people walking in unholy shoes. For us to continue enjoying His love, we must undo what we have done; pour out the unholy things and fill our minds with His words. God loves the sinner but He hates his sins. He loves the unholy but hates his unholiness. An unholy mind makes an unholy man.

> I beseech you therefore, brethren, by the mercies of God, that ye present your bodies a living sacrifice, holy, acceptable unto God, which is your reasonable service. And be not conformed to this world: but be ye transformed by the renewing of your mind, that ye may prove what is that good, and acceptable, and perfect, will of God

(Romans 12:1-2).

Though we're in this world, we must choose not to be of this world. We have to constantly renew our minds by the power of the Holy Spirit and depart from iniquity and every appearance of the evil one. We're no longer under the authority of the devil. We have a brand new Master who is Christ Jesus, the author and finisher of our faith.

The Bible makes it clear that without holiness, no man shall see God (Hebrews 12:14). It doesn't matter how long you have been in the church, how many positions you hold, how high up there you are or how much tithe and offering you give. If you're not holy, you're just a minister in unholy shoes, lifting up unholy hands to a holy heaven. Your sacrifices of praise are not acceptable before the Lord.

I urge you brethren according to God's Word, "Wherefore gird up the loins of your mind, be sober, and hope to the end for the grace that is to be brought unto you at the revelation of Jesus Christ; As obedient children, not fashioning yourselves according to the former lusts in your ignorance: But as he which hath called you is holy, so be ye holy in all manner of conversation; Because it is written, Be ye holy; for I am holy" (1 Peter 1: 13-16).

33
FAITH is HONEST

I was at the store with very little money left on me, forcing me to buy only the very necessary things. (Which by the way is a good lesson I learnt in the school of adversity.) I saw a sweatshirt and decided to get it for my oldest son, not because it was financially convenient; but because he needed it. The sweat cost $15. I picked two other items, totaling about $21 and headed for the cashier. For some devilish reason, the sweat didn't scan and the cashier didn't notice. She scanned the other items and gave me a total of $5.95.

In a time of desperate need, that was a good opportunity for me to cheat. But I know the God I serve. Cheating will not do me any good. It will only add to my problems. Right there, I told her there was a mistake. She added the $15 and I paid the correct amount and went home rejoicing in another victory over Satan. This may not apply to you. But whatever your case may be, God would have you honest as you profess your faith in Him.

Each time I watch talk shows these days, I'm sore at how people can proudly and publicly talk of their dishonesty–talking about shoplifting, fornication, adultery, sex outside marriage, wives and husbands cheating on one another.

When these things happen amongst people who don't claim to know the Lord, it won't come as a surprise. But when these same things occur amongst brethren, then it's a problem. How can one profess to be a believer, claim to have faith in God and smile at dishonesty, which seems to be the order of the day? Christians, who know the God they serve must not engage in the 'if you can't beat them, join them' race. It's the devil's slogan and should not be mentioned among people of faith.

Faith Is Honest

A need arose among the early body of believers. The disciples grew in number but contrary to expectation, some of the new believers complained that their widows were being neglected.

> And in those days, when the number of the disciples was multiplied, there arose a murmuring of the Grecians against the Hebrews, because their widows were neglected in the daily ministration ... Wherefore, brethren, look ye out among you seven <u>men of honest report,</u> ... whom we may appoint over this business (Acts 6:1-4).

The men to be chosen had to be men of honest report, not just anyone. They were to be trustworthy individuals. If God can't trust us in little things, how do we expect Him to put us in charge of big stuff? When Christians are counted along with men and women who 'mistakenly' bring office stuff home, how then do they preach godliness to unbelievers in the same office? If a pastor cheats on his wife, on what ground does he rebuke a member that is caught in adultery? When the head is crooked, the body can never be straight. Unfortunately, the sin of one single member can go a long way to cause problem to the whole body. The dishonesty of one family member will affect every one in that family, directly or indirectly.

In the Old Testament, we read about Achan.

> But the children of Israel committed a trespass in the accursed thing: for Achan, the son of Carmi... took of the accursed thing: and the anger of the LORD was kindled against the children of Israel (Joshua 7:1-2).

It is obvious from this verse that Achan was the dishonest man. He stole the accursed things. But the Lord was angry at the whole race. The sin of one person led to Israel's defeat by the inhabitants of Ai. When he stole and hid the accursed things, he thought he could play some hanky-panky game with God and get away with it. No one does it and succeeds. The Bible clearly states that your sins will find you out (Numbers 32:23). Unfortunately, the repercussion may not be yours alone.

> So Joshua sent messengers, and they ran unto the tent; and, behold, it was hid in his tent, and the silver under it.... And Joshua, and all Israel with him, took Achan the son of Zerah, and the silver, and the garment, and the wedge of gold, and his sons, and his daughters, and his oxen, and his asses, and his sheep, and his tent, and all that he had: .... and burned them with fire, after they had stoned them with stones. And they raised over him a great heap of stones unto this day (Joshua 7:22-26).

A single man stole; a whole race suffered; an entire family perished. How sad and pathetic?

Parents, what do you say when your child brings home things that don't belong to him? Do you rebuke or relax? It may be the beginning of a family feud that you'll never be able to figure out. Do you have accursed things in your wallet, things that are not yours; but you rejoice at keeping them? And you still wonder why you gather and never have; you still wonder why you sow and never reap? The Lord is warning you. Don't bring a curse upon your life. Stand for truth when convenient and when not convenient.

Remember Ananias and Sapphira, partners in greed than grace? They were dishonest to the body of believers. Little did they realize they were lying to the Holy Spirit and their end was death. The Bible says, "There is a way that seemeth right unto a man, but the end thereof are the ways of death" (Proverbs 16:25).

When you go to the store and just by share mistake, you're over changed, what do you do? Do you go home rejoicing or do you go back returning? When you're put in charge of money, do you turn everything in or do you keep back part of it for your own use? You're not doing it to man. You're grieving the Holy Spirit of God that dwells inside of you.

If truly you profess to know the Lord, honesty is mandatory. When you cheat, you sin. And the Bible says the wages of sin is death (Romans 6:23). If you're in need, talk to your heavenly Father. He has promised to supply all your need according to His riches in glory by Christ Jesus. But you have a part to play. Being in need is not an excuse for dishonesty, either to God or to men. We're to provide for honest things, not only in the sight of the Lord, but also in the sight of men (2 Corinthians 8:21). It does not matter if others around us are dishonest. When we do the right thing, we win them over and show them the right way. We don't correct dishonesty by being dishonest. And greater is He that is in us than he that is in the world (1 John 4:4).

Finally brethren, whatsoever things are true, whatsoever things are honest, whatsoever things are just, whatsoever things are pure, whatsoever things are lovely, whatsoever things are of good report; if there be any virtue, and if there be any praise, think on these things (Philippians 4:8).

34
FAITH HOPES

There are three gifts in the Bible that abide together and cannot be separated; faith, hope and love. As children of God, we cannot have one and be void of the other. People of faith must strive to possess the three. I don't see how a person can have faith and be hopeless. When we abide in the Lord and dwell according to His words, our hope will be endless.

People hope for many things in life. But the hope of this world is not the hope of believers. We don't hope for temporal things but for things that are eternal. Temporal things are things we can see with our visible eyes. They don't last forever. They may make happy for a while, but they cannot give joy. When we're done with our journey here, we leave them behind. They are servants that outlive the master.

Houses, cars, and education are good things to wish for and good things to have. But by the time you're done having them, a vacuum of dissatisfaction is still left and you begin to wonder, why do I seem to have it all and still feel like I lack it all. That's because you have placed your hope on things of no eternal value.

> For we are saved by hope: but hope that is seen is not hope: for what a man seeth, why doth he yet hope for? But if we hope for that we see not, then do we with patience wait for it (Romans 8:24-25).

As believers and people of faith, we hope for heavenly things and not things that are here today, gone tomorrow. Heaven is full of treasures for us. If you believe in the Lord Jesus, be rest assured that your faith and hope in Him is not in vain.

Apostle Paul said, "We give thanks to God and the Father of our Lord

Jesus Christ, praying always for you, Since we heard of your faith in Christ Jesus, and of the love which ye have to all the saints, For the hope which is laid up for you in heaven, whereof ye heard before in the word of the truth of the gospel; If ye continue in the faith grounded and settled, and be not moved away from the hope of the gospel, which ye have heard, and which was preached to every creature which is under heaven; whereof I Paul am made a minister; To whom God would make known what is the riches of the glory of this mystery among the Gentiles; which is Christ in you, the hope of glory" (Colossians 1:3-5, 23, 27).

This was not for the Colossians alone. These words are for us as well. We should never allow anything to move us away from the hope of the gospel; so that at the end, we may be able to lay our hands on the hope that is laid up for us in heaven and hear our Daddy say, "well done, thou good and faithful servant, enter thou into the joy of thy Lord" (Matthew 25:21).

What are some of the things believers hope for? The first and the most important is the return of our Lord and Savior. By faith we believe that Jesus came, died for our sins and resurrected on the third day. By faith we should also believe that He's coming back again to take us to be with Him. One of these days, soon and very soon, the Lord is coming for the elect. His coming is closer than we think and "If in this life only we have hope in Christ, we are of all men most miserable" (1 Corinthians 15:19).

I don't want my hope in Christ to end in this life. I'm so eager to see the One who gave His life for me. I have a question for Him; what did I do to deserve such a sacrifice? How could He offer His pure and sinless life for a sinful, wretched, and unclean life like mine? I hope to see the shoulders that carried the cross, the head that wore the crown of thorns, the prints of the nails in His hands, the scars of the stripes on His body, and the mouth that cried, "It is finished." I want to touch Him, feel Him, kiss Him, just wrap myself around Him and say, I LOVE YOU JESUS. Heaven is going to be full of joy.

> Paul, a servant of God, and an apostle of Jesus Christ, according to the faith of God's elect, and the acknowledging of the truth which is after godliness; In hope of eternal life, which God, that cannot lie, promised before the world began (Titus 1:1-2).

Eternal life with God awaits believers who hope to forever be with the Lord. He has promised it and He cannot lie. His promises are sure.

Believers must also hope for a reunion with their loved ones who have preceded them to glory.

> But I would not have you to be ignorant, brethren, concerning them which are asleep, that ye sorrow not, even as others which have no hope. For if we believe that Jesus died and rose again, even so them also which sleep in Jesus will God bring with him.... Then we which are alive and remain shall be caught up together with them in the clouds, to meet the Lord in the air: and so shall we ever be with the Lord. Wherefore comfort one another with these words (1 Thes. 4: 13-18).

Do you weep because of your loved ones that have gone to be with the Lord? Be comforted, hope and weep no more. For soon you will be reunited with them in a land where the profession of an undertaker is completely unrecognized; for in heaven no one dies and no one will ever be buried. There, there will be no more tears; for He who wept for mankind will wipe away all tears from our eyes. Soon you will meet them and part no more. And so shall you ever be.

Do you hunger for food and thirst for water? Put your hope in Jesus, for He's the bread of life and the fountain of living water that never runs dry.

Do you have an ailment in your body? Sorrow no more. He who healed all diseases knows exactly how you feel. He had gone through it all.

Definitely there will be times when we just don't understand what is going on in our lives, when we struggle with little success, while others around us, who don't know the Lord, succeed with little struggle and all hope for something better totally evades us. Don't you fret, brother; don't you fret sister. The Lord knows, the Lord understands. Help will come, just hope in Him. Your days of heartache and heartbreaking, sorrow and struggle, troubles and tears are almost over. The Bible says, "Blessed is the man that trusteth in the LORD, and whose hope the LORD is" (Jer.17:7).

When you hope in the Lord, you're in for blessings. Just hold on hoping on. And I pray that the God of hope will fill you with all joy and peace in believing, that you may abound in hope by the power of the Holy Spirit. Amen.

35
FAITH is HOSPITABLE

Hospitality is a gift that all Christians should desire to have. I believe that though not all are hospitable, but all can be hospitable because the Bible wants us to be.

Be kindly affectioned one to another with brotherly love; ... given to hospitality (Romans 12:10-13).

While we strive to keep our other spiritual gifts, Paul advised that we add the gift of hospitality to them. In fact hospitality is one of the qualifications that a bishop must have on his spiritual resume if he wants to be a truly ordained bishop.

This is a true saying, if a man desire the office of a bishop, he desireth a good work. A bishop then must be blameless, the husband of one wife, vigilant, sober, of good behaviour, given to hospitality, apt to teach (1 Timothy 3:1-2).

For a bishop must be blameless, as the steward of God; not selfwilled, not soon angry, not given to wine, no striker, not given to filthy lucre; But a lover of hospitality, a lover of good men, sober, just, holy, temperate (Titus 1:7-8).

The book of Hebrews specifically talks of those who through hospitality entertained angels without knowing it.

Be not forgetful to entertain strangers; for thereby some have entertained angels unawares (Hebrews 13:2).

This particular verse is talking about Abraham and his wife, Sarah who trusted God for a child for a long time. The year of their breakthrough came when they entertained three men, not knowing they were angels

(Genesis 18:1-16).

Hospitality is a voluntary act and doesn't wait to be asked. It enjoys doing it. I love having people in my house, just cook some food and set it on the table. I don't have to wait for a birthday or thanksgiving to invite people over for lunch. I just love to do it. Call it my gift, I accept. I don't know if I've ever entertained angels, but I know I've entertained men and women of God who rained blessings of prayer on my house before they left. We don't need a huge amount of money to call a few friends and just share some cookies and grapes together on the table.

Hospitality has rewards. Nothing we give goes unrewarded. When Abraham volunteered to entertain those men of God, I bet he didn't know it was going to be for a miracle. When the woman of Shunem volunteered to entertain prophet Elisha, nobody asked or forced her to do it (2 Kings 4:8-17). Little did she realize that would be the end of her long-term barrenness. She even went a little farther by providing sleeping accommodation for him.

I'm sure these people never thought their hospitality would bring fertility to their dead reproductive systems. They did it without grudges or murmurings. It came from willing hearts. They were happy doing it. The Bible recommends hospitality done without grumbling.

Use hospitality one to another without grudging (I Peter 4:9).

At the appointed time set by God, both of them had joy put in their hands. Why? Because they were hospitable. They had money, they had wealth. But because they entertained the men of God with what money could buy, they got what wealth could never supply. They got children. Oh the gift of hospitality, how good and rewarding. If you lack it, ask it from God.

36
FAITH is HUMBLE

Our Lord and Savior Jesus Christ is our perfect example of humility. To be humble in the simplest sense means to be empty or void of pride. The spirit of pride is of the devil and it's should not be mentioned of a believer. The Bible says, "Humble yourselves in the sight of the Lord, and he shall lift you up" (James 4:10).

When we come before the Lord in humility, He hears us. But when we act like the Pharisee, then we miss our blessings.

> And he spake this parable unto certain which trusted in themselves that they were righteous, and despised others: Two men went up into the temple to pray; the one a Pharisee, and the other a publican. The Pharisee stood and prayed thus with himself, God, I thank thee, that I am not as other men are, extortioners, unjust, adulterers, or even as this publican. I fast twice in the week, I give tithes of all that I possess. And the publican, standing afar off, would not lift up so much as his eyes unto heaven, but smote upon his breast, saying, God be merciful to me a sinner. I tell you, this man went down to his house justified rather than the other: for every one that exalteth himself shall be abased; and he that humbleth himself shall be exalted (Luke 18:9-14).

Jesus used this parable to teach that humility is necessary in everything we do; whether we're praying to God or dealing with men. It doesn't matter how educated we are; it's irrelevant how rich we may be. When we claim to know God and have faith in Him, then we need to function as His children. Self-justification is an act of pride and when we walk in that path, we're on a

Faith Is Humble

detour to doom.

Our Savior never acted according to His position of greatness, but according to His perception of it. His washing of the disciples' feet (John 13:1-17) was humility practicalized. It was to prove that greatness lies in servanthood and to demonstrate a God who came to serve and not to be served. If Jesus did this for His disciples, what reason do we have to be proud?

If anyone had any reason to be proud, Mary the mother of Jesus did.

An earthly woman who carried the heavenly King in her body and felt God the Son move in her womb.

She went through labor pains to bring the Lord into the world and shed her blood on the baby who would shed His blood for her and the whole of human race.

She delivered the boy who would one day become a man and deliver the world from their sins.

She was the first of human race to hold the Lord and kiss the 'Immanuel,' God with us.

She nursed the Almighty with her breasts and changed the soiled diaper of the God that would change our spiritual dilemma.

She took care of Jesus in the day and carried Jehovah at night.

She admired the curls as she stroked her fingers through His hair.

She watched the Savior take His first faltering steps and saved Him from falling who would save her from her fall.

She held the Healer to her chest when His temperature ran high.

She felt the pains when He bruised His knees.

She bathed the Lord and clothed the Messiah.

She pampered Him when crying and rocked Him to sleep when drowsy.

She heard the first words of the Great I Am.

She fed the baby who would one day feed the hungry and gave water to the Child who would one day quench the thirst of the thirsty.

She wondered as 'Wonderful' wiggled in her hands and peacefully smiled back as the Prince of Peace opened His toothless mouth.

She saw Him grow His first milk tooth and watched Him shed His last.

She knew hers was not an ordinary baby. He was perfectly human, yet perfectly Divine.

She held and admired the little hands of her little baby, not knowing she would one day watch those hands spread on the cross and pierced with nails.

She checked Him when wrong and praised Him when right and before she realized it, her boy of yesterday had become a man.

She knew all along that there was something different about her baby of thirty years. Though she had other children, He astounded and excelled them all. There was something He had that the others lacked. And yet she was never proud about it.

She knew the One who turned water to wine could not be anything less than Wonderful.

She knew He was going to become a King but never thought His crown would be made of thorns.

She saw Him restore sight to the blind and witnessed Him heal the sick. Perhaps she was there when He fed the five thousand with five loaves and the four thousand with seven loaves.

She could even have been there when He raised Lazarus from the dead.

Which mother would not be proud of all these achievements in the life of her son? But rather than let loose like a chicken out of a cage, Mary remained cool and calm. Not once did she brag about her special place with God. She was humble all through. Is it any wonder she was highly favored among women?

As the boss in your office, congratulations. The question is not how high up there, but how humble over there are you? The Lord is calling you to a Spirit of humility, for by so doing you show forth the Jesus you profess to your unbelieving employees and those around you who are weaker in the faith. That's not to give room for undue behavior. Even Jesus rebuked workers of iniquity. Godly humility is not an absence of secular authority, but an evidence of spiritual maturity. We don't close our eyes to evil pretending to be humble. That amounts to false humility and the Bible condemns it (Col. 2:18).

And as an employee, how humble are you? You're very skilled in the job, there's no doubt about it. But trust me, that's no reason for you to be rude or unruly to those who are over you. If truly you profess to have faith in the living God, you're to be subject to authority. Remember one of these days, it may be your turn to be the boss and you won't like for anyone to override your authority. Be humble unto your boss, as you will want your employee to be humble unto you. And as you do that, riches, honor and life will be your portion.

I

37. FAITH is IMPORTUNATE — 147

38. FAITH has INTEGRITY — 151

39. FAITH INTERCEDES — 154

37
FAITH is IMPORTUNATE

Importunity is an act of persistence, a conviction not to give up on one's pursuit, a determination to continue until the desired end is achieved. This is essential to our faith if we intend to get anything from God. People in the secular world do all they can to lay hands on their desires. How much more should we–the citizens of heaven–refuse to leave our Father's presence until He gives us the desires of our hearts? A faith that cannot persist is a faith that cannot progress. If all you do is give up when you don't get an answer, you'll never get an answer.

The faith heroes in the Bible are there because they never gave up. They were persistent in asking; consistent in desiring and insistent on getting.

Prophet Daniel had been fasting and praying for the sins of his people, with no results for twenty-one days.

> In those days I Daniel was mourning three full weeks. I ate no pleasant bread, neither came flesh nor wine in my mouth, neither did I anoint myself at all, till three whole weeks were fulfilled (Daniel 10: 2-3).

Daniel didn't give up. He persisted. Does that mean God delayed the answer or that He refused to hear Daniel's plea? No. God had already granted the request the first day Daniel started praying. But the devil, the prince of Persia, stood in the way of the angel that was bringing the good news (10: 10-13). But because Daniel knew the importance of persistence, he refused to be discouraged until he got his breakthrough. He knew that waiting begets getting and to leave was to loose.

Attributes Of A Working Faith

People got their miracles from Jesus because they didn't leave Him until they got what they wanted. A woman of Canaan who had a demon-possessed daughter came to Jesus.

> Then Jesus went thence, and departed into the coasts of Tyre and Sidon. And, behold, a woman of Canaan came out of the same coasts, and cried unto him, saying, Have mercy on me, O Lord, thou son of David; my daughter is grievously vexed with a devil. But he answered her not a word. And his disciples came and besought him, saying, Send her away; for she crieth after us. But he answered and said, I am not sent but unto the lost sheep of the house of Israel. Then came she and worshipped him, saying, Lord, help me. But he answered and said, It is not meet to take the children's bread, and to cast it to dogs. And she said, Truth, Lord: yet the dogs eat of the crumbs which fall from their masters' table. Then Jesus answered and said unto her, O woman, great is thy faith: be it unto thee even as thou wilt. And her daughter was made whole from that very hour (Matthew 15:21-28).

This woman had many reasons to be discouraged and walk away from Jesus. She must have heard a lot about His miracles and deliverances. I doubt if she ever thought she was going to get the kind of treatment she got. Jesus didn't answer her a word. How come? He answered the others. So why was He not answering her despite her crying and pleading? And to worsen her dilemma, His holy disciples suggested He should send her away.

If I entered a church and asked the pastor to pray for me, I would feel terrible if he refuses to say anything. But I would feel humiliated if his elders and deacons ask him to send me away. For a moment, I think I'll forget about prayer because I want to know what I did to deserve such a horrible treatment.

This woman's case was worse. She was in the presence of the Savior. She had no other place to go. At least I can leave the church and go back home, get on my knees and talk to my Lord. I can even find another church. She didn't have that choice. No other option was left for her. He was the only solution to her problem. The disciples, who could have pleaded for her pleaded against her. But she didn't give up. She worshipped Him and asked Him to help, only to be given a more terrible shot.

I can just picture myself in the position of this woman. If Jesus would not do anything about my case, He should at least not call me a dog, a little one for that matter. I'm a person of small stature. Well not really small. I just don't fall to the big group. I'll sure feel bad if anyone calls me a little girl at this age, much less a little dog.

Thank God for people of faith, who are our examples today. These things are in the Bible for us to read and learn. This woman didn't give up. She was completely importunate. She was bent on getting her miracle. It didn't bother her a bit what the Lord said to her. As far as she was concerned, it was nothing compared to the magnitude of her problem. This is the only way we can get from God. We must never allow circumstances to hinder our goal.

Distractions will definitely show up. People will discourage us and tell us we're wasting our time. No we're not. A time wasted in the presence of God is a time well wasted. If wasting my time worshipping and serving my Savior is wrong, I don't want to be right. I would rather waste my entire life in the house of God than waste one second with the devil. This woman got her miracle because she refused to pay attention to distractions. No wonder Jesus described her faith as great.

We cannot relent in faith and expect a favor from God. We must carry on, we must press forward. The battle of faith is not an easy battle. There's a tendency to get discouraged and give up. But the battle is never over until it is over. God is not deaf to our requests. It may have to do with getting the good news of Jesus to somebody else. Only the Holy Spirit can convict and convert the lost. But we have the commission to communicate the word to a lost world.

There's an evangelist in my country. Before he came to Jesus, he was sentenced to ten years in prison for armed robbery. While there in the prison, an inmate who had accepted Christ decided to share the gospel with him. He would go to his cell time after time to give him a tract. This man would refuse. But the friend won't give up either.

When two heady spirits are in for a battle, the Holy Spirit will always win. Finally, he took the tract from him, not to read it, but for two reasons: one, to stop the inmate from coming back; two, to use it for smoking. But he was about to have an encounter with the Lord Jesus. That night, he couldn't sleep. He tried all he could, but sleep refused to come. He got the tract from underneath his pillow, thinking he would fall asleep while reading.

The story? The conversion of Saul of Tarsus, a hardened religious fanatic, who met with the Lord on the road to Damascus and became an evangelist for Jesus. The story deeply touched him and there inside his prison cell, he surrendered his life to Jesus. Today, he's one of the great evangelists in the country. That's because some years back, somebody refused to give up.

If only we can be more persistent in our witnessing, may be the world would have been more evangelized than it is today. And if only we can be more importunate in our faith, may be we would have been more blessed than we are today. Teach me, Oh Lord to be importunate in my faith. Won't you pray the same?

38
FAITH has INTEGRITY

Integrity is the quality of sound moral uprightness and principle; it's the attitude of a man who says what he means and means what he says. He doesn't say yes when he means no and doesn't say no when he means yes. His communication is "Yea, yea; Nay, nay: for whatsoever is more than these cometh of evil" (Matthew 5:37).

The Word of God encourages us, as people of faith, to be men and women of integrity, believers who can stand the test of time when others around them go a different direction; Christians who will run far from sin even when it appears to be pursuing them; children of God who will not allow earthly gains to rob them of their heavenly glory; to be elects who can stand by their words and be taken for their words at any given time; to be people who can be trusted both in little things and big matters.

Lord, who shall abide in thy tabernacle? who shall dwell in thy holy hill? He that walketh uprightly, and worketh righteousness, and speaketh the truth in his heart. He that backbiteth not with his tongue, nor doeth evil to his neighbour, nor taketh up a reproach against his neighbour. In whose eyes a vile person is contemned; but he honoureth them that fear the LORD. He that sweareth to his own hurt, and changeth not. He that putteth not out his money to usury, nor taketh reward against the innocent. He that doeth these things shall never be moved (Psalm 15:1-5).

We serve a God of orderliness, quality and integrity. He wants those He can trust to bear His good name, no matter what the situation is. People who profess to have faith but lack integrity cannot abide in His tabernacle and dwell in His holy hill. Heaven doesn't recognize them, earth doesn't reckon with them.

After his brothers sold him into slavery, Joseph (Jacob's son) ended up in Egypt, in the house of Potiphar, a man of high repute under Pharaoh's command and the captain of his guard. Because his presence brought blessings to his master, Joseph was put in charge of everything in the house. But Potiphar's wife fell in love with Joseph's beauty and desired to have sexual relations with him. She made a mistake. Joseph was a man of integrity who would not allow sexual lusts to sever him from his Savior's love. He refused to sin against God (Genesis 39:9) because though his master didn't know what was going on, God knew. How hard and difficult this must have been for Joseph. He had every good chance to fall. But integrity always makes the difference between the believer who is tempted and the believer who yields to temptation. Joseph was tempted but he didn't yield to temptation. He would rather suffer than surrender. This was a battle between a Belial and a believer.

Standing for integrity is not a joke, neither can anyone claim it's easy. The devil is very cunning and he knows the best time to visit any man or woman of integrity. He knows the best time to attack any Christian. He will bring opportunities across your way at a time most difficult to refuse. He tempted Jesus with food after forty days and forty nights of fasting. What time could be better to tempt a believer with food than when he or she has just finished marathon fasting?

The devil knew that was a prime time in Joseph's life. He would be in his early twenties. He had been separated from family and friends for a few years. Any normal functioning man of his age would be tempted to rush at this free deal. But not Joseph, a man of faith, a man of integrity.

Faith Has Integrity

    Whether yours is as hard as Joseph's or not, stand for integrity in everything and God will honor you. He honored Joseph. Though he ended up in prison, but even right there he received God's favor (Genesis 39:21-23).

    When you stand in your integrity for truth, venue will be no barrier to your blessings. God will honor you regardless of place or race. If Joseph had satisfied his desires, if he had failed in his integrity, he would have been killed. Today, you can read his story and learn because he stood for his faith. You too can stand so that sometime to come, others will read your story and learn. The Bible says, "The just man (and woman, pardon me for being jealous) walketh in his (her) integrity: his children (her children) are blessed after him (her)" (Proverbs 20:7). Walk in your integrity and your children will live to enjoy the fruits you have sown.

39
FAITH INTERCEDES

To intercede is to go before the Lord, not for yourself, but for someone else. It is praying on behalf of that other person who may or may not be aware you're praying for him or her. I pray for people that request me to do so. But I also pray for those who don't even know I'm praying for them.

As a family, we pray together all the time. But I doubt if my husband and my children have an idea how much I intercede on their behalf once they leave the house for the day. I use the time they spend at school and at work to pray for them and seek God's protection, favor, and grace to follow them everywhere they go. I ask the Lord to chase evil away from them and if in any danger, He should deliver them. I go round each room and pray over each person by name, claiming God's promises for them: they're heads and not tails, they would be above and not below, they would lead and not follow, they would lend and not borrow (Deut. 28:12, 13). His blessings would pursue them and overtake them; whatever they set their hands on to do shall prosper and that includes my children's academic performances. But more importantly, the love of the world would not take the love of the Lord from their hearts and all the days of their lives, they shall be giants in His vineyard.

No matter how holy and how spiritual you're, you still need someone to uphold you in prayer. The pulpit needs to intercede on behalf of the pew, so the people can be filled with the power of God when they hear the messages. The pew needs to uphold the pulpit in prayer that God may continue to anoint His preachers and pastors, so they can preach the true and undiluted Word of God. One cannot do without the other. No pastor ever preaches to an empty church and no congregation ever listens to the wall preach to them.

Faith Intercedes

Otherwise, there will be need for an intercessor to pray for their deliverance. Brothers need sisters; children need parents. It goes on and on and so shall it be till the Lord returns.

Intercession is scriptural. Moses on many occasions interceded on behalf of the children of Israel. When he went up to Mt. Sinai to receive the Ten Commandments, the Israelites got tired of waiting for his return and made another god in form of a golden calf. God's anger was kindled against them. But Moses stood in the gap to seek the face of Jehovah (Exodus 32:1-14). Moses interceded; God relented His anger.

We all have difficult people around us. People that are just naturally hard to please. Even amongst Christians, there are those that aren't so easy to get along with. They need your prayers. You never know the reason for their actions. People get on the edge for one reason or the other. Whatever the case may be, let's learn to uphold others in our prayers.

In Antioch, Herod Agrippa was reigning. After killing James with the sword, he laid hold on Peter and put him in prison. And to make sure he couldn't get away, he put four squads of soldiers in charge, to watch him. I know a squad consists of at least four soldiers. Which means he had at least sixteen soldiers watching over one soul. What could a single man do to free himself from sixteen soldiers? Not sixteen men, sixteen soldiers. But watch the power of intercession.

> And when he had apprehended him, he put him in prison, and delivered him to four quaternions*of soldiers to keep him; intending after Easter to bring him forth to the people. Peter therefore was kept in prison: <u>but prayer was made without ceasing of the church unto God for him.</u> And when Herod would have brought him forth, the same night Peter was sleeping between two soldiers [what a place

to sleep], bound with two chains: and the keepers before the door kept the prison. And, behold, the angel of the Lord came upon him, and a light shined in the prison: and he smote Peter on the side, and raised him up, saying, Arise up quickly. And his chains fell off from his hands. And the angel said unto him, Gird thyself, and bind on thy sandals. And so he did. And he saith unto him, Cast thy garment about thee, and follow me. And he went out, and followed him; and wist not that it was true which was done by the angel; but thought he saw a vision. When they were past the first and the second ward, they came unto the iron gate that leadeth unto the city; which opened to them of his own accord: and they went out, and passed on through one street; and forthwith the angel departed from him. And when Peter was come to himself, he said, Now I know of a surety, that the LORD hath sent his angel, and hath delivered me out of the hand of Herod, and from all the expectation of the people of the Jews (Acts 12:4-11).

Intercession works wonders. When intercession is in session, every action of the enemy goes into a recession. As faith intercedes, flesh recedes. Intercession moves the hands of God and puts His angels to work. It gives peace to the persecuted in prison and sets the captives free. It shakes the powers of heaven and shatters the plans of hell. The power of intercession, no amount of guard posts or iron gates can stand in its way. It's real, it's strong, it's reliable.

No wonder apostle James said, "Is any sick among you? let him call for the elders of the church; and let them pray over him, anointing him with oil in the name of the Lord: And the prayer of faith shall save the sick, and the Lord shall raise him up; ... Confess your faults one to another, and pray one for another, that ye may be healed. The effectual fervent prayer of a righteous man availeth much" (James 5:14-16). Praying for a sick person to receive healing is an act of intercession.

Brethren can also intercede for the forgiveness of sins for another brethren. If a sister confesses her trespass to you, you're supposed to pray and not mock her behind. The only saints who cannot fall are those under the ground. As long as you still stand above the ground, you can fall.

Wherefore let him that thinketh he standeth take heed lest he fall (1 Corinthians 10:12).

The day you begin to see yourself as one who cannot fall, that's the beginning of your downfall. Therefore pray and intercede for others who have fallen and the Lord will use them to lift you up when it's your turn.

*Set of four

J

40. FAITH has JOY 159

40
FAITH has JOY

Most of the time, people mistake happiness for joy. It's good to be happy. There's nothing wrong with it. But happiness never lasts. That's because it only comes when we get what we want. People get happy on their wedding days. I was happy and I'm happy still. But just like any other marriage, there have been so many gloomy days in between, days I wished I never got married.

Joy on the other hand, is far deeper than just a temporal state of excitement. A new home will make anyone happy. But people move into new homes, seem all happy, only to loose their peace after a while. Definitely the Bible wants us to be happy. Children of the Most High are to be happy that they have God as Father. But joy far outweighs and outlives happiness.

The joy of the LORD is your strength (Nehemiah 8:10).

Joy gives us strength in the face of persecution and temptation. The Bible tells us to count it all joy when we fall into temptations because the trying of our faith will lead to patience (James 1:2-3).

Looking unto Jesus the author and finisher of our faith; who for the joy that was set before him endured the cross, despising the shame, and is set down at the right hand of the throne of God (Hebrews 12: 2).

Jesus endured the cross for the joy set before Him. What joy? The joy that He was going to be crucified? No! The joy that He was going to die? No! It was the joy of the completion of His mission. The only reason He came was to die for the sins of the world, so we can be reconciled unto the Father. And that was finally done on the cross. His crucifixion was a mark of victory.

Happiness laughs at success, but joy smiles at the storm. When faced with trials and tribulations, the joy of the Lord is to be our strength. Nobody can be happy during tribulation or persecution. Jesus compared a person in tribulation to a woman in labor.

> A woman when she is in travail hath sorrow, because her hour is come: but as soon as she is delivered of the child, she remembereth no more the anguish, for joy that a man is born into the world. And ye now therefore have sorrow: but I will see you again, and your heart shall rejoice, and your joy no man taketh from you (John 16: 21-23).

A woman in labor is not a happy woman. I've been through it, so I'm talking practicality. (Remember there's nothing like epidural in my country.) There's no way anyone can be in such pain and be happy. But there was always this thought behind my mind–'I'm going to have a baby.' The moment my baby was handed over to me, I found it difficult to remember the pain I went through for that baby to come. All I wanted was to cuddle my little bundle of joy and give glory to God.

Happiness can be taken away from anybody. Fire can cause damage to that which makes us happy. Flood can put a sudden end to the source of our excitement. But our joy no one can take. Joy will watch the house on fire and still give glory to God. It will burst into laughter when the enemy of the good news is inflicting pains on the body. Even when it means we have to die for the cause of Christ, we do so rejoicing that eternity with Jesus is awaiting us.

Prophet Isaiah gave an excellent description of the joy of the redeemed.

> Therefore the redeemed of the LORD shall return, and come with singing unto Zion; and everlasting joy shall be upon their head: they

shall obtain gladness and joy; and sorrow and mourning shall flee away (Isaiah 51:11).

When joy comes, sorrow flees. The Bible confirms in the presence of the Lord, there is fullness of joy and at His right hand are pleasures for evermore (Psalm 16:11). Our faith in God must make our joy radiate to others around us. Unfortunately, many Christians are guilty of that. We come to church, nagging and frowning.

I was at the church on a Wednesday evening for Bible study. As I tried to park, I saw another empty parking slot and decided to back out so I could move closer to the building. Meanwhile, a lady pulled up behind me. I could tell from my mirror that she was aggravated by the one-minute delay. So I decided to get out of her way. I didn't realize how much I had provoked her until she zoomed past me. For a while I could not believe she was coming for Bible study. The anger was so visible that even my boys remarked the look on her face. If that were my first time going to a church, I don't think I would ever attempt to go back. Who knows how many souls she has sent back because of her attitude? After the service, I went and apologized to her. She explained that she was coming straight from work. But she definitely felt bad that I had to come and apologize to her.

Brethren, whether we're coming from work or home, eating or drinking, reading or writing, let us strive to show to others the joy in our faith. A faith without joy cannot share Jesus with others. We cannot give what we don't have. When the Bible asks us to rejoice always (1 Thes. 5:16), it means to rejoice always, whether the weather is good or bad. It's telling us to be joyful even when doing so may not make sense.

Rejoice when you loose a loved one in the Lord, not because you're happy at the loss, but because you know that soon you will see that person again. Rejoice when you have no food to eat, not because you don't feel the hunger, but because you know the bread of life will send help from above. Rejoice when people hate you because you always mention the name of Jesus, for soon they will come to recognize that your Jesus indeed is Lord.

Be joyful in winter, for soon it'll be spring and life will return to every dead situation in your life. Be joyful in spring, for soon the summer will come and the warmth of His love will fill your home and brighten your heart. Be joyful in summer, for soon it'll be fall and every tree of sadness and sorrow in your life will wither away. Be joyful in autumn, for soon it'll be winter and angels from the realms of glory will fill your world with glad tidings. Be joyful in season, be joyful out of season. And if truly you have faith in God, again I say rejoice.

K

41. FAITH is KIND   164

41
__FAITH is KIND__

I had my daughter in 1997. We were living in Columbus, Ohio. One evening we went to KFC and from there went to Meijers (Pronounced Myers) to get some groceries. On our way back around 9.p.m., the vehicle suddenly stopped. My girl was only a few months old. Initially we thought it was the engine oil. My husband ran to a nearby gas station, while I stood on the roadside waving vehicles down for help. I can't remember the number of vehicles that ran away for fear of someone who might be waving them down for evil. I don't blame them. It was dark and I'm black.

Finally, a man stopped because he saw me carrying a baby. Though the police came few minutes later, that man determined not to leave us there. He went home and called his wife. None of them left until we got the car off the road. And even after the ordeal, he asked the police to go while he and his wife took us home. The whole ordeal lasted about one hour. But up till today, their kind gesture remains fresh in my memory. [In case you get hold of this book, thanks Jack and Maria for being so kind; and to the police that helped us that night, you are awesome.]

An act of kindness by many people's understanding of the word, is done to someone you love or at least know. That's not true. There are people I've never known in my life who have shown unexpected kindness to me. I just mentioned the couple that helped us when our vehicle stopped. I never met them before in my life. In fact, we never saw them again after that night, though we called to thank them. As people professing to have faith in God, we need to show kindness to people around us.

Rahab was a harlot. But the Bible says she did not perish with them

Faith Is Kind

that believed not, because she received the spies –who were men of God–with peace (Hebrews 11:31). She was kind to them. If a harlot could be wise enough to find her way to faith haven, what will be the excuse for us who are not harlots? Apostle James said, "Likewise also was not Rahab the harlot justified by works, when she had received the messengers, and had sent them out another way?" (James 2:25).

Let's not think that the Word of God supports harlotry or lying. NEVER! What makes her case unique is that a harlot of all persons, was least expected to do what she did. There are believers who would not spare a cup of water for a fellow brethren and yet, they want God to recognize their contributions to the church. Rahab obtained a promise of safety and security from the evil to come, because of her kindness. She saved her life and that of her entire household. And who would ever have thought that the Savior of the world would come through the lineage of the savior of messengers: "And Salmon begat Booz of Rachab; and Booz begat Obed of Ruth; … And Jacob begat Joseph the husband of Mary, of whom was born Jesus, who is called Christ" (Matthew 1:5, 16).

In fact, we may not be the recipients of our kind acts. But generations to come will live to reap the fruits of our labors of kindness. When Jonathan acted kind to David, he had no idea his lame son Mephibosheth would be the one to enjoy the fruits long after his death (2 Samuel 9). Apostle Paul said for us to be kind to one another (Ephesians 4:32), as we have the opportunity, do good to all men (Galatians 6:10), and even those enemies who least deserve our kindness, we're to feed them if they hunger and give them drink if thirsty (Romans 12:20). Apostle Peter admonished us to add kindness to godliness (2 Peter 1:7).

Let's not be hearers and readers of the word only, but also doers

fulfilling the law (James 1:22). Our God has an everlasting kindness on us. So why won't we show kindness towards another? If indeed you have faith in God, then I strongly admonish you to add kindness to it. After all, isn't it because of God's unmerited and undeserved kindness that we're joint heirs with His Son Jesus?

L

42. FAITH LEADS   168

43. FAITH is LIGHT   171

44. FAITH LOVES   180

42
FAITH LEADS

    Leadership comes in various ways. There are leaders over nations, cities, communities, households, churches and even small groups up to Christian cell groups. As we have presidents over nations, we also have husbands over households–some good, some evil and the rest in-between. But the kind of leadership I like to consider is faith based. These were leaders who acted based upon their faith in God. They were leaders either appointed by God or moved by the power of the Holy Spirit to lead.

    Deborah was a Judge but more importantly, a prophetess in Israel. As a prophetess, she was inspired to give Barak a message from God.

    And the children of Israel again did evil in the sight of the LORD, when Ehud was dead. And the LORD sold them into the hand of Jabin king of Canaan, … And the children of Israel cried unto the LORD: for he had nine hundred chariots of iron; and twenty years he mightily oppressed the children of Israel. And Deborah, a prophetess, the wife of Lapidoth, she judged Israel at that time. … And she sent and called Barak the son of Abinoam out of Kedeshnaphtali, and said unto him, Hath not the LORD God of Israel commanded, saying, Go and draw toward mount Tabor, and take with thee ten thousand men of the children of Naphtali and of the children of Zebulun? And I will draw unto thee to the river Kishon Sisera, the captain of Jabin's army, with his chariots and his multitude; and I will deliver him into thine hand. And Barak said unto her, If thou wilt go with me, then I will go: but if thou wilt not go with me, then I will not go. <u>And she said, I will surely go with thee: notwithstanding the journey that thou</u>

Faith Leads

takest shall not be for thine honour; for the LORD shall sell Sisera into the hand of a woman. **And Deborah arose, and went with Barak to Kedesh. And Barak called Zebulun and Naphtali to Kedesh; and he went up with ten thousand men at his feet: and Deborah went up with him (Judges 4:1-10).**

Though this message was from God, Barak was scared to go to war, not unless Deborah followed him. He had no confidence in himself. I'm surprised that a man who was void of self-confidence could repose confidence in a woman, especially when it had to do with a war. Sure Deborah had a strong personality but that wasn't the reason for her acceptance to go with Barak. She was a woman of faith. She was confident that God would give them victory. She knew God would do what He had always done in the past. That was the power of faith.

Our God is no respecter of sex, age or height. What He can accomplish through a giant, He can also accomplish through a dwarf. He can make a David do what a Saul cannot do. All He's asking is our availability, not our ability. In fact, if ability were God's standard for choosing a leader, no one is qualified, for there's none able to do God's work and definitely none strong enough to withstand the enemy of our soul, the devil. But when we make ourselves available for His task, then He makes us able for the task.

Joash was alive when God bypassed him and used his son Gideon to save Israel from the hand of the Midianites. Though the least in his father's house–a poor house in Manasseh–yet God said to him, "Go in this thy might, and thou shalt save Israel from the hand of the Midianites: have not I sent thee? Surely I will be with thee, and thou shalt smite the Midianites as one man" (Judges 6:14, 16).

That might that you call little is all God needs to use you for great

things. Leadership is not something we do by our own valor or knowledge. God is not asking us to help Him do the job when He puts us in positions of leadership. He's capable of doing His job, but He needs men and women of faith He can assign as overseers. We need to accept our inability and ask that He impart His ability into us. And that's where faith comes in. Flesh says, 'I can't do this job, so I quit.' Faith says, 'I know I can't do this job, but "I can do all things through Christ which strengtheneth me" (Philippians 4:13). Therefore I shall do it "as of the ability which God giveth: that God in all things may be glorified through Jesus Christ" (1 Peter 4:11).

Has God placed you in a position of leadership, oh man and woman of faith? The power to succeed has been given to you. Just hold on to your faith in God. Even Jesus was not a leader without problems. He had enemies from within and without. But He didn't allow the actions of men to decide for Him. He led with authority. Don't look at yourself as unfit. If God says you're fit, you're fit. Lead as one who has the backup of the Holy Spirit and you will not be put to shame.

43
FAITH is LIGHT

December 24, we were in church for the Christmas candle light service. Every person had a candle. When it was time to light the candles, all lights in the sanctuary were put out and the whole place turned dark. I could not see the person in my front. But with one lit candle lighting another, everything changed within a few minutes. I could see the person in the third row in front. What made the difference? The lights from the candle dispelled the darkness.

How best can we describe light? I consider it as a non-existence or an absence of darkness. The importance of light cannot be overestimated. Before creation, the Bible says the whole earth was without form and was covered with darkness (Genesis 1:2). And before God created any other thing, He created light (Genesis 1:3). For light to precede everything ever created tells how important it must be to the heart of God. Even science admits if there's no light, there's no life.

After Jesus had been baptized in the Jordan River, the first event that took place was His confirmation as the light of the world.

> And Jesus, when He was baptized, went up straightway out of the water: and, lo, the heavens were opened unto him, and he saw the Spirit of God descending like a dove, and lighting upon him (Matthew 3:16).

As Christians, we live in a world of utter spiritual darkness. Whether we like it or not, we're part of the system. But we can make a difference by lighting up the dark places. That doesn't mean we take candles with us everywhere we go or walk around with flashlights in our hands. But we serve a God of light and believe in His Son, Himself the Light. We can make a difference by shining the light of the gospel, the light of God's Word into the dark hearts and minds of those that are still in spiritual darkness. Many are wallowing in their sins and spiritual blindness. They can't see unless someone shows them the way. He who must lead the blind must have eyes. And he who will rescue out of darkness must have light.

As believers, the Bible calls us the light of the world. For that light to be seen by those in the dark, we have a part to play.

> Ye are the light of the world. A city that is set on an hill cannot be hid. Neither do men light a candle, and put it under a bushel, but on a candlestick; and it giveth light unto all that are in the house. Let your light so shine before men, that they may see your good works, and glorify your Father which is in heaven (Matthew 5:14-16).

How can we make our lights shine before men?

❖ Light makes manifest and reveals the truth. Workers of evil hate light and love darkness because their deeds are evil (John 3:19-20). It's easier for them to hide their evil deeds when it's dark to avoid being caught and brought to justice.

In the book of Kings, two harlots both had babies three days apart (I Kings 3:16-21). In the mid of the night, one harlot slept on her child. The child died. She replaced her dead son with the living son of her partner. But there was one thing that helped the other woman identify her true son, the morning light. The evil was done in the night but the truth was revealed in the light. That's exactly what God wants us to be to the dark world.

When we speak and spread the infallible, undiluted and non-compromising Word of God, the Word of truth, the Word that we heard and accepted, it dispels the lies of Satan and brings the truth out in Jesus and reveals the secrets of darkness to those dwelling therein. It lets those in bondage see the horror they're in. Many of them are in darkness out of sheer ignorance. They don't even know it's dark. It takes knowing bad to recognize good, and it takes knowing darkness to appreciate light. If you have never seen light, darkness won't make any difference. So how can they understand their spiritual dilemma unless someone takes the pain and the initiative to show them the difference? Christians, we have a job to do.

Jesus said we don't light a lamp and put it under a bushel. It has to be strategically and 'mountainously' positioned so others can see and benefit from it. As the light of the world, we have known the truth of the gospel. But there are others who haven't heard. Christians and people of faith, it's our duty to share the word with them, to tell them the truth, to let them know there's something better than darkness. The disciples never ceased to tell the truth, even when the enemies of the gospel didn't want to hear. That's the same adamant attitude we have to develop and maintain.

❖ Light does not ask permission to shine. It shines without paying any attention to darkness, completely irrespective of its obstruction. Whether evildoers want to hear or not is of no relevance to the preaching. The gospel must be preached, the truth must be said, the light must continue to shine to every dark places. We have to tell them how we were once in that same bondage (Ephesians 5:8) and how the truth has made us free (John 8:32).

Anyone who has ever been an unbeliever was once in darkness. I've been there and I know the difference between then and now. Before I came to know the Lord, I knew there was something different about the believers. There was something they had that I lacked. They had the Light and I was groping in darkness. Now that I've come to the Light, I cannot and must not keep it to myself. A believer that fails to share his or her faith with another person is nothing but a spiritual failure. He or she is a lamp hidden under a bushel. His or her light is hidden and therefore of no benefit to the darkness around it.

❖ Going back to the candle light service, the lighting of candles started with just one candle. The moment that candle was lit, all eyes turned towards that direction. Why? It drew people's attention to itself. As men and women of faith, we have to draw unbelievers to us by our good works. Just as light is very pleasant to have and attracts life to it, so must those who know us be attracted to our faith.

Anywhere we are, others must see the difference in our actions and attitudes. There are many hurting souls out there who are dying in darkness. They need help to get out of their misery. When there's no light and everywhere is dark, a lot of bad things come with it. So it is with people in darkness. A lot of unimaginable evil things befall them and they have no solutions. We're the only solution left for them.

One particular night, the lights in our neighborhood went out. I was in the parlor with my children. The moment the darkness set in, there was confusion, insecurity, and uncertainty. That's the way it is with the people in spiritual darkness. Everyday of their lives is graced with confusion, uncertainty and insecurity. That's why many of them get fed up with life and either commit suicide or end up in prison. Unfortunately, many don't know what to do, where to go or who to approach. When we make ourselves available for their help, a confidence for trust will be built in them, knowing that they have someone with whom they can share their heartaches.

The only thing that saved us that night was a small flashlight. It made a great difference. Darkness is never of help to light. But light, no matter how small, is always a ready help in darkness.

Faith Is Light

Our faith must prove to the weak in mind there's power in the name of Jesus and help at the foot of the cross. Even if it's a little faith, let it make a difference in your neighborhood or wherever God has placed you. Let the good word be evidenced in your good works.

❖ Light knocks out darkness. When we drive in the night, we need light to see in the dark. As we approach a dark area, the light knocks out the darkness and we get a clearer vision of the road. Once in the faith and true to God's Word, darkness cannot stand in our way. His Word will be our guide to lead the way. He has promised to go before us and make the crooked places straight, break in pieces the gates of brass, and cut in sunder the bars of iron (Isaiah 45:2).

As children of the Almighty, we're going to face mountains, walk on crooked paths, and encounter gates of bronze and bars of iron. They're all metaphorical of the powers of darkness. They will attack us, cross our paths and even attempt to hinder our eternity with God. But when we remain strong in the faith, we're insured and protected in the blood of Jesus. The power of darkness is no match for the faith of a child of God. Just as a small flashlight in hand will make a difference when going through a dark path, so also a child of God must make a difference where evildoers and evil spirits operate.

On many occasions in the Bible, children of light encountered evil spirits. But the man of faith always prevailed. Demons have no power over the faith of a Christian. They're of darkness and we're of light. The two cannot dwell together. There's no communion between light and darkness. When light appears, darkness disappears. When light comes, darkness flees. When a child of God is around, principalities and powers have to bow and recognize the authority. We have to boldly and confidently assert our authority and nullify their powers. Christians living in the same house with a worker of darkness must always be a threat, not to the individual, but to the evil spirit living inside the person. Our prayers must constitute a spiritual disturbance to them. They can only function when we're not around.

An evangelist in my country was traveling in a vehicle with his driver. On the way, a young lady waived them for a ride. The evangelist knew there was something not right about her but still decided to give her a ride. She entered and they proceeded. Not too long after, she asked to be dropped off. "Why?", the evangelist asked. He knew the problem with her. She was feeling uneasy staying in the same vehicle with the man of God. She didn't want her secrets exposed. Every attempt to start off a conversation with her failed. She just wanted to be out of the vehicle. Holy Ghost fire was burning on her body. She felt threatened by the power of light because she was of darkness.

This should be the testimony of us Christians. When children of darkness are around us, they must feel uncomfortable and uneasy. Our presence must constitute a hindrance to their operation.

❖ Light brings warmth to the body. As people of faith, we're to bring warmth and revival to the dark and boring world of unbelievers. In our work place or anywhere we are, God wants us to display a spirit of joy that others will see and be moved to ask what the secret is. And then we'll be able to tell them we serve a God of all joy, the true Light who is Jesus Christ.

Others must know us as peculiar, no grumbling, disputing or trouble making people, always bubbling with joy. That's not to act dumb and join in ungodly practices. But that our light ought to put out their dark practices when we hold fast the Word of God, to keep us blameless and harmless, and to make us shine in a crooked and perverse generation. We cannot claim to be in the faith and be in bondage of darkness.

In conclusion of this topic, let's see the parable of the rich man and

Lazarus.

> There was a certain rich man, which was clothed in purple and fine linen, and fared sumptuously every day: And there was a certain beggar named Lazarus, which was laid at his gate, full of sores, And desiring to be fed with the crumbs which fell from the rich man's table: moreover the dogs came and licked his sores. And it came to pass, that the beggar died, and was carried by the angels into Abraham's bosom: the rich man also died, and was buried; And in hell he lift up his eyes, being in torments, and seeth Abraham afar off, and Lazarus in his bosom. And he cried and said, Father Abraham, have mercy on me, and send Lazarus, that he may dip the tip of his finger in water, and cool my tongue; for I am tormented in this flame. But Abraham said, Son, remember that thou in thy lifetime receivedst thy good things, and likewise Lazarus evil things: but now he is comforted, and thou art tormented. And beside all this, between us and you there is a great gulf fixed: so that they which would pass from hence to you cannot; neither can they pass to us, that would come from thence (Luke 16:19-26).

Many times I've tried to see somebody outside in the night. When the lights are off and the inside of the house is dark, there's a clear vision of the person in the light. Remarkably, the person in the light will not be able to see who is in the dark. The Bible says, "The people which sat in darkness saw great light" (Matthew 4:16).

As men and women in this world, we're all on a trip. At one time or the other, that trip will end and we have to go back home. When that happens, there are only two destinations we can call home, heaven or hell. Those who are in the faith will end up with Daddy and Brother Jesus in heaven. And

Attributes Of A Working Faith

those who choose to follow Satan will end up with him in hell, and so shall it be forever.

One thing however is sure. In hell, it's absolute darkness (Matthew 8:12). In heaven, it's absolute light. No darkness shall ever appear for the Bible says, "And the city had no need of the sun, neither of the moon, to shine in it: for the glory of God did lighten it, and the Lamb is the light thereof" (Revelation 21:23). And just as a person in darkness sees him who is in the light, so will citizens of hell see us in heaven, but we will never see them.

In the above parable, the rich man saw Lazarus in Abraham's bosom. There's no record that Lazarus saw him and I believe he did not. If I get to heaven and see my unbelieving father in hell, I'll definitely be sad and shed tears. But the Bible says, "<u>And God shall wipe away all tears from their (our) eyes</u>; and there shall be no more death, <u>neither sorrow</u>, <u>nor crying</u>, neither shall there be any more pain: for the former things are passed away" (Rev. 21:4).

The moment we cross over to our Paradise, it won't matter what we went through here. It is all over. No more sorrowing, crying or weeping. Our last laugh shall turn out the best. But those in hell will continue to see us and wish they had chosen and walked the way of light. They will beg us for mercy that's too late to offer. They will wish they too can enjoy the freedom we enjoy. That freedom does not just come. We chose it and you too can choose it.

There's only one way to freedom, and that is knowing the truth before it's too late. The truth is not found in darkness but in the Light, which is Christ Jesus. If you don't have this Light, it's never too late to put out the darkness in your life and accept Jesus as your Lord and King. Let Him have the control of your life and His light will continue to shine in your way. The night is far spent, the day is at hand. Therefore cast off your works of darkness, and put

on the armor of light (Romans 13:2).

44
FAITH LOVES

God had demonstrated to us the act of perfect love. "For God so loved the world, that he gave his only begotten Son, that whosoever believeth in him should not perish, but have everlasting life" (John 3:16). But it appears like these days, there's an unfortunate use of the expression LOVE. People no longer seem or care to know the difference between love and like. There's a visible lack of love for other people and that unfortunately has spread to the body of believers.

We smile at each other, we claim to love God, and we confess our faith in Jesus. The question is, do we love one another? If we profess to know God and claim to love Him and have faith in Him, how come we can't be like Him in love? What kind of a faith do you have towards God if you lack in love towards your brother or sister?

Beloved, let us love one another: for love is of God; and every one that loveth is born of God, and knoweth God. He that loveth not knoweth not God; for God is love (1 John 4:7-8).

It's not possible to love God and hate men–that's loving the potter and hating his clay. The two are inseparable. Apostle Paul wrote, "But let us, who are of the day, be sober, putting on the breastplate of faith and love; and for an helmet, the hope of salvation" (1 Thes. 5:8). We of the day are believers in the Lord. Our breastplate of faith is incomplete without love. The two must go together. In his letter to Philemon, Paul wrote, "I thank my God, making mention of thee always in my prayers, Hearing of thy love and faith, which thou hast toward the Lord Jesus, and toward all saints; … For we have great joy and consolation in thy love, because the bowels of the saints are refreshed by thee, brother" (Philemon 4-7).

Brother Philemon knew the secret of faith and love. He knew that faith with love equals refreshing. We can't have faith in God and love Him without extending the same love to others. That will make us spiritual liars and hypocrites.

If a man say, I love God, and hateth his brother, he is a liar: for he that loveth not his brother whom he hath seen, how can he love God whom he hath not seen? (1 John 4:20).

There's no hide and seek in the law. If you claim to love God, if truly you're a believer in Christ, if indeed you have faith in Jesus, you have to love your brethren. Otherwise, you're not of God.

Faith and love form a bunch with hope. I call them conjoined triplets because they're inseparable, but love weighs more than the other two.

Though I speak with the tongues of men and of angels, and have not charity*, I am become as sounding brass, or a tinkling cymbal. And though I have the gift of prophecy, and understand all mysteries, and all knowledge; and though I have all faith, so that I could remove mountains, and have not charity, I am nothing. And though I bestow all my goods to feed the poor, and though I give my body to be burned, and have not charity, it profiteth me nothing. ... <u>And now abideth faith, hope, charity, these three; but the greatest of these is charity</u> (1 Corinthians 13:1-13).

This is the best sermon any preacher can give on the subject of love. But no matter how much faith a preacher has, if he lacks love, even his message of love will be of no effect. If Paul lacked in love, his preaching on love would have rendered him a liar. You can't be fervent in faith and be lacking in love. It avails to nothing and has no life.

I remember the case of a dear sister in the Lord. She had been married for about twelve years but no child. Hers wasn't a case of barrenness. She would get pregnant but never carry it to term. And that went on year after year. Then she had a vision that she should invest her love for a child in the life of another child.

Meanwhile, another sister in another city had a baby and died at childbirth. She took the child and gave her all the love she would give her own baby. They were strangers to each other but that didn't hinder her from doing what God wanted her to do. Within fifteen months, she got pregnant and for the first time in her marriage, she carried a baby to full term. By the time the girl hit two years, she gave birth to a boy. That was because she gave her love in faith.

Does that minister to you oh barren? God is asking you to love other children. If you can't love other children, how can you love your own? Don't assume you're going to have fault-free children. It doesn't matter how spiritual you are, some of them will just run you crazy. They'll suck the patience out of your loins. But you know what? God has given them to you for a purpose. While you don't make them take over the control of your life as to loose your parental discipline, you still make them feel appreciated and loved. Invest your love in any child that comes your way and by this time next year, you'll be holding your own baby. Receive it in Jesus' name.

> For in Jesus Christ neither circumcision availeth any thing, nor uncircumcision; but faith which worketh by love (Galatians 5:6).

I envy your faith, brother. I respect your faith, sister. I wish I could have the kind of faith you have, pastor. But God is asking, do you love others as Christ loved the church or even as you love yourself? For without love, your faith is bleak and weak.

*Love

M

45. FAITH has MEASURE	184
46. FAITH is MEEK	193
47. FAITH is MERCIFUL	195

45
FAITH has MEASURE

Measure? Does it mean faith has length and breadth? No! The Bible says, "For I say, through the grace given unto me, to every man that is among you, not to think of himself more highly than he ought to think; but to think soberly, according as God hath dealt to every man the measure of faith" (Romans 12:3).

There are different measures of faith, and every man has been given a measure, either great or small. He who claims not to have faith in God does so out of his ignorance. God is not in anyway responsible for any man's lack of faith.

While we know that God is no respecter of persons but definitely, there are people who're stronger in faith than others. Barak was a man of faith. But he admitted Deborah was stronger than him. That was why he would not go to war unless Deborah followed him.

Faith played key roles in the various healing miracles recorded in the Bible. When the two blind men came crying after Jesus, He touched their eyes and said to them, "According to your faith be it unto you" (Matthew 9: 29). Though we have no idea how big or small their faith was, but it definitely played a role in their healing.

Let's consider the different measures of faith outlined in God's Word.

1.<u>Common Faith</u>: When Paul wrote to Titus, he addressed him as his true son in the common Faith (Titus 1:4). By common faith he wasn't implying a faith everyone picks up on the street. Faith can be seen in two different ways. We talk of people who have enough faith to move mountains–that's faith exercised. Believers in the Lord Jesus also address themselves as people of faith–that's faith expressed and that's the common faith. Go to any part of the world, believers in Christ are the same.

I meet believers from other parts of the world. Of course they speak different languages and I just look when they talk. But one thing remains constant. When it comes to Jesus, we all have the same attitude. The faith of an American believer is not different from that of a German. I'm from Nigeria and I know what I'm talking. The excitement here is the same over there. I've never heard of missionaries who go to other countries and come back confused because the people have a different Jesus. If that happens, the truth is they don't have Jesus. They're just being plain carnal.

In the Corinthian church, there were divisions amongst the believers. Some said they were of Appolos, some of Paul and others spiritual enough said they were of Jesus. But Paul told them there could be no division in the body of Christ. "For other foundation can no man lay than that is laid, which is Jesus Christ" (I Cor. 3: 11). It's just one Christ and you're either for Him or not. There's nothing like dual spiritualism in Jesus.

When Christ laid down His life, He did so for all, not just a sect or a particular race. The Bible doesn't say for God so loved the English people or the Latin America. It says, "For God so loved the world, that he gave his only begotten Son, that <u>whosoever</u> believeth in him should not perish, but have everlasting life" (John 3:16). The faith that the white has to believe in Him is the same as that of the black. Of course the name Jesus may be called in different dialects but the message of the Cross is the same. Jesus is the same everywhere.

The faith of the apostles of old is not different from that of ours today. I've never heard of a race or nationality where the Lord's Supper is referred to as the Lord's breakfast. I know some churches may be more rigid than others as to insist on having it only at night. But whether taken in the morning or at midnight, the Lord's Supper is the same. We all trace it back to the last meal He had with His disciples while on earth, and which He commanded to be done in remembrance of Him. We share a common faith and a common salvation in Jesus, whether Gentiles or Jews, slaves or free.

2. <u>**Great Faith**</u>: On two different occasions, Jesus used this term for people in the Bible. The first was the centurion in Matthew 8:5-13. The second was the woman of Canaan in Matthew 15:21-28 or Syrophenician woman in Mark 7: 26. From these two passages, there are two qualities of a great faith: humility and importunity.

The centurion was a man of high estate and the least expected to do what he did. After all, he wasn't the only rich man in his days. The rich young ruler who came running to Jesus left His presence sad because he could not give to the poor, much less a servant. There are many other rich men mentioned in the Bible, but none went to Jesus pleading on behalf of an ordinary servant. But the centurion didn't function as a master to be served, but as a master who could serve others, including those under him. Inspite of his wealth, he didn't see his servant as a poor servant but a precious soul who deserved to live and not die. Isn't that what Jesus did for you and I? He never saw us the way we were. We were supposed to be hung on the cross for our sins but Jesus took it upon Himself to do that for us, so that we will live and not die. Our poor wretched souls were more precious to Him than His very own life.

The centurion also displayed remarkable humility in his approach to Jesus. Though himself a man of authority, yet he recognized that of Jesus as higher. He who had others under him became completely self-abased to

Faith Has Measure

Jesus. He believed that though he had authority over his servants, Jesus had authority over everything–men and women, demons and diseases, powers and principalities, animate and inanimate, visible and invisible, living or dead. And distance was never a barrier to His authority. His words spoken from afar would do the same job as those spoken from near.

In the case of the woman of Canaan, her importunity made her faith great. She was undaunted and not easily discouraged. There's no record of Jesus ever snubbing any who came to Him for mercy. But in this woman's case, yes it happened. Her patience was tried, her faith was tested. But through it all, she remained resolute and undistracted. The trial of her faith, being much more precious than of gold that perisheth, though it be tried with fire, was found unto praise and honour and glory (1 Peter 1:7). It came out proved and improved. She didn't allow the words of Jesus or those of His disciples to bother her. Even after she was called a dog, she turned the humiliation into a humor. One who desires to have a great faith must be ready to possess these qualities.

3. <u>Full Faith:</u> To be full is to be void of space. When a person is said to be full of faith, I believe that's the highest degree anyone can get from the Believers School of Faithology. Anything above full will be a spillover, thus a waste.

The Bible describes Stephen as a man full of faith and the Holy Spirit (Acts 6:5). There was no way he could have gone through his experiences if he lacked a full faith. For only such a faith can stand such a test of time. Stephen did great signs and wonders among the people. But just as it was with our Savior, he was persecuted and accused of blasphemy. How does it feel to be risking one's life for a set of people only to discover they don't even appreciate your efforts?

The core of the matter is, when we get full of faith, we become void of self. We put on the image of our Savior and are ready to tell the truth no matter what the outcome is. We firmly stand against any opposition to the gospel. That doesn't mean we hate our persecutors. We just won't give in to them. And though our tongues they may remove from our mouths, the truth they cannot remove from our minds. They may take our life, but they cannot take our Lord.

Stephen didn't allow fear to grip him. He said what needed to be said. He rebuked them to their face. No wonder he saw the heavens opened. Only a full-grown faith like that of Stephen would see the heavens opened and pray forgiveness for his enemies even while they were taking his life. When you ask for this kind of faith, be ready for that kind of forgiveness.

4. <u>Little Faith</u>: Just as we differ in shape and stature, we also differ in faith. Some have great, others have little. What are the things that make a believer to be of little faith? (Read Matthew 6:25-30; 8:23-26; 14:22-31 and 16:5-12.)

From these different accounts, I can identify four traits of believers with little faith.

➢ <u>Anxiety</u>: This is evident from the first one. Jesus taught His disciples (and is teaching all believers) not to be anxious about the day that had not arrived. They were getting worried over their physical needs and He had to straighten them out, to stop allowing their concern for tomorrow rob them of their comfort of today. Not that we should have no plans for the future. But we must always remember we have no control over the next minute of our lives.

People we see by 1p.m may be dead by 1.30.p.m. The Bible compares our lives to vapor (James 4:14), here now, gone the next moment. When we get unnecessarily worried, we give room to the tormenting spirit of anxiety. It leaves us unhappy and instead of a good night's sleep, we develop a growling nauseating stomach.

➢ <u>Doubt</u>: Doubt is the exact opposite of trust. It's easier for us to read the account of Peter walking on water and condemn him for doubting. We all have our moments of looking at the sea instead of focusing on the Savior. Many times we pray in faith and then turn around and wonder if it's actually possible. We wonder if God can indeed do what we request.

No matter how much faith we have, occasions will come up for us to question the reality of a dry land in the midst of our Red Sea. We find it hard to believe that ordinary seven hallelujahs can bring down a wall like that of Jericho. But if God truly is the Creator of the whole universe (and I believe He is), what else in that creation will He not be able to handle? If He can be merciful enough to provide for the birds of the air and the lilies of the field, how come we simply can't trust Him to do the same for us that are made in His image?

There's the tendency in man to doubt the availability of what we cannot see. If only we trust Him who has promised to supply all our need according to His riches in glory (Philippians 4:19), then we will have less cause for doubt.

➢ <u>Fear:</u> Fear paralyses our faith. When we allow fear to take over, it cripples us in the Spirit and for a moment, we forget that He who could still the waters can also still our fears. When the tempest arose, the disciples got fearful and allowed their situation to blind them to their Savior, who was right there in the boat. If He could peacefully sleep in the midst of the waves, He could also still the waves. The same thing happened to Peter. He got fearful of the sea and for a moment forgot the Savior.

When waves of life rise against us, let's remember the promise of God that says, "When thou passest through the waters, I will be with thee; and through the rivers, they shall not overflow thee" (Isaiah 43:2).

➢ <u>**Forgetting Past Blessings:**</u> One of the ways the devil easily gets at us is to make us forget the things God had done and focus on what we think He needs to do.

When Jesus asked His disciples to beware of the leaven of the Pharisees and Sadducees, they thought He was asking them not to eat the bread. Could be He wanted to punish them for their forgetfulness? No! They didn't understand that Jesus was inferring the doctrine of the Scribes and the Pharisees, and not the physical bread that goes into the mouth. These disciples were there when Jesus fed the five thousand with five loaves and the four thousand with seven loaves. He who did that could command bread out of the stones for them and they would eat and still have left over.

A little faith nags over a present need and forgets that the God who did it then will do it now. He's still the same God. He doesn't change. Yesterday, today, and forever Jesus is the same (Hebrews 13:8). If He could feed five thousand, He could feed twelve.

5. <u>**Strong and Weak Faith**</u>: If there's a strong faith, then there's a weak faith. That implies two different strengths in regard to faith. The two examples given by apostle Paul clearly explain the differences.

> And being not weak in faith, he considered not his own body now dead, when he was about an hundred years old, neither yet the deadness of Sarah's womb (Romans 4:19).

This was talking about father Abraham.

> Him that is weak in the faith receive ye, but not to doubtful disputations. For one believeth that he may eat all things: another, who is weak, eateth herbs (Romans 14:1-2).

From these two passages, we get two descriptions of strong faith. The first has to do with a test of faith; and the second is based on one's religious conviction. As individuals, we react to things differently. Abraham was a man of strong faith. He stood the test of time. We read his story without pausing and asking, if I were to be in that same situation, would my faith have remained strong as his? The Bible says, "hope deferred maketh the heart sick" (Pro. 13:12).

When a man of Abraham's age has no child, it's frustrating. But it was even more frustrating when God assured him he would have a child, and be the father of many nations and for twenty-five candid years, the child never showed up. That's enough to weaken any man's faith. But Abraham refused to be discouraged. He remained strong. He saw the hand of God in everything. To him, barrenness was no excuse for bitterness. There's no record of him ever complaining about Sarah's barrenness. It's even remarkable that he could still have relationship with her as to produce a child. He didn't consider himself biologically dead to make a baby; neither did he think that of his wife. Anything short of this is a weak faith.

The second part is a weak faith that stems from a person's religious conviction. A weak faith easily sees something wrong with his action. There are people who by nature are religiously rigid. They have dos and don'ts. Definitely there's right and wrong when it comes to one's belief in Jesus. There are certain things a true child of God should never attempt to do or be forced to do. We have the Bible as our guide.

But when it comes to doctrinal issues, caution must be applied. If someone has faith strong enough to eat anything, it's okay for him. But he has no right to make fun of him whose faith doesn't go beyond eating herbs. He has to accommodate the weaker without being pushy in any way, for by so doing, we build ourselves up in the faith. We all have the same Lord, but not

Attributes Of A Working Faith

the same measure of faith.

Having considered the different types of faith there are, suffice it to say that all you need is faith like a grain of mustard seed to move a mountain. That's like having faith like a grain of sand, just one grain to move Mt. Everest. Amazing, isn't it?

46
FAITH is MEEK

Gentleness is not the same as meekness. The Bible differentiates them: "But the fruit of the Spirit is love, joy, peace, longsuffering, gentleness, goodness, faith, meekness, temperance: against such there is no law" (Galatians 5:22-23). And of course both are different from quietness. I know quiet people who not only don't know the Lord, but are also as proud as peacock and only a 'd' short of the devil.

As men and women of faith, we're not to act unduly to others who're either weaker in the faith or have no faith at all. Some qualities of meekness must show forth in a man of faith. The Bible describes Moses as the meekest man on earth (Numbers 12:3).

When God called him to lead the children of Israel out of Egypt, Moses didn't know they were going to give him that much headache. A journey that should have lasted at most eleven days (Deuteronomy 1:2-3) lasted forty years because of their ignorance. He was eighty years when God called him. By the time he died, he was one hundred, twenty years. He spent each day of forty years leading a bunch of ingrates out of bondage. And though at no time did God ever leave him without instructions, he was meek all through. Not once did he allow spiritual pride or feelings of superiority to take over his heart. I describe him as an ordinary man with extra-ordinary meekness.

Apostle Paul said, "I THEREFORE, the prisoner of the Lord, beseech you that ye walk worthy of the vocation wherewith ye are called. With all lowliness and meekness, with longsuffering, forbearing one another in love" (Ephesians 4:1-2). As children of God, let's endeavor to be meek in all our dealings, so people around us will know that indeed we're of the faith we profess.

When we find others in fault, meekness must super impose judgment. Not for us to be blind to evil practices among the brethren, as this would tarnish the name of God. But the Bible commands that the restoration must be done in the Spirit of meekness.

> BRETHREN, if a man be overtaken in a fault, ye which are spiritual, restore such an one in the spirit of meekness; considering thyself, lest thou also be tempted (Galatians 6:1).

There's no way we can successfully restore a straying sheep by chasing it with a stick. You only drive it further. Condemnation would not in any form or manner restore a straying brother or sister to the faith. We have to apply wisdom and meekness to win him or her back to the fold. After all, there's no one above straying so long we're still in this flesh. We are all what we are by God's grace. It didn't happen in a day. We all grew up to the stage.

> To speak evil of no man, to be no brawlers, but gentle, shewing all meekness unto all men. For we ourselves also were sometimes foolish, disobedient, deceived, serving divers lusts and pleasures, living in malice and envy, hateful, and hating one another (Titus 3:2-3).

If only we can always remember that once we were spiritually blind, now we can see; but we did not see of our own power, Christ gave us sight. May be then we shall able to deal in meekness with those that are less spiritual than we are.

47
__FAITH is MERCIFUL__

Mercy is refraining from harming or punishing offenders, enemies, persons in one's power; kindness in excess of expectation. That was what Jesus did for you and I that today we can be called children of God. We were offenders from the Garden of Eden.

When the first Adam fell, God showed us kindness in excess by sending His only begotten for the propitiation of our sins. The justification we have in Christ is mercy undeserved. God didn't deal with us according to the gravity of our sins. He through His mercy restored us to Himself.

Blessed be the God and Father of our Lord Jesus Christ, which according to his abundant mercy hath begotten us again unto a lively hope by the resurrection of Jesus Christ from the dead (1 Peter 1:3).

If we enjoy so much a grace from Him, we ought to show mercy to others. Once we surrender our lives to Jesus, the changes must show forth. We cannot claim to be new but continue to act old.

Woe unto you, scribes and Pharisees, hypocrites! for ye pay tithe of mint and anise and cummin [whatever that means], and have omitted the weightier matters of the law, judgment, mercy, and faith: these ought ye to have done, and not to leave the other undone (Matthew 23:23).

A man of faith has nothing to be proud of if he has no mercy. He's nothing but a hypocrite parading as a priest. The Bible says for us to "Put on therefore, as the elect of God, holy and beloved, bowels of mercies, kindness, humbleness of mind, meekness, longsuffering" (Colossians 3:12). We're to put on mercy. When we lack it, we feel spiritually naked.

There are instances of men and women who showed mercy to others in the Bible, even when such didn't by any yardstick deserve it.

King Saul was an archenemy to the man of God David. After his defeat of the giant Goliath, Saul got jealous and from then on sought to kill him. He made several attempts but failed. For a man whose life was being sought for death, one would think he too would seize any opportunity he had to take the life of his enemy; but not David. He was not only a man of faith; he was a man of mercy, who would not take the life of him that sought after his life.

When the need arises for us to show mercy, feelings have to step aside for faith. For he who acts by feelings is not perfected in faith. If Jesus had acted according to His feelings, He would not die on the cross. Imagine being put to death by the people you came to save. The Bible says, "Whoso rewardeth evil for good, evil shall not depart from his house" (Proverbs 17:13). But this can only happen if we show mercy to the undeserved. God will avenge us on them. Naturally the flesh will want to react. But we must step aside and let God be God. To your faith, add mercy and just as he avenged David over Saul, God will avenge your case over your enemy.

N

48. FAITH NEVER DOUBTS   198

49. FAITH NEVER LOOKS BACK   200

48
FAITH NEVER DOUBTS

Doubt is one of two things that any strong faith in the Lord must <u>never</u> do. It's a terrible disease that eats deep into the faith of believers. It shakes the anchor of our spiritual strength and twists the arm of our belief. Satan knows the power of doubt and he would do anything to bring it to our minds at a time we need to strongly hold on to our faith.

You say there's no one who doesn't doubt. That's absolutely correct. But the truth is when that happens, it's no longer faith in operation but flesh manifesting in fear.

When Jesus asked Peter to come walking to Him on water, Peter had enough faith to get on the water. But at one point, he doubted his ability. And just at that very moment, he began to sink.

And immediately Jesus stretched forth his hand, and caught him, and said unto him, O thou of little faith, wherefore didst thou doubt? (Matthew 14:31).

It was by faith that Peter got on the water. But when flesh told him he would sink, fear gripped his mind and for a moment, he doubted the word of the One who said to him, "Come." Doubt took his eyes off the ability of the Savior and instead made him see the abnormality of the sea. When we allow doubt to take our eyes off the Lord of our life, we're heading for the bottom of the ocean.

Jesus said, "Verily I say unto you, If ye have faith, and doubt not, ye shall not only do this which is done to the fig tree, but also if ye shall say unto this mountain, Be thou removed, and be thou cast into the sea; it shall be done" (Matthew 21:18-21). When we allow doubt to take over our thoughts, it paralyzes our faith.

Apostle James said, "If any of you lack wisdom, let him ask of God, that giveth to all men liberally, and upbraideth not; and it shall be given him. But let him ask in faith, nothing wavering. For he that wavereth is like a wave of the sea driven with the wind and tossed. For let not that man think that he shall receive any thing of the Lord. A double minded man is unstable in all his ways" (James 1:5-8).

He compared the doubting mind to the wave of the sea. We know what the wave of the sea does. I've been to the beach a few times in my life. I love the way it rolls up and down. One moment, it appears to be getting closer. The next moment, it's gone. When I read this verse, I then understood that one who has that kind of faith could never get anything from God. One moment, it's on, the next moment it's off. One moment, it's moves forward. Before you know it, it's drawing back. We have to be stable, nothing doubting.

Does that mean we would never doubt? No. Sure there will be times when we'll be tempted to think that God no longer hears our prayers. It's nothing but the devil's trick to lure us away from our blessing. A true faith must put doubt aside, for faithful is He who has called us (1 Thessalonians 5: 24) and has promised to never leave us nor forsake us (Hebrews 13:5).

49
FAITH NEVER LOOKS BACK

I was in the track team in my high school. I ran both short and long distances. During that time, I learnt one important lesson especially when running the long distance. The moment I looked back and saw that somebody was getting close to me, I got discouraged and that got me weak. But if I kept my focus on the front and put in all my energy, though I may not be first, I would definitely make it to the finish line without quitting in-between.

The end of a race is never at the back. The ribbon is always in front. Any aspiring athlete will strive to make it to the finish line, not go back to the starting point. Or better still. When we drive, the focus is always on the front. I don't see how anyone can be driving and be looking back at the same time. Before he knows it, he's going to hear a loud noise. The same principle applies to our faith. Once we accept Jesus into our lives, looking back is dangerous. The end of our journey is not at the back. We have a finish line and that is heaven.

Coming to the Lord is a step of faith that's not done on a trial and error basis. Salvation is not a football game to be tried out. If you want to follow Christ, if truly you want to have the faith you see in the lives of other Christians, you must be willing to give up what they gave up. Again I say it, salvation is not a bed of roses. Many people come to Christ expecting pearls. When they find nothing but persecutions, they put their gear in reverse.

When you come to Christ, you must be prepared for times that mountains will surface but the challenge to speak the word may not be as easy as it sounds. For there are times the word will be spoken and the mountain will not move immediately. And there are times it may simply never move if

God so wills it remains. What do you do? Going back is not an option, for that makes you unworthy and unqualified for the race.

When Paul gave his life to Jesus, he went through the most horrible times any man of God can go through (2 Corinthians 11:22-33; 2 Corinthians 12:7-10). Paul didn't come to Christ because of poverty. He was a trained lawyer. He spoke the fluent languages of his days. But when he came to the faith, he had every good reason to look back inspite of all his sufferings. At the same time, he knew that looking back meant destruction for him, both here and there. Faith requires a great deal of forward moving and no backward looking.

I've been in the world before and I know there's a difference between my life then and my life now. For me, looking back is not an option. My husband was formerly a Muslim. He knew what it meant when he accepted Jesus. For over thirty years now, he has not looked back. We both have decided to follow Jesus without turning back. Not that there were no discouragements and distractions along the way. But looking back will not be of any help. Our hereafter is more important to us.

As we go in our journey of faith, the decision to continue must always override the temptation to relax. I believe I'll be worse than before if for any reason I look back. Paul said, "Not as though I had already attained, either were already perfect: ... Brethren, I count not myself to have apprehended: but this one thing I do, forgetting those things which are behind, and reaching forth unto those things which are before, I press toward the mark for the prize of the high calling of God in Christ Jesus" (Phil. 3:12-14).

When God was going to destroy Sodom and Gomorrah, two angels warned Lot to take his wife and daughters and flee to the city of Zoar and they must not look back. Lot's wife heard but she did not heed. She knew she wasn't supposed to look back but she did. She looked back to all they had left behind. She looked back to possessions that were going to be destroyed. She forgot the promises of God for their future. Rather than move forward, she looked backward. She missed it. She became a pillar of salt. She lost it here and lost for eternity.

Our Lord warned, "In that day, he which shall be upon the housetop, and his stuff in the house, let him not come down to take it away: and he that is in the field, let him likewise not return back. Remember Lot's wife" (Luke 17:31-32). And I also say to you, remember Lot's wife. Don't look back.

O

50. FAITH OBEYS   **204**

50
FAITH OBEYS

As sweet as obedience can be when observed, it's one of the most difficult aspects of faith. Not that we want to deliberately disobey, but the flesh is always at war with the Spirit when it comes to obedience. Even in the ordinary relationship between parents and children, husbands and wives, masters and servants, people we can see with our physical eyes, obedience is not an issue to be taken lightly.

I have two teenage boys and I can honestly tell you they have no problem with most things save obedience. The kind of music we love they hate. The ones we hate they love. True they know they have no choice but to respect our presence. They can't listen to just anything or watch any nonsense. But I won't deceive you; it's a tug of war. If that can happen with people we see, how much more with the God we don't see? Most of the time, He tests our obedience to know if we love Him and more importantly to know if we're still in the faith.

There's no doubt that Abraham wasn't only a man of faith; he was also a man of perfect obedience. Even in the most difficult times, Abraham obeyed God. To him, obedience was not a matter of choice, but an obligation.

<u>By faith Abraham</u>, when he was called to go out into a place which he should after receive for an inheritance, <u>obeyed</u>; and he went out, not knowing whither he went (Hebrews 11:8).

When God called him to get out of his father's house, he was seventy-five years old. He had no direction of any type to guide him in the journey. How happy would you feel if God asked you to pack your bags and baggage and just head out of your house, knowing not where you're going?

Faith Obeys

Yours may not be as hard as Abraham's because you have the freeway. Abraham had nothing but a desert to go through. With a vehicle or an airplane, you'll get to your destination in good time. The father of faith only had his two feet, and may be a camel. But of how much importance would a camel be in a journey that would last months, possibly years?

You can stop at rest areas and get some refreshments; he had to hunt just to feed the battalion that went with him. If for any reason you get tired, you can take your time to lodge in a hotel. He had no choice but to pitch tents at different places so he and his people could rest. If you get sick on the way, you can check in to a hospital. All Abraham could do was trust the God who called him out. And may be put some herbs together, no measurement, no hygiene, no potency accuracy.

In case of danger, your cell phone will be of great help. Or at least, you can use the pay phone to call the emergency. The only thing Abraham could do was expect the best and settle for the worst. Hey don't forget you have the road map handy; but the man of God had nothing to follow. But he knew that the One who called him out has the whole world in the palm of His hand. He would direct his paths through the unknown pathless desert.

Abraham went on a journey that you and I would never dare to go. Yet, he obeyed. Don't tell me he didn't know it was going to be rough. When you think of his age, you'll realize only an obedient faith can do what he did. God didn't tell him where he was going. God only said He would show him. So there was the problem of uncertainty as to how long the journey itself would last. Though I've never traveled through the desert, but I don't think a journey through the desert of those days could be pleasant in any way. Abraham went through it obediently, not whining, not nagging. On top of it all, he had no child. Two barren old couple traveling on a journey, taking with them all they had, but lacking what they loved.

And as if that wasn't enough. The long awaited promised child finally arrived and with him came the greatest test of faith any normal human being will abhor to be subjected to. After several years of hoping for a son, Isaac was born. Imagine the joy of having a child at the ripe old age of hundred years. Then imagine the sorrow of having to take the life of that child with your own hands.

And it came to pass after these things, that God did tempt Abraham, and said unto him, Abraham: and he said, Behold, here I am. And he said, Take now thy son, thine only son Isaac, whom thou lovest, and get thee into the land of Moriah; and offer him there for a burnt offering upon one of the mountains which I will tell thee of (Gen. 22: 1-2).

Now that he had been instructed to go and offer him, would he still remain the promised child? A dead child can no longer be considered an heir.

Brethren, when we're ready to faithfully obey God, asking questions won't do us any good. God doesn't need to seek your opinion before He asks you to do. He's not interested in what you think about His command. He's an autocratic King reigning from His kingdom on high. When He asks you to do, you have to do. If you don't do, you die. That may sound intellectually unrealistic. But it's the gospel truth. Disobedience to God is a sin and the Bible says, "The wages of sin is death" (Romans 6:23). Abraham knew the word and obeyed the Lord's command.

And Abraham rose up early in the morning, and saddled his ass, and took two of his young men with him, and Isaac his son, and clave the wood for the burnt offering, and rose up, and went unto the place of which God had told him. Then on the third day Abraham lifted up his eyes, and saw the place afar off (Genesis 22:3-4).

This is the most difficult part of the passage to me. He lifted his eyes and saw the place afar off. I can just picture what would be going through his mind at that particular moment, thinking of his son Isaac and his wife Sarah. Though the Bible is silent about Sarah at that stage, I'm convinced beyond doubt that Abraham only disclosed his mission to Sarah, not his vision. Sarah possibly only knew he and Isaac were going on a journey, to go and sacrifice.

I can't imagine my husband telling me the Lord had instructed him to go and offer any of our children as burnt offering. He would sure have to speak to me too. In Sarah's case, it was worse. This was an only child. She had him at a very old age of ninety years. Abraham didn't bother to think of what Sarah would do when he got back home. It didn't matter what the men that followed him would think of him. He didn't even care what his friends would say if they heard that he had 'killed' his child, his promised child whom he waited twenty-five years to get. He simply obeyed God.

Was it that Abraham didn't have sad feelings? I don't think so. But his faith was tougher than his feelings, for it would take men with such tough faith to get going when the going gets tough. A faith that obeys is a faith that obtains. No wonder Abraham obtained his son Isaac.

How about Noah? When God asked him to build an ark there was no sign of rain (Genesis 6). But Noah didn't try to reason it out with God. God said it, he believed it and that settled it. If Noah had disobeyed, he and his household would have perished.

Fellow believers, we need to learn to obey God in everything. When it comes to obeying God, human reasoning has to be put aside. A ninety-year-old woman is humanly impossible to have a baby. But faith in God always defies all human knowledge.

Peter had been a fisherman longer than Jesus had been a fisher of men. He knew all about fishing. When Jesus asked him to launch his net into the deep, human reasoning told Peter that the time of the day wasn't appropriate to dip into the deep.

> And Simon answering said unto him, Master, we have toiled all the night, and have taken nothing: <u>nevertheless</u> at thy word I will let down the net. And when they had this done, they inclosed a great multitude of fishes: and their net brake. When Simon Peter saw it, he fell down at Jesus' knees, saying, Depart from me; for I am a sinful man, O Lord (Luke 5:5-6, 8).

Nevertheless is a term of submission or humility as in the case of Jesus. You have a better knowledge than the person giving you instructions. But you still do what he asks you to do, either out of obedience or humility. Peter had worked all night and caught nothing. It must have been such a boring trip to the sea. Not because he didn't know how to fish. That trip was God's plan. God had to first de-robe him of his occupational pride. He had to teach him to be submissive to the new Master he was about to have. And because Peter simply obeyed Jesus, boredom gave way to blessing. Not only did he catch physical fishes. From that day forward, he caught spiritual fishes.

The power to obey is embedded in us. We've no excuse not to obey. It has nothing to do with hierarchy. Of what use are priests, pastors and preachers who can't obey the laws of God? He who cannot obey God in faith should not exhort men in the faith.

> And having in a readiness to revenge all disobedience, when your obedience is fulfilled (2 Corinthians 10:6).

In other words, if your obedience is not complete, you're not qualified to condemn somebody else's disobedience.

Faith Obeys

And hereby we do know that we know him, if we keep his commandments. He that saith, I know him, and keepeth not his commandments, is a liar, and the truth is not in him (I John 2:3-4).

When we obey Him, it's then we keep His commandments. Though there may be times our obedience will make us appear like fools. Imagine marching around a wall in silence (Joshua 6:1-20). Why? To bring the walls down. Sounds very crazy. But believe me it's as crazy as putting a knife to the throat of a child you waited a quarter of a century to have. There's no way you can escape unwanted comments if truly you want to be obedient. It's all part of being a child of God. People will ridicule you for being too honest. That's okay. Just keep on being obedient. At long last, they who have laughed at you will laugh with you.

I also want to mention that our obedience to God should never be at the expense of our obedience to civil authorities. When we obey authority, we bring glory to the name of God. Does that mean we obey even when it's wrong? No. But as long as it doesn't negate our faith, we're to obey authority. Jesus was not afraid of any man's authority, but two times, He displayed respect for authority. (Read Matthew 17:24-27 and 22:15-22.)

If Jesus obeyed authority, on what spiritual ground do we stand to disobey those in authority? The Bible says, "Let every soul be subject unto the higher powers. For there is no power but of God: the powers that be are ordained of God. Wherefore ye must needs be subject, not only for wrath, but also for conscience sake. For for this cause pay ye tribute also: for they are God's ministers, attending continually upon this very thing. Render therefore to all their dues: tribute to whom tribute is due; custom to whom custom; fear to whom fear; honour to whom honour" (Romans 13:1, 5-7).

We're to display the quality of obedience to authority not only in taxes but also in everything that doesn't in any way infringe on our religious belief. And not only government authority. I believe it should extend to any authority, whether authority over the church, or the home, the school or the office. God wants us to respect and obey authority. In closing this topic, I love to end with the words of the apostle Peter.

> Submit yourselves to every ordinance of man for the Lord's sake: whether it be to the king, as supreme; Or unto governors, as unto them that are sent by him for the punishment of evildoers, and for the praise of them that do well. For so is the will of God, that with well doing ye may put to silence the ignorance of foolish men: As free, and not using your liberty for a cloke of maliciousness, but as the servants of God (1 Peter 2:13-16).

Let us remember to always submit to authority for the Lord's sake.

P

51. FAITH is PATIENT	212
52. FAITH is PEACEFUL	214
53. FAITH is PENITENT	217
54. FAITH is POSITIVE	220
55. FAITH has POWER	224
56. FAITH PRAISES GOD	228
57. FAITH PRAYS	231
58. FAITH PREVAILS	235
59. FAITH is PURE	239

51
FAITH is PATIENT

Since the time we've been in the United States, we've lived in two states, Ohio and Tennessee. The speed limit in Ohio is 65mph on the freeway. Within neighborhoods, there are 45mph, 30mph and even lower. And I remember I always had a problem with other drivers on the road. They were always passing me.

Then we moved to Tennessee. The speed limit on the freeway is 70mph. Yet, people will be passing us. Is it because we're too slow? No. They're too fast. Keeping within the limit is impossible for them. They believe if they do, they'll never get to where they're going. Why? Because they're in a hurry. The reason? Impatience. I only have one question for them. Where in the world are they going?

Unfortunately, some of us are like that in our journey of faith. We're so much in a hurry for breakthroughs, blessings and miracles; so much so that we feel God is too slow. No He's not. We're impatient. The bitter truth is we can never out fast Him. No matter how fast we believe we are, He's faster. Before you get to where you're going, He's there because He's Omnipresent. He's everywhere, every time.

People get in car wreck because of impatience. When we're in a hurry in our faith, we get a spiritual wreck. We miss the blessings that God has in stock for us. The Bible tells us to imitate men and women who through faith and patience obtained God's promises for their lives (Hebrews 6:9-12). They patiently waited, knowing that "He is faithful that promised" (Hebrews 10: 23).

Patience is easier preached than practiced. Some of us will have to pray for patience just to get through a daily devotion that will last only thirty minutes. How much more wait for twenty-five years for a promise? But we must be patient if we must receive from Him. God has a set time for every promise. While our patience will not make it happen later than it should, our impatience will not make it happen faster. God doesn't operate on the same calendar we have.

> But, beloved, be not ignorant of this one thing, that one day is with the Lord as a thousand years, and a thousand years as one day (2 Peter 3:8).

By the time you finish counting one thousand, He has just counted one. So why hurry? He knows what you need and at His own appointed time, He will accomplish it. "My brethren, count it all joy when ye fall into divers temptations; Knowing this, that the trying of your faith worketh patience" (James 1:2-4). There's no way we can escape a test of faith. A faith not tested is a faith not trusted. And we can only pass that test if we're patient. Today we read and learn about Abraham because he was patient in trial and tribulation. He knew he could not help God accomplish His work. So also we can't help God accomplish His purpose for our lives.

Not only in receiving promises, even in our dealings with others, we must be patient. "And the servant of the Lord must not strive; but be gentle unto all men, apt to teach, patient" (2Timothy 2:24). The moment you accept Christ, you're a servant of God. It's true there are ordained ministers. But anyone that propagates the gospel and preaches the word of the kingdom to others is God's servant. Getting the word across to unbelievers requires patience. An unbeliever does not understand the message. We have to patiently explain why we believe what we believe. And I know that with more patience, we shall win the world for the Lord.

52
FAITH is PEACEFUL

Back in the high school, I knew a passage of the Bible that talked about peace. You can easily guess what that was. "Blessed are the peacemakers, for they shall be called the children of God" (Matthew 5:9). I knew the verse very well and so did many of my schoolmates. But if you asked where it was in the Bible, then you messed me up. Do I even know it now? (Just teasing.) I knew the verse so well but understood it so little. That's exactly the case with many Christians.

Many of us know this passage and say it often. But when we come to the real meaning of what Jesus is teaching us, when it comes to the practicality of real peace making, it's more than we think. It's not just implying settling a dispute between two people, which was the way I understood it then. It involves giving up our own right for the sake of peace without giving up our faith.

People have no problem recognizing you as a Christian. That's easily noticeable from the way you talk and walk. But when it comes to the issues of peace, they find it hard to believe that the same you, who preached to them yesterday, are fighting them today because of your dog or cat. You say Jesus didn't teach you to be stupid. Yes, you're right. He didn't. But He asked you to turn the other cheek when you're hit on one (Matthew 5:38-39).

When Jesus pronounced blessing on the peacemaker, He knew it's not an easy thing. He knew it would take some self-denial to make peace with the one who doesn't want to see you. It's always the case when we try to make peace with a person, that's the time the devil will send his agents to come and make trouble with us. We then have to choose between making trouble and making peace.

Our refusing to make trouble is not an evidence of fear. It's a display of peaceful faith. It's not that we don't know what to say to our troublers. In fact, most of the time, we know what to say to hurt them more than they know what to say to hurt us. But we won't. It may initially appear they won but their end is never good.

How do people know you in your neighborhood, as a peacemaker or a peacebreaker? One reinforces your faith, the other ruins it. That's why the Bible tells us to pursue peace at all cost. "For he that will love life, and see good days, let him refrain his tongue from evil, and his lips that they speak no guile: Let him eschew evil, and do good; let him seek peace, and ensue* it" (1 Peter 3:10-11). Peace is never within easy reach. We have to continuously stretch to get it. And by so doing, we sow the fruit of righteousness.

Faith also gives us peace during the trials of life. Not that we don't feel the pangs of the thorn, but the grace of the Lord will be sufficient to bear it (2 Corinthians 12:10). When we loose loved ones, faith steps in and peacefully reminds us that they're just a distance away. By the time they look back, we shall be standing right behind them before Jesus. The parting won't be for long. Instead of confusion, we shall have comfort.

We serve the Prince of Peace. He gives us peace in the good times, peace in the bad times, peace when the going is rough, peace when it's smooth, peace to pass through the valley of the shadow of death and fear no evil, because we know He's with us; peace when we have no means to meet our needs, for we know God shall supply our need according to His riches in glory by Christ Jesus; peace to fear no accident on the road, peace to fear no crash in the air, peace to fear no derailment of the train and peace to fear no shipwreck on the sea.

It's the peace that only Jesus can give and only we can choose not to have. The peace that your doctors cannot understand and your physicians cannot fathom, for they don't know how somebody in your condition can still be smiling when hurting. It's the peace that makes us smile at the storm and laugh at a loss. It reminds us not to fuss over what we didn't bring into this world and will sure not take out. "Great peace have they which love thy law: and <u>nothing</u> shall offend them" (Psalm 119:165). For as long as we love His law, He'll never fail. He'll continue to keep us in peace, because our mind is stayed on Him (Isaiah 26:3).

If you don't have this peace we're talking about, it's never too late to ask for it. That you're still breathing is a proof that God is giving you a second chance. Surrender the control of your life to the Giver of peace, the Lord Jesus Christ our Savior. He alone is the Prince of Peace. Any other one aside from Him gives nothing but problems. Eternal peace of the coming King rest with you.

*Pursue

53
FAITH is PENITENT

Penitence is repentance on the part of a sinner who falls but later realizes his wrongdoing. He feels sorry for listening to Satan's voice and takes the necessary step to be reconciled with God, "For godly sorrow worketh repentance to salvation" (2 Cor. 7:10).

I know there are highly spiritual Christians. I respect them and wish I could be like them. But is any Christian above temptation? I don't think so. "Wherefore let him that thinketh he standeth take heed lest he fall" (1 Corinthians 10:12). Which means if you think you're above falling, you're making a mistake. No matter how high you're in the pinnacle of faith, the devil can bring you down. It happened in the days of the Bible and it still happens today. But penitence makes the difference between a believer that falls and he that remains fallen. As children of God, we should strive not to fall to temptation. But if it happens, then we need to retrace our steps back to our Savior.

A good example is David. David was a man of faith. It was by faith he defeated Goliath. But then he fell: from the lust of the eyes to the lust of the flesh, to adultery and finally to murder. It's unfortunate how the devil will do anything to make one sin lead to another if care is not taken. When we're not where we're supposed to be, we'll find ourselves where we don't want to be. A pastor, when he's supposed to be in church but stays home for no genuine reason other than watch the football game, will end up watching television to his perdition. The devil knows your weakness and he'll bring the right stuff your way.

At a time he was supposed to be with his men in battle, David was resting and having a nice sleep at home. By the time he woke up, Satan presented him with an irresistible figure.

> And it came to pass in an eveningtide, that David arose from off his bed, and walked upon the roof of the king's house: and from the roof he saw a woman washing herself; and the woman was very beautiful to look upon. And David sent and enquired after the woman. And one said, Is not this Bathsheba, the daughter of Eliam, the wife of Uriah the Hittite? And David sent messengers, and took her; and she came in unto him, and he lay with her; for she was purified from her uncleanness: and she returned unto her house. And the woman conceived, and sent and told David, and said, I am with child (2 Sam. 11:2-5).

UFOs come in all sexes, sizes, and shapes. Bathsheba was a UFO, Undignified Female Object. And David himself was a UFO, Unclothed Female Observer. The devil is a master planner for the slack in soul. Just at the time Bathsheba shamelessly displayed her nakedness, the devil woke David from sleep and took him to the top of the roof to go and behold. Instead of taking his eyes off, he went from looking to lusting. He sent to have her brought. Since she was an undignified personality, it was no problem for David to lay with her.

Bathsheba got pregnant and to cover his evil act, David ordered that Uriah (Bathsheba's husband) be put in the war front where he could easily be slain. How apathetic and unreasonable of someone God described as a man after His heart (Acts 13:22). His was a grievous offence that one would wonder if he deserved to be forgiven. But God is merciful. When we come to Him repentant, he forgives our sins and we receive justification, just as if we had never sinned. When David realized his mistake, he repented of his sins and wrote the Psalm 51 in penitence.

Any sinner that comes to His presence repentant will leave His presence reconciled and renewed. Let's not allow our past to hinder our present and rob us of our future. Let's return to our Maker in penitence. And if we have committed any trespass, He's willing to welcome us back home, just like the prodigal son.

54
FAITH is POSITIVE

1996, I was pregnant with our third child. We already had two boys and in all honesty, it didn't really matter to me what the third one turned out to be. All I wanted was a healthy baby. But one morning–just to appear funny–I passed a joke. My husband was in front of the mirror and I said I don't think I really care whether a boy or a girl. I remember him saying something like don't you have faith. This one is a girl. Period!

Though there was nothing we could do. The baby was formed, case closed. But that's the kind of faith God wants us to have. We need to positively affirm our desires and perceive them as real, though we're yet to receive them. In our own case, we could not change the sex of the baby. But don't tell me God could not. He put the baby there in the first instance. He was the potter of the clay in my womb. If He chose to remodel it, who in the world could query Him?

When God asked Abraham to go and offer his only son Isaac as a sacrifice, I don't want to believe he wasn't disturbed. But Abraham was a man of positive faith.

And Abraham said unto his young men, <u>Abide ye here with the ass; and I and the lad will go yonder and worship, and come again to you</u> …. And Isaac spake unto Abraham his father, … Behold the fire and the wood: but where is the lamb for a burnt offering? <u>And Abraham said, My son, God will provide himself a lamb for a burnt offering:</u> so they went both of them together (Genesis 22:5-8).

The journey took him three days. God didn't stop him on the way. He traveled three sad and miserable days to go and take the life of his own son.

Faith Is Positive

It must have been a tense period for Abraham. Nobody wants to sacrifice his child. I don't and I'm sure you don't either. But a positive faith hopes for the best to come out of the worst situation. Two times Abraham made positive statements of faith. He never said anything negative. He was undoubtedly positive that God would provide a replacement for Isaac.

The Shunammite woman in the book of Kings, at the most unrealistic period of her life exercised a remarkable positive faith. Her only son, whom she got after a long period of barrenness died. While on her way to go and inform the man of God Elisha about the child's death, he spotted her from a far distance and sent his servant to inquire what the problem was. Note her reply.

> So she went and came unto the man of God to mount Carmel. And it came to pass, when the man of God saw her afar off, that he said to Gehazi his servant, Behold, yonder is that Shunammite: Run now, I pray thee, to meet her, and say unto her, Is it well with thee? is it well with thy husband? is it well with the child? And she answered, <u>It is well</u> (2 Kings 4:25, 26).

Under such a pressure, this woman declared, "It is well." Does it mean it was well for her son to die? NO! Remember this was her only child. She was past age when she gave birth to the boy. But she knew that the God who gave her the boy was not a killer. He was just testing her faith. And when the worst had obviously happened, she declared, "It is well." Though that didn't seem to make any sense, but that's what it takes to have a positive faith.

When Moses saw the Red Sea, he knew it was a sea. He wasn't blind. But he knew that if God took them out of Egypt, He would not back out at the Red Sea. When God asked him to go and lead His children out of Egypt, destruction was not included in the instruction. He didn't deliver them out of bondage so He could drown them in the waters. He said He would take them to the Promised Land, not the Red Sea. And that was what Moses held on to. He was positive that He who saved them from bondage would take them to the Promised Land.

The woman with the issue of blood affirmed her healing even before she got near Jesus. The Bible says, "For she said within herself, 'If I may but touch his garment, I shall'–not I may– 'be whole'" (Matthew 9:21). This was a faith soliloquy.

Negativity cannot stay in the same house with faith. The two don't go together. One is a cat, the other is a rat. Let's learn to positively hold on to our faith and even when it seems unrealistic to do so, let's be positive.

Our faith in Jesus is another thing we need to positively affirm. The devil is never tired of paying us visits. But we have to firmly remind him of our stand in Jesus. He needs to hear us say it time and time again that we know Him whom we believe. When he tells us we can never be healed, we need to remind him we were healed by the stripes of Jesus (1 Peter 2:24) long before the illness started. When he tries to make us feel unworthy and unforgiven, then he needs to hear us affirm that we have been forgiven by God for Christ' sake (Ephesians 4:32); and we are His royal priesthood (1 Peter 2:9). The positive affirmation of our faith confirms our beliefs and affrights our fears.

I don't know that for which you have been trusting the Lord. We may never meet on this planet earth. But as you go through life in your journey of faith, always remember to positively affirm your miracle even before you get results. You cannot make it happen because you're not God. But be positive when you act and ask in faith. That's not to make me sound holier than thou. I've said it before and I'll continue to emphasize it throughout the book. I have my moments of fears and doubts. But let's work as a team and together we shall be a threat to the devil's domain.

55
FAITH has POWER

My second son is a football player. I asked him how power applies to the game. He said power has a lot to do with it because the bigger has advantage over the smaller. But if the smaller has more strength than the bigger, then he has better advantage. Why do we need power? To tackle someone who is stronger in force or fist, shape or stature.

In the spiritual realm, we need power to carry us through the journey and that power lies in our faith. There are evil forces and principalities that we have to wrestle with. And without faith, we can do nothing. Fear gives problems but faith gives power. The moment we accept Jesus into our lives, fear has to give way to faith. "For God hath not given us the spirit of fear; <u>but of power</u>, and of love, and of a sound mind" (2 Timothy 1:7). Our power comes as a result of the infilling of the Holy Spirit.

Following the healing of the lame man at the temple gate, a great revival broke out at Solomon's porch. Five thousand souls were saved. For that generation, that was a remarkable number. The elders, rulers and Sadducees got jealous and arrested Peter and John. Why? Because they didn't understand the power behind their action. The Bible says, "And when they had set them in the midst, they asked, By what power, or by what name, have ye done this?" (Acts 4:7). Since they didn't have that kind of faith, they could not comprehend that kind of power.

We can do wonders when we don't allow our faith to "stand in the wisdom of men, but in the power of God" (1 Corinthians 2:5). He has called us, He will also equip. When He ordains, He also sustains. Today, believers don't need to wait in the upper room. The power comes with the confession of our faith.

The Bible says, "the prayer of faith will save the sick" (James 5:15). What happens when a prayer of faith is offered for the sick? There's a discharge of power. The power goes forth and renders the power of sickness sterile.

The book of Acts records that "God wrought special miracles by the hands of Paul: So that from his body were brought unto the sick handkerchiefs or aprons, and the diseases departed from them, and the evil spirits went out of them" (Acts 19:11-12). Wow! That was because the power of faith from him was transferred to the handkerchiefs and aprons. He believed that even in his absence, his faith would work wonders.

Jesus wasn't physically present in all His miracles. There were times He only sent the word and signs followed. But those were not ordinary words. They were words charged with His healing power. He said, "whosoever shall say unto this mountain, Be thou removed, and be thou cast into the sea; and shall not doubt in his heart, but shall believe that those things which he saith shall come to pass; he shall have whatsoever he saith" (Mark 11:23). Does that make us magicians commanding inanimate objects to move? Not in any sense. But when we command the mountain to move by faith, power goes forth and discharges the work as ordered. This is not talking of a mountain visible to the eyes; but problems that refuse to go. Anything that stands as a blemish to the reality and glory of God in our lives is a mountain.

We intercede in faith on behalf of somebody and later hear the testimony of his or her deliverance or miracle. It's the power that goes forth from our prayer and establishes the miracle. People sit in their living rooms and receive healing just by watching TV. The healing power is not coming from the set but from the faith of the person praying at the other end, which cannot be hindered by anything, not even electricity.

When we plug our iron, power doesn't come from the iron itself. It comes from the contact it has with the electricity. When electricity flows into the iron, it receives power and generates heat. This is also true of our faith. The moment we profess to have faith in Jesus, we become connected with heavenly electricity. Power flows automatically into our system and we become spiritually charged, hot enough to straiten out any rough spots of demons and diseases.

One of the most difficult things to do is preach or win souls. But when we receive the Holy Spirit just like the disciples on the day of Pentecost, the power to preach enters into us. We become energized and ready for action. The disciples didn't do anything of their own accord. Their power lied in their faith. Nothing got them discouraged. But that didn't happen until they received the Holy Spirit.

Assembled together with His disciples after His resurrection, Jesus commanded them to remain in Jerusalem and wait for the Father's promise of the Holy Spirit (Acts 1:8).

The promise of the Holy Spirit? What for? To give us power to be witnesses unto Him in Jerusalem, and in all Judea and Samaria, going from America to the Muslim dominated country of Afghanistan, from Britain to Germany, from the artic region all the way down to the coast of Africa.

We shall receive power. Power, not to condemn, but to convict; power, not to be silent, but to speak; power, not to pronounce judgment, but to preach Jesus. Power, enough for a Daniel to stand in opposition to a dictator; power, enough for a Gabriel to preach to a gambling governor; power, enough for a Peter to tell the good news to a president; power, for a John to tell a Judge what it means to exercise justice; power to make a Stephen bold enough to reprove the atrocities of a senator.

Yes! We shall receive power. Power to be in jail and sing 'all hail'; power to know that His grace is sufficient for us inspite of the thorn in the flesh; power to see the crown of righteousness behind the cross of ridicule.

Yes! We shall receive power. Power for us to know that to live is Jesus, and to die is gain; power to preach and do His will in season and out of season; power to look unto Jesus, the author and the finisher of our faith.

We shall receive power. Power to heal the sick, power to raise the dead; power to remain loyal until Daddy bids us welcome home, good and faithful servant; enter into the joy of thy Lord. We shall receive POWER. Only speak in faith. Remember, there's power in your faith.

56
FAITH PRAISES GOD

If we're to consider this topic from human perspective, praises are easier offered when things go smooth. And the opposite is the case when things go topsy-turvy. We find it extremely difficult to lift up our hands and sing praises when we've just been diagnosed with a terminal illness.

When a loved one has just died, the flesh naturally finds it hard to sing praises. And even when we do, some will judge our actions insane. But the biblical truth is, if we truly claim to have faith in God, then we have to praise Him <u>all the time</u>. He has chosen us for that purpose; that we may sing His praises. The Bible calls us "a chosen generation, a royal priesthood, an holy nation, a peculiar people; that ye should shew forth the praises of him who hath called you out of darkness into his marvellous light" (1 Peter 2:9).

When we receive miracles, we show our gratitude and tell the world of our salvation by singing praises to our Redeemer. A faith good at receiving should also be good at praising.

When Hannah received her miracle, she didn't stop there. She sang praises to the Lord (1 Samuel 2). After the Israelites crossed the Red Sea, Moses sang to the Lord (Exodus 15:1-18). After Mary had been told the greatest news of all time, that she was going to be the mother of the Savior of the world, she composed a song (Luke 1:46-55). After their victory, Deborah and Barak sang praises to the Lord (Judges 5). When the lame man received his healing, the Bible confirms, "he leaping up stood, and walked, and entered with them into the temple, walking, and leaping, and praising God" (Acts 3: 8).

Our praises should have nothing to do with our condition. Though we're not to be drunk with wine, wherein is excess; but we're to be filled with the Spirit; Speaking to ourselves in psalms and hymns and spiritual songs, singing and making melody in our heart to the Lord; Giving thanks always for all things unto God and the Father in the name of our Lord Jesus Christ (Ephesians 5:18-20). Spiritual intoxication is no sin. We're to praise God in season and out of season. It should be to us what air is to our lungs. When we fail to do it, we feel spiritually suffocated. We live by it. It's part of our system. We cultivate it as a habit.

When we're locked up in prison for the sake of the gospel, we praise Him like Paul and Silas did in Acts 16. It will break us loose from the chains of the evil one. Yours may not be physical chains. But if you're bound by the pangs and pains of life, you're in a spiritual prison. Praises will cause a heavenly earthquake that will shake and break you loose from the chains of Satan. And those who don't know what had happened will run to you and ask what they can do to be saved.

Our praises are contagious. People will want to be like us when they notice we're always singing and never down in the Spirit. That was what happened to the jailers. Had Paul and Silas not sung praises to God in a prison of all places, the jailers would never have been saved. No wonder the Bible says, "Praise ye the LORD: for it is good to sing praises unto our God; for it is pleasant; and praise is comely" (Psalm 147:1).

Isn't it amazing that many of the choruses we sing today were composed by people like you and I, some of them written during the deepest and unspeakable agonies and tragedies in the lives of the writers? The Lord has a great delight in our praises. He wants to hear our voices. Our praises are anti-dotes to our pressures.

When we praise, pressures panic. Unwanted strangers in our bodies will fade away and be frightened out of their close places (Psalm 18:45). We feel light in the Spirit and an inexplicable relief fills our hearts. I've tried it several times and I can assure you it works.

And the best thing about praises is, it's the only thing we do here and continue hereafter. There's no other job we shall do in heaven but just to sing and sing and sing. Can you picture yourself singing for ten thousand years only to be told you have just begun? You might as well start practicing it here, so by the time you get there, it's part of you. Are you burdened down in the Spirit? I suggest you praise the Lord.

57
FAITH PRAYS

Prayer and faith go together. By faith we believe that God is, by prayer we communicate with Him. When we have faith, it helps us to pray. When we pray, we must have faith that our prayers will be answered. Faith propels us to pray and prayer builds us up in the faith. The Bible says for us to pray "in the Holy Ghost" (Jude 20).

Praying in the Holy Ghost doesn't mean we should only speak in tongues when we pray. But we're to pray in the power of the Holy Spirit to strengthen our faith and dispel all fleshly thoughts that may tend to distract us. It helps us "Hold the mystery of the faith in a pure conscience" (1 Timothy 3:9). We focus on the Father so much so that we get connected with heaven.

It's true there are times we want to pray and some unwanted thoughts will show up from nowhere. Such should be rebuked and brought into captivity to the obedience of Christ. And of course there are times we're so weak that we can't utter a word. When that happens, the Holy Spirit Himself will take over. The Bible says, "Likewise the Spirit also helpeth our infirmities: for we know not what we should pray for as we ought: but the Spirit itself maketh intercession for us with groanings which cannot be uttered" (Romans 8:26). It's a great relief to know that the Holy Spirit is interceding on my behalf.

Prayer has nothing to do with spiritual status. No matter how high up you are in the Spirit, you still need to pray. If Jesus prayed, what excuse have we not to pray? A pastor too big to pray is a pastor too weak to preach, for his power is commensurate to his prayer. He does not resemble his Jesus.

Three times the Lord prayed for the cup of death to pass Him over. There's nothing wrong with persistence in prayer, and even repeating the same words. Such times cannot but come, times we feel short of words because of the agony in our hearts. All you need do is say the words you can remember. Daddy understands. We're His children. He's never tired listening to us, even in our most silent moments. In fact, our prayer is His delight. "The sacrifice of the wicked is an abomination to the LORD: but the prayer of the upright is his delight" (Proverbs 15:8). King Solomon said, "The LORD is far from the wicked: but he heareth the prayer of the righteous" (Proverbs 15:29). Don't ever succumb to the thought that God is not hearing you. The answer may not come by your own timing, but delay is not denial.

It's true there are times we don't get what we ask for. That's because God knows it's not going to do us any good. The end of it is regret. It was not impossible for God to avert the crucifixion of His only begotten Son. But if He did, you and I will not be saved. Our prayer is supposed to be a petition to God, not a persuasion. While it's okay to be particular in our request; it should never be to that end we feel we have to make God do what we want Him to do. In any case, God will only do what He will do.

Praying to God should not be at good times only. Even when we stray from the commandment of God, we must never think that He will not listen when we pray. If we call in true penitence, He will hear. When Jonah disobeyed God, he was forced to lodge in the Fish Motel for three days. But when he called on the Lord from the inside of the fish, He heard and forgave him (Jonah 2:1-2).

God is Omnipresent. It doesn't matter where we are, He will hear us. From inside the belly of the fish, God heard Jonah. Whatever posture we maintain, as long as it's the best for us to glorify God, God will listen. He deals with the sincerity of our heart, not the posture of our body. If God heard a prayer offered inside the fish, how will He not hear when we pray inside the pool? Many times I've prayed sitting on the commode. Does it really matter to God? Absolutely not. If I pray in the church and have no faith, of what use is my prayer? It will not go beyond the ceiling. But with my faith in God, prayers I offer to Him inside the bathroom are as effectual as those I offer inside the bedroom.

Wherever we are, in whatever position we find ourselves, one thing we must always do: pray. He knows what to do with our situation. He knew about it even before we ask. He understands our languages and dialects. Even when we speak the same language but mean different things, He still understands. He won't give to an American what He will give to a British when they both request for a pair of pants. He knows the British needs the American underwear and the American needs the British trousers. When one requests a plaster and the other a band-aid, you're both asking the same thing, only in different terms. (God sure has a sense of humor.) Ours is to pray in faith and believe that He has the best in mind for us.

There may be times we will need the help of a few people to stand with us in prayer. I've requested the help of fellow believers in prayer before and wonders have happened. Only let's be careful whom we pick, not such as will serve as discouragements to us. The disciples in the Gethsemane could not pray for themselves, much more pray with Jesus. The Bible says their eyes were heavy. People whose spiritual eyes are heavy cannot be of any good to us in times of desperate need. They in fact need to be prayed for.

Above all, let's bear it in mind that our prayer is vital to our faith as much as our faith is to our prayer, for it's only with prayer that we can resist the devil.

Be sober, be vigilant; because your adversary the devil, as a roaring lion, walketh about, seeking whom he may devour: Whom resist

Attributes Of A Working Faith

stedfast in the faith (1 Peter 5:8-9).

Resisting the devil cannot be done in the power of the flesh. We have to watch and pray. If we don't pray the devil off our lives, he will prey off our lives. Whether we're leaders of a church or ordinary members, let's remain grounded in the faith and be prayerful; for then and only then shall we not become preys to Satan.

58
FAITH PREVAILS

To prevail is to gain the advantage or mastery over something or someone; it is to triumph. As believers in Christ, we're faced with challenges from day to day. We wrestle with forces, seen and unseen. We meet with people who are no more than agents of Satan and nothing we do is ever right. It's a spiritual war. But when we have faith in God, we shall prevail.

There are children of God in the Bible who prevailed over forces visible to the eyes. Let's take a look at the encounter of David with Goliath.

> And it came to pass, when the Philistine arose, and came, and drew nigh to meet David, that David hastened, and ran toward the army to meet the Philistine. And David put his hand in his bag, and took thence a stone, and slang it, and smote the Philistine in his forehead, that the stone sunk into his forehead; and he fell upon his face to the earth. <u>So David prevailed over the Philistine</u> with a sling and with a stone, and smote the Philistine, and slew him; but there was no sword in the hand of David (1 Samuel 17:48-50).

David prevailed over Goliath not because of his fist, but because of his faith. If fist were to do it, he didn't have the fist to fight the giant. When we put our trust in God, we need not rely on our strength to prevail. All we need is our faith: "For the weapons of our warfare are not carnal, but mighty through God to the pulling down of strong holds" (2 Corinthians 10:4). Because David's confidence was in God (1 Samuel 17:45), God supplied the needed strength and skill to overcome the enemy. We can never prevail when we fight the battle of the spirit in the power of the flesh. Things of the Spirit must be handled by faith.

Attributes Of A Working Faith

There's another interesting case of a prevailing faith. The Bible records that Jacob prevailed against an angel, in fact against God. Against God? Huh! Well, let's see.

> And he rose up that night, and took his two wives, and his two womenservants, and his eleven sons, and passed over the ford Jabbok. And he took them, and sent them over the brook, and sent over that he had. And Jacob was left alone; <u>and there wrestled a man with him until the breaking of the day</u>. And when he saw that he prevailed not against him, he touched the hollow of his thigh; and the hollow of Jacob's thigh was out of joint, as he wrestled with him. And he said, Let me go, for the day breaketh. And he said, I will not let thee go, except thou bless me. And he said unto him, What is thy name? And he said, Jacob. And he said, Thy name shall be called no more Jacob, but Israel: <u>for as a prince hast thou power with God and with men, and hast prevailed.</u> And Jacob asked him, and said, Tell me, I pray thee, thy name. And he said, Wherefore is it that thou dost ask after my name? And he blessed him there. <u>And Jacob called the name of the place Peniel: for I have seen God face to face</u>, and my life is preserved (Genesis 32:22-30).

When I first read this story, I was completely puzzled. My own understanding of wrestling back then was two men involved in a power challenge. One won, the other lost. So how could a man win God in a fight? But thank God for the Holy Spirit that enlightens our weak understanding. The wrestling being described there is that of importunity in request.

Following the 'bowl of soup' episode, the relationship between Jacob and his brother Esau broke down. Jacob ran away from home to his uncle Laban. God later instructed him to go back and return to the land of his fathers. But the feud between him and his brother still haunted his soul, thus making him fearful to face him. But since he desperately wanted to make up with his brother, the only option he had left was to seek God's face for favor and divine intervention, so by the time he would see his brother Esau, all Esau would see in him would be the glory of God, against which no one can fight.

He therefore took it upon himself to wrestle in the presence of God all night, not in fight, but in prayer. The clay cannot overcome the potter. He who created Jacob was Master over Jacob's strength and soul, no matter how strong he was. Jacob wrestled in prayer all night, travailing before the Almighty for a blessing. In his ordeal, the angel of God appeared to him. When God sends His angel, they come in different forms. There were instances of angels that came in flesh and blood, such as could be touched, having direct contact with men of God. And just like Jacob, those men didn't realize they were angels until the angels left their presence.

We must never believe that Jacob prevailed against God the way David prevailed over Goliath, in the raw sense of the word 'prevail.' That Jacob refused to leave the presence of God until blessed will be a better analogy. He had an encounter with God's angel. He refused to depart from him until the angel pronounced a blessing upon him. He wrestled vehemently in the Spirit. He had enough faith to carry him through the night. And the result? He met with his brother's favor.

As people of faith, circumstances will arise in our lives that will require wrestling in the Spirit to overcome. Many Christians are going through tough times. Each day is a battle. Cases of children going against parents, husbands and wives living like cats and rats, pastors and congregation always at loggerheads. We that are supposed to be enjoying the goodness of God are living like poppers; sicknesses and diseases force to go to the hospital with no

Attributes Of A Working Faith

money to pay for doctor's visit.

These are spiritual battles that cannot be fought carnally. They must be handled with a prevailing faith, a faith that will refuse to leave until blessed, persisting through the night till the break of day. Why? Because a faith that comes to His presence without persisting will leave His presence without prevailing. The strength to prevail has been given to you. Are you willing to prevail?

59
__FAITH is PURE__

One of the greatest marks of a true child of God is the ability to maintain a pure heart in an impure world. We're living in a world that's full of junks and a true Christian, one who claims to have faith in God, cannot and should not participate in them. We must strive to keep our hearts pure from filthy things that would hinder our relationship with the Lord. When we purchase pure water from the store, we don't get home and dilute it with ordinary tap water. Doing so would rid it of its purity. That's how it should be with our faith.

Faith in God is for people who mean business with Him. The moment you sign up for Him, you must sign off the world. We live in the world all right, but we don't have to be of the world. People of the world do things that we can't afford to do. The love of money is taking the love of God from their hearts. They'll do anything, tell any lie, and even kill, all in an attempt to get rich quick. We're to purify ourselves because the One who called us is pure.

> And every man that hath this hope in him purifieth himself, even as he is pure (1 John 3:3).

The Lord that we profess is holy and pure. No pollution or impurity can dwell with Him. Worldly things are impurities to our faith. That's why the Bible says for us to "Love not the world, neither the things that are in the world. If any man love the world, the love of the Father is not in him. For all that is in the world, the lust of the flesh, and the lust of the eyes, and the pride of life, is not of the Father, but is of the world. And the world passeth away, and the lust thereof: but he that doeth the will of God abideth for ever" (1 John 2:15-17).

Impurities separate us from Daddy. It puts us outside of His will and we become alienated from His love. We become like pure water mixed with mud, not fit for drinking or cooking. We cannot stand in His presence defiled and contaminated and expect to receive anything from Him.

Who shall ascend into the hill of the LORD? or who shall stand in his holy place? He that hath clean hands, and a pure heart; who hath not lifted up his soul unto vanity, nor sworn deceitfully. He shall receive the blessing from the LORD, and righteousness from the God of his salvation (Psalm 24:3-5).

An impure heart is a heart filled with idols of all forms, deceit, lust, adultery and the like. As citizens of heaven, we cannot be part of such things. To do so is to fall short of His glory. No wonder apostle Paul advised us to hold the "mystery of the faith in a pure conscience" (1 Timothy 3:9).

How about false doctrines? Peter called them pollutions from which we have been set free (2 Peter 2:18-22). Once we profess our faith in God, we must stay completely extricated from them because going back to them will get our already purified hearts spiritually stained and contaminated. We soil our white garments of faith with red oil. No amount of oxyclean will make it white as it was. Faith and impurity cannot co-exist. Let's keep a good distance from anything that will hinder us from God. And as we draw close to Him, He'll draw close to us.

Q

60. FAITH QUICKENS   242

60
FAITH QUICKENS

To quicken is to bring life back into something that has been considered dead and hopeless. And if you would agree with me, nothing has done that as good as faith in the Almighty Jehovah.

So now are we saying that faith can make life return into a dead body? You got it; faith, if put into action can make life return into a dead, stinking body. The faith of one person can bring life back into the dead body of another. It was Elijah's faith in God that brought life back into the dead body of the Zarephath widow's son.

And it came to pass after these things, that the son of the woman, the mistress of the house, fell sick; and his sickness was so sore, that there was no breath left in him. And she said unto Elijah, What have I to do with thee, O thou man of God? art thou come unto me to call my sin to remembrance, and to slay my son? And he said unto her, Give me thy son. And he took him out of her bosom, and carried him up into a loft, where he abode, and laid him upon his own bed. And he cried unto the LORD, and said, O LORD my God, hast thou also brought evil upon the widow with whom I sojourn, by slaying her son? And he stretched himself upon the child three times, and cried unto the LORD, and said, O LORD my God, I pray thee, let this child's soul come into him again. And the LORD heard the voice of Elijah; and the soul of the child came into him again, and he revived. And Elijah took the child, and brought him down out of the chamber into the house, and delivered him unto his mother: and Elijah said, See, thy son liveth. And the woman said to Elijah, Now by this I know that thou art a man of God, and that the word of the LORD in thy mouth is truth (1 Kings 17:17-24).

What do you call a child in whom there was no more breath? Dead, isn't it? That was a hopeless case both for the child and the mother. After providing for the servant of God practically out of nothing, the Lord increased her supplies, but her only son–whose father was already dead–died. But what happened when Elijah laid upon him? The dead child received life. Because of his faith in the living God, he did what he would not have ordinarily attempted to do. It was not his religion that gave him the confidence to stretch over the body of that boy; it was not even his title of a prophet. It was his faith in God, pure and simple.

Another incident.

Apostle Paul was having an all night prayer. (What we call night vigil in my country.) He preached through the night until a brother fell off the window and died. Let's read it.

> And upon the first day of the week, when the disciples came together to break bread, Paul preached unto them, ready to depart on the morrow; and continued his speech until midnight. ... And there sat in a window a certain young man named Eutychus, being fallen into a deep sleep: and as Paul was long preaching, he sunk down with sleep, and fell down from the third loft, and was taken up dead. And Paul went down, and fell on him, and embracing him said, Trouble not yourselves; for his life is in him. When he therefore was come up again, and had broken bread, and eaten, and talked a long while, even till break of day, so he departed. And they brought the young man alive, and were not a little comforted (Acts 20:7-12).

Satan wanted to disrupt God's plan by bringing confusion into the souls of the hearers of the word, instead of the conversion of their souls. But he made a mistake. The preacher was a man of faith. By his faith in God, life came back into the dead body. I'm not in any way insinuating that preachers preach till heads fall off windows before they stop. But as believers, God can do with us what He did with them. That faith was not of Elijah or Paul. That faith was of God, the same God you and I worship and believe. God can wrought through us what He did through them.

However, this is not the only way our faith brings life into a dead situation. There are thousands out there walking about with dead issues in their lives. They have no idea what to do. They have gone to all and sundry, but nothing seems to work. They have given up all hope. Yes, that's a dead Eutychus, that's a dead child for a lonely mother.

As people of faith, what does God expect of us? He wants us to quicken their 'deads' by imparting the words of life into their dead situations: dead achievements, dead marriages, dead wombs, dead jobs, dead anything. When we meet with them, let's not only listen to their problem. Most of the time, we do too much of listening to people talk of their problems than we do telling them about the only solution to that problem, faith in the Lord Jesus Christ.

Some of us even add death to death by telling them how many people we know who have the same problem, but have given up hope. That doesn't sound like faith. Faith doesn't discourage, it encourages. Yes, you're the consultant for all those around you. In your work place, in your church, in your neighborhood; people come and tell you their problems. But instead of solution, all you have offered so far is destruction. Because of your bad advice, hopes have been dashed, marriages have been broken, homes have been scattered. And you still claim you're a Christian. Well, I have no idea what kind of faith you have, but not the kind I'm talking about here and definitely not the kind Christ wants us to have.

There are people who are living with children that are totally dead to obedience. Nothing the parents say ever goes. They have given up all hope on that child. Trust me, that's a dead situation. As a person of faith, speak life into that house. Join hands with them and pronounce the words of revival, the words of hope, the words of repentance into the life of that child. Call the child's name and pronounce the Spirit of God to enter into him (her) and convict him (her). Remind God that He heard the prayer of Elijah, He heard that of Paul. So He has no choice but to hear yours. That son (daughter) is the work of God's hand and He has said, "Ask me of things to come concerning my sons, and concerning the work of my hands command ye me" (Isaiah 45:11). He has given us the audacity to do, so do it. After all, you are what you are because God <u>quickened</u> you, who were dead in trespasses and sins (Eph. 2:1). Be unto others what God has been to you.

If you found yourself in a dead church, don't leave until you have made an effort to bring life therein. God may have sent you there for that purpose. It's true there are ministers who are so consumed in their own spiritual arrogance and nothing will make them take advice from 'an ordinary church member.' They believe God will not tell a member what He has not told them. Wrong. God can use anybody to bring revival to anything. You stand in the gap. If they don't listen, you'll be free of all guilt and the records will show that you did the best you can.

God can use you to change the whole world if you take the pains to speak life into just one dead life. When one receives a miracle, he (she) will be a living testimony to others of what God can do through one soul and through that single soul, millions will come to know the Lord. And when that happens, won't you be glad that it took you, because of your faith in God, to do that?

R

61. FAITH is REALISTIC 247

62. FAITH RECEIVES 251

63. FAITH REPROVES EVIL 255

64. FAITH RESTITUTES 259

65. FAITH is RIGHTEOUS 262

61
FAITH is REALISTIC

Regardless of what I'm going through, I believe in confessing positive about my situation. I know God will work everything out for the glory of His name. But there's one thing I never do; I don't make myself believe the problem is not there all in the name of faith. That's like getting myself confused. Anytime I go before Daddy to ask His help, I have to be real in my plea. If I have a headache, I tell Him I have a headache but I know He's greater than my headache. One of the qualities of faith is reality.

Many people in the Bible that trusted God for miracles first faced the reality of their situation before seeking help. They knew they had a problem beyond human solution and it would take the hand of the Divine to be victorious. And when they sought help, they laid their problems bare and open before the One who had all solution in His control. They didn't pretend there was nothing when there was something.

When Abraham was trusting God for Isaac, he knew what his problem was and he was realistic about it. Sure he knew that God was able to make him fruitful. That not withstanding, he faced the reality of his barrenness.

> After these things the word of the LORD came unto Abram in a vision, saying, Fear not, Abram: I am thy shield, and thy exceeding great reward. <u>And Abram said, LORD God, what wilt thou give me, seeing I go childless,</u> and the steward of my house is this Eliezer of Damascus? <u>And Abram said, Behold, to me thou hast given no seed:</u> and, lo, one born in my house is mine heir (Genesis 15:1-3).

Though a man of indisputable great faith, he still made the pain of his barrenness clear to God. He didn't mince words. He was straight in his reply.

When the Israelites got stuck at the Red Sea, Moses their leader–a man of faith–never acted like the Red Sea wasn't real or that the armies of Pharaoh were not coming behind. Of course there was a Red Sea that they had to cross; and there was the Pharaoh's army coming from behind. He faced the reality of the situation. There's no single verse in the Bible where he told the children of Israel to pretend that the Sea wasn't real or the armies were just mere imaginations.

And Moses said unto the people, Fear ye not, stand still, and see the salvation of the LORD, which he will shew to you to day: <u>for the Egyptians whom ye have seen to day, ye shall see them again no more for ever</u>. The LORD shall fight for you, and ye shall hold your peace (Exodus 14:13-14).

This was a reality of faith. Of course they saw the Egyptians. There was no doubt about that. The problem was as real as their bondage back in Egypt. That they could not move forward made it even more real. Moses was realistic about the situation. But because of his faith, he knew the God who took them out of Egypt would not forsake them at the Red Sea. He already told them He was taking them to the Promised Land, which obviously could not be the Red Sea. Faith says I see this problem but I know God is greater than my problem.

How about Jabez? When his mother gave birth to him, she named him Jabez saying, "Because I bare him with sorrow"(1 Chronicles 4:9). Each time people called him, they emphasized sorrow in his life. But when Jabez got tired of being a sorrow, he didn't pretend the problem was not real. Of course it was. That was why he asked God to remove the pangs of pain from his life, to turn his situation around for good. The Bible says he was more honorable than his brothers. But Jabez knew there was no honor in sorrow. He faced the reality of the evil that his mother pronounced upon his life. He was fed up with it. The honor was no honor when it carried sorrow with it. It was that reality that led him to call on God to erase the evil, to remove the pain of sorrow, to restore the honor and make him honorable indeed. He had faith in God. But he was realistic.

How many of the people that came to Jesus pretended they had no problem? As many as came to Him for healing faced the reality of their circumstances. Not because they had no faith, but because faith doesn't call black white. Many Christians are suffering in silence because of unrealistic faith. Nobody prays with or for them because they make people believe they have no problems.

I can understand if we don't want to make a political campaign of our situations. When I talk to people, I first accept there's a problem. Then I declare my victory over the problem. When I go before the Lord, lying to Him won't do me any good. I have to be real. If I'm in pain, I come to Him, 'Lord, I am in pain. I need a relief.' He will know I mean business with Him. Faith is not an elimination of reality, but a validation of trust in time of trouble.

If we have to speak to the mountain, it has to be real. How can you speak to unreality? Jesus didn't say, 'you know what, when you see the mountain, just pretend it's not there'. He said if you shall speak to the mountain, it would hear you and obey you. That means I've got to first admit the reality of the mountain, then I command it to be removed. If I speak to the sickness in my life, it will hear and obey. But I've got to admit I'm sick. If I speak to the barrenness in the life of that sister, it will hear and be removed. But that sister has to admit she's barren. And then we go before the Lord and command the spirit of barrenness to be cast into the sea.

Attributes Of A Working Faith

When we come before the Almighty, let's open up unto Him. If we can't be open to Him, He will be closed to us. And if we seek the help of another brethren in prayer, let's be realistic. When we come empty and naked, we shall leave full and clothed.

62
FAITH RECEIVES

A faith that prays and asks, also receives. The Bible says, "Ask, and it will be given to you; ... For everyone who asks receives" (Matthew 7:8). God wants us to ask so we can receive. Abraham and Sarah asked for a child. God didn't forget them. At His own most appointed time, He remembered them. They didn't miss out. The Bible says, "Through faith also Sara herself received strength to conceive seed, and was delivered of a child when she was past age, because she judged him faithful who had promised" (Hebrews 11:11).

Zacharias and Elizabeth trusted God for a child. Because of their faith, God honored them and they received John the Baptist (Luke 1:57).

Hannah trusted the Lord for a child. God honored her faith and she who was barren received the great prophet Samuel (1 Samuel 1:20).

Rachel believed God for the fruit of the womb. She became the mother of Joseph, the second in command to Pharaoh in the land of Egypt (Gen. 30:22-24).

When Jesus came down from the mountain, a leper came and worshipped Him, saying "Lord, if thou wilt, thou canst make me clean" (Matthew 8:2). Because of his faith, his leprosy was cured. He received a brand new skin.

A centurion came to Jesus and pled on behalf of his paralyzed servant. According to his faith, Jesus sent the word and his servant received healing that very moment (Matthew 8:5-13).

The woman with the issue of blood touched the hem of Jesus' garment. Because of her faith, she received her healing (Matthew 9:20-22).

Two blind men yelled after Jesus for their sight to be restored. They had faith in Him and didn't relent until they got to Him. Because of their faith, they received their sight (Matthew 9:27-30).

A woman of Canaan refused to give up in spite of all the ridiculing and humiliation she received. She pled and persisted on behalf of her demon-possessed daughter. She received her desire. Her daughter was made whole (Matthew 15:21-28).

The father of an epileptic came to Jesus and pleaded on his son's behalf. Though the disciples could not cast it out, he wasn't discouraged. And because of his faith, his son was healed of epilepsy (Matthew 17:14-20).

Two other blind men came to Jesus as He and His disciples were getting out of Jericho. They were sitting by the road when they heard that Jesus was passing by. They cried out for Him to have mercy on them. Of course they knew the right person to call. They were calling the source of all mercy. The multitude restrained them but they refused to yield. Jesus had compassion on them and touched their eyes. Because of their faith, they received their sight (Matthew 20:29-34).

In Capernaum, four men carried their paralytic friend to Jesus. Because there was no way through the door, they uncovered the roof and let him down to get close to the great Healer. Their friend received his healing both physical and spiritual (Mk. 2:3-12).

Ten lepers met Jesus while passing through Galilee on His way to Jerusalem. They lifted up their voices to Jesus and begged for mercy. Jesus asked them to go and show themselves to the priests. On their way, they received their healing (Luke 17:11-14).

Jairus, a ruler of the synagogue in Capernaum, came and fell at Jesus' feet and earnestly begged that He come and lay His hands on his sick daughter. While still in the presence of Jesus, news came that his daughter had died. This was the worst news of his life, but it came to him at the best place in his life. There's no better place to receive news of death than in the presence of the One who had conquered death. Jesus heard and followed him to his house. Because of his faith, his 'Talitha cumi' from the dead. He received his dead daughter back to life (Mark 5:21-24; 35-43).

The Bible says, "Women received their dead raised to life again" (Hebrews 11:35). Mary and Martha of Bethany sent to Jesus and informed Him of their brother Lazarus' sickness. Though their brother died before Jesus came, yet because of their faith, they received their brother back to life (John 11:1-44).

By faith we receive victory over the workers of iniquity. Elijah single-handedly stood against four hundred, fifty prophets of Baal. Because he feared the Lord and resented evil, he received victory over the prophets of Baal (1 Kings 18:20-40).

When we fear Him and depart from evil, we shall have victory in every area of our life. We'll call on Him and He will answer. You don't have to be on mount Carmel to have an encounter with Baal prophets. They're everywhere. Yours could be living right next door to you. He could be living in the same house with you. He or she may be working in the same office with you. How about your unbelieving friend who loves everything about you except the name of Jesus? He or she is a Baal prophet. Ask for God to touch him (her) and prove that He indeed is God. And you shall receive him (her) to His kingdom.

Following His resurrection, Jesus asked His disciples to wait in Jerusalem for the promise of the Father, which is the Holy Spirit. The power that comes from Him, evident in speaking of tongues or new language, is one

Attributes Of A Working Faith

of the things we shall receive when we give our lives to Jesus. If you don't have it, then you need to ask for it. Cling to God in faith and do His will, and you shall receive favor, victory, healing and power. And in addition to all these earthly benefits, you shall receive eternal benefits that will serve you here and carry you there, if you don't loose heart.

63
FAITH REPROVES EVIL

Rebuke and reprove are sometimes used interchangeably. There are two ways faith reproves evil: rebuking the evil spirit out of a person's life; and reproving or exposing the evil deeds of another person.

While Jesus taught inside the Capernaum synagogue, a man with an unclean spirit, upon seeing Him cried out "Let us alone; what have we to do with thee, thou Jesus of Nazareth? art thou come to destroy us? I know thee who thou art, the Holy One of God." The Bible says, "And Jesus <u>rebuked</u> him, saying, Hold thy peace, and come out of him" (Mark 1:24, 25).

The spirit of sickness is of the devil. When Jesus went to Simon's (Peter) house, his wife's mother was sick with fever. The Bible records Jesus stood over her and rebuked the fever. It left her immediately and she served them (Luke 4:37-39). You say but Jesus did all these. That's true. But He said, "Verily, verily, I say unto you, He that believeth on me, the works that I do shall he do also; and greater works than these shall he do; because I go unto my Father" (John 14:12).

There were instances when Paul rebuked evil spirits in the Bible.

And it came to pass, as we went to prayer, a certain damsel possessed with a spirit of divination met us, which brought her masters much gain by soothsaying: The same followed Paul and us, and cried, saying, These men are the servants of the most high God, which shew unto us the way of salvation. And this did she many days. But Paul, being grieved, turned and said to the spirit, I command thee in the name of Jesus Christ to come out of her. And he came out the same hour (Acts 16:16-18).

Attributes Of A Working Faith

This was an act of rebuke by a man of faith. You too can do it.

There is the second part of reproving evil because we feel uncomfortable with it. It negates the profession of true faith. We show a form of hatred towards a person's evil and ungodly act. Only there's a difference in the way the hatred is shown. While we hate the evil, we must show Godly love towards the evildoer. The show of hatred should be demonstrated in the spirit of love. Not because we love his evil deeds, but because we hate his eternal condemnation.

Jesus never hated sinners but He reproved their sinful deeds. Loving other brethren is not an excuse to take our eyes off their wrongdoings. While we do not stand judgmental, at the same time we're not to condone sin.

When the Scribes and Pharisees brought the woman caught in adultery to Jesus, they were judgmental of her action and wanted to stone her to death, since that was their law. Jesus reproved them, not because He supported that woman's immorality; but because the value of her life far outweighed the gravity of her sin. After all, the accusers themselves were guilty sinners who should be stoned to death for their various atrocities. They never saw their own problems. He who cannot be reproved cannot reprove. They were not wrong in their accusation, for indeed hers was a sinful act. But they were guilty of their approach.

As children of God, we're to be light in a world of darkness. Our light must expose the works of darkness. Apostle Paul said, "For ye were sometimes darkness, but now are ye light in the Lord: walk as children of light: (For the fruit of the Spirit is in all goodness and righteousness and truth;) Proving what is acceptable unto the Lord. And have no fellowship with the unfruitful works of darkness, <u>but rather reprove them</u>" (Ephesians 5:8-11). While we continue to tolerate an evildoer in love–perhaps this will bring a change of heart unto repentance–there must be a level of intolerance for the sinful acts.

When God instructed Saul to go and utterly destroy Amalek, he disobeyed. God sent Samuel to him with a sharp rebuke.

> And Samuel said, Hath the LORD as great delight in burnt offerings and sacrifices, as in obeying the voice of the LORD? Behold, to obey is better than sacrifice, and to hearken than the fat of rams. For rebellion is as the sin of witchcraft, and stubbornness is as iniquity and idolatry. Because thou hast rejected the word of the LORD, he hath also rejected thee from being king .... And Samuel said unto him, The LORD hath rent the kingdom of Israel from thee this day, and hath given it to a neighbour of thine, that is better than thou (1 Samuel 15:22-28).

This was a powerful and frantic rebuke from God through Samuel to king Saul. In rebuking or reproving a fellow believer (or even an unbeliever), fear must be put aside. Depending on how serious the offence, we may need to fast and pray before taking any step, for not all rebukes and reproofs are taken lightly. We have to prepare for opposition and confrontation. We don't know why Saul seized and tore the edge of Samuel's robe. Could be he wanted to put up some confrontation. Obviously he didn't like the reproof. He was a scorner that loveth not one that reproveth him (Proverbs 15:12).

Faith in God cannot accommodate bad practices. Much as we are to respect other people, it must not be at the expense of the truth. The Bible says, "Them that sin rebuke before all, that others also may fear" (1 Timothy 5:20). "For there are many unruly and vain talkers and deceivers, specially they of the circumcision: Whose mouths must be stopped, who subvert whole houses, teaching things which they ought not, for filthy lucre's* sake ... Wherefore rebuke them sharply, that they may be sound in the faith; Not giving heed to

Attributes Of A Working Faith

Jewish fables, and commandments of men, that turn from the truth" (Titus 1:10-14).

As followers of Christ, we cannot close our eyes to evil, big or small. God will not hold us blameless if we fail to reprove. As we show love we also show them the Lord. Our Lord never stopped loving evildoers, but He hated their evil deeds. It's good for us to refrain from evil. But it's expedient that we reprove such as bring shame to the name of our God. And when we're reproved by God, let's accept in the Spirit of humility. For he whom the Lord loves, He also chastens.

*Monetary gain

64
FAITH RESTITUTES (RESTORES)

A man had stolen some window glasses from the school where I taught back home in my country Nigeria. Years later, he met with the Lord and the spirit of disturbance came upon him. He was sorry for his past bad act. He didn't stop there. He brought new glasses back to replace the ones he originally stole. That was a spirit of restitution.

When we profess Jesus as Lord and Savior, people look forward to seeing changes in our character, our ways of life, and our attitudes. Unfortunately, there's something under the dress that nobody can see except God. As unbelievers, many of us had done things that can never be taken back. When we asked for forgiveness, God wiped them out of the book of remembrance. He will remember them no more. We're eternally free. And now the big question–how about those things that can still be returned to whom or where they belong?

As Jesus passed through Jericho, he met Zacchaeus, a tax collector. And Jesus entered and passed through Jericho. And, behold, there was a man named Zacchaeus, which was the chief among the publicans, and he was rich.... And when Jesus came to the place, he looked up, and saw him, and said unto him, Zacchaeus, make haste, and come down; for to day I must abide at thy house... **And Zacchaeus stood, and said unto the Lord: Behold, Lord, the half of my goods I give to the poor; and if I have taken any thing from any man by false accusation, I restore him fourfold** (Luke 19:1-8).

Zacchaeus had wrongfully taken from other people to enrich himself. When he met the Lord he felt convicted. But he didn't stop at conviction.

He proceeded to restoration and returned fourfold of all he had <u>**wrongfully**</u> **taken.**

You cannot be in the faith and have in your possession those items that don't belong to you: office pens, school computers, church property, library books, state money, store items that were shoplifted. How about all the tax money you have withheld? Did you declare the right amount? God will not overlook them. It's mandatory for you to restore them back to where they belong, for without that your faith is at stake. No amount of prayer can save you. You have to undo what you have done.

Ezekiel was sent by God as watchman to preach a message of restoration to the house of Israel.

> Therefore, thou son of man, say unto the children of thy people, The righteousness of the righteous shall not deliver him in the day of his transgression: as for the wickedness of the wicked, he shall not fall thereby in the day that he turneth from his wickedness; neither shall the righteous be able to live for his righteousness in the day that he sinneth. ... Again, when I say unto the wicked, Thou shalt surely die; if he turn from his sin, and do that which is lawful and right; <u>If the wicked restore the pledge, give again that he had robbed,</u> walk in the statutes of life, without committing iniquity; he shall surely live, he shall not die. None of his sins that he hath committed shall be mentioned unto him: he hath done that which is lawful and right; he shall surely live (Ezekiel 33:12-16).

It doesn't matter how righteous you think you are. It has to do with that one iniquity that you know but fail to do something about. The accuser of the brethren will point it out on that great day and make that property to stand before you as condemnation. That money you borrowed and purpose

Faith Restitutes (Restores)

in your heart not to refund will be a witness against you on the judgment day. The number of souls that have been saved through you will be astounded to see you heading a different direction. Why? Because you did not return the pencil you took from the store; because you failed to return the money back to the church purse; because of the page you ripped off the library book. You got it whole and returned it maimed. Would you rather loose eternity with Jesus because of a worthless commodity?

The Bible says, "for the things which are seen are temporal; but the things which are not seen are eternal" (2 Corinthians 4:18). Whatever it is you have today is temporal. But your soul is eternal. God loves you and He would not have you perish. The question is, would you have yourself perish or not? Remember, the world is temporal, heaven and hell are eternal. And the choice is yours.

65
FAITH is RIGHTEOUS

Righteousness is an attitude of uprightness and justice. It is to stand for truth in a world full of lies. It's not always easy. In fact most of the time, it's hard. For when you strive to be orderly in the midst of disorderliness, you end up being out of order; since disorderliness is the way of the heathen. That however is not enough reason for a Christian to join in the unrighteous wagon. Unequal yoke does not apply to marriage alone. It extends to every area of life where the wind of God blows and people breathe in His air free of charge.

God loves to see His redeemed children practice righteousness in everything they do. The Bible says, "The way of the wicked is an abomination unto the LORD: but he loveth him that followeth after righteousness" (Proverbs 15:9). When we're righteous, we receive the favor of His love.

Righteousness is not something we negotiate with God, to do or not to do. Half righteousness is as evil and abominable before God as unrighteousness. It's true we live in an unrighteous world. But that is not peculiar to our age. It started right from the Garden of Eden after our first parents disobeyed God.

By faith Abel offered unto God a more excellent sacrifice than Cain, by which he obtained witness that he was righteous, God testifying of his gifts: and by it he being dead yet speaketh (Hebrews 11:4).

Cain was Abel's brother and the first human being born in accordance with the natural ordinance of God. But why did he take the life of his brother Abel? Because Abel offered a righteous and acceptable sacrifice to God. God is not a beggar to whom we throw the left over. We either give or we don't.

David said he would not give to God that which would not cost him something (2 Samuel 24:24). Our giving to God has to come from a willing heart. We must be happy doing it. It's not that Cain did not give, but he did not give an excellent sacrifice. We give God what is right, not what is left.

Righteousness puts our prayers in good standing with the Lord. "The effectual fervent prayer <u>of a righteous man</u> availeth much" (James 5:16). "For the eyes of the Lord are over the righteous, and his ears are open unto their prayers" (1 Peter 3:12).

Righteousness opens the prayer line with a power that the devil and his co-hort cannot withstand. In every way and in everything, we must deny unrighteousness. We must forsake the way of the world. We're not having a second chance to pass through this world. "And as it is appointed unto men once to die, but after this the judgment" (Hebrews 9:27). This is the only opportunity we have to be righteous before our Maker. God is not going to force anyone to be righteous, just as He won't force anyone to accept Jesus as Lord and Savior. But the choice has been given to us to determine to stay righteous in an unrighteous world.

Though there are temptations all around us; God will not excuse our unrighteousness based on temptations. He has given us the grace to overcome them. Even Jesus was tempted but He never yielded to temptation. The men of God of those days had enough cause to be unrighteous. Yet, we read testimonies of their righteousness.

When the winds of life blow against you, God will give you the strength to stand and the grace to press forward. You just stay righteous and He will take care of the rest.

S

66. FAITH is SALT	265
67. FAITH SEEKS GOD	274
68. FAITH SOWS TO GOD'S KINGDOM	278
69. FAITH SPEAKS GOD'S WORD	282
70. FAITH is STEADFAST	285
71. FAITH SURRENDERS TO GOD'S WILL	287

66
FAITH is SALT

To address this topic, I shall divide it into two parts: one, how the faith of the speaker of the word can be salt to the hearer of the word; and two, how the faith of a believer can be salt to someone else.

How can the faith of the speaker of the word be salt to the hearer?

1. <u>Salt Penetrates.</u> When salt is applied to an open wound, there's a penetrating effect. It doesn't just stay on the surface doing nothing. It sinks deep into the wound to start the work of healing.

The message of the gospel, like salt, has a penetrating effect in the heart of the hearer. "So then faith cometh by hearing, and hearing by the word of God" (Romans 10:17). The Word of God when spoken sinks into the heart of the hearer. By faith we speak the word, by faith the hearer believes it. It's one thing to speak the word, it's another thing for the spoken word to enter into the hearts of those being addressed. But when it does enter–that is, when it penetrates–the Holy Spirit takes over and produces the next quality.

2. <u>Salt Pierces.</u> The moment salt touches a wound; it pierces through and causes a burning sting.

Following the descent of the Holy Spirit on the disciples, they spoke in different tongues. The crowd that gathered to see them assumed them to be out of their minds. Peter used that as an opportunity to launch his first sermon.

> Now when they heard this, they were pricked in their heart, and said unto Peter and to the rest of the apostles, Men and brethren, what shall we do? (Acts 2:37).

These people heard the words but didn't stop at hearing. The words caused a discomfort in their spirit by cutting into their hearts and convicting them of their sins. Then they asked what they could do to be saved.

Once the word of faith penetrates into the heart and pierces through the spirit, a sense of guilt for sins comes alive. There's a feeling of discomfort with the old and sinful life and a yearning to start a new life with the Lord. That's because "the word of God is quick, and powerful, and sharper than any twoedged sword, <u>piercing</u> even to the dividing asunder of soul and spirit, and of the joints and marrow, and is a discerner of the thoughts and intents of the heart" (Hebrews 4:12).

I've been through it. There were things I did before I knew the Lord that I never considered sinful. In fact, those who were not doing them were either stupid or ignorant. But when I came to the truth of the gospel, it had a gradual penetrating and piercing effect on me. I began to see those same things as sinful, one after the other. I was pierced in my spirit, pierced to that extent that I had a second baptism. I felt guilty about my first one and I realized I needed to have it done again. Six months pregnant with my first child, I was re-immersed in water, this time unto Christ.

<u>3</u>. <u>Salt Purges.</u> The burning effect of salt on a wound lasts a few seconds and stops gradually. That's a purging process to get rid of any infection that might have occurred.

When I came to my senses about my past sins, I began to think on how to get them out of my life and not go back to them. This has not been easy. It has taken me years to be what I am today. But God has been faithful in purging me one day at a time.

The same thing applies to any soul that is touched by the stinging truth of the gospel. After hearing and accepting that truth, a step must be taken towards renouncing the old and embracing the new. The Bible says, "<u>Purge</u>

<u>out therefore the old leaven</u>, that ye may be a new lump" (1 Corinthians 5:7).

Making a conscious effort to forsake old sins is a spiritual purging of an old leaven and the secret lies in reading God's Word. It cannot be done in the power of this flesh, for our flesh has a sinful nature embedded in it. But when faith is applied, the Holy Spirit takes over. A brand new vessel of honor comes alive and the works and things of the Kingdom will be of more interest than any earthly attractions.

> If a man therefore purge himself from these, he shall be a vessel unto honour, sanctified, and meet for the master's use, and prepared unto every good work (2 Timothy 2:21).

4. <u>Salt Purifies</u>. This is another unique quality of salt. It not only gets the unwanted stuff out, it cleanses the filth left behind; thus making for a better healing process.

After renouncing my old ways of living, I struggled with guilty feelings about the past. That was the filth from my old life. But as I grew in the faith, I realized I needed not feel guilty for a sin God had already forgiven me. I began a purifying process by attending Bible study classes, reading the Word of God on daily basis, filling my heart with Scripture verses. As I drew near unto Him, He drew near unto me and took care of my concerns. His Word cleansed me from my past sins and purified my heart from doubled-mindedness (James 4:8). Then I understood better what God's true forgiveness actually means. I now feel closer to Him than when I first accepted Him.

The other type of filth is the urge to want to go back to the old instead of clinging to the new. When an individual embraces the new life, there'll still be traces of the old life and He (she) feels like doing what has been renounced. The devil is not going to give up on a prostitute who embraces the new life in Jesus. He wants her back. She will constantly have that urge to go back.

That's because she's not yet totally clean. But the Word of God is always there as an anchor. If you're battling filth from past sins, get yourself soaked in His Word. He will cleanse you and make you a brand new creature.

5. <u>Salt Protects</u>. An open and untreated wound is always a happy zone for flies, not for good but to impair the healing process. If meat is left uncovered, flies make their living off it by depositing infectious germs. But when salt is sprinkled, it prevents the invasion of flies, thus protecting from contamination.

A believer, new or old in the Lord is a devil's target. Satan is the believer's archenemy and he's never happy at the conversion of any soul. He'll attempt to draw the soul back to his messy past by suggesting ungodly thoughts into the mind. He's the truth thwarter and gospel twister, who makes lies appear easy by making truth appear difficult. That's why we must never get complacent with our faith.

The Bible says for us to gird up the loins of our mind, be sober, and hope to the end for the grace that is to be brought unto us at the revelation of Jesus Christ; As obedient children, not fashioning ourselves according to the former lusts in our ignorance: But as he which hath called us is holy, so are we to be holy in all manner of conversation (1 Peter 1:13-16). It's only by so doing that a believer can remain strong and steadfast. When we allow the Word of God to serve as antidote to the ministrations of the devil, His Spirit will lift up a standard against the evil thoughts.

And just as salt protects from contamination by preventing flies from getting on the meat, the Word will prevent any spiritual impurity that may want to set in, thus protect the heart from its effect. And though the faith is tried, it shall remain unshakable.

6. <u>Salt Preserves</u>. Salt serves as a preservative to keep food from spoiling or rotting.

Coming to Jesus is a battle, not against flesh and blood that we can hold and touch; but against principalities and powers that most of the time, we can neither see nor touch. However God's Word is full of promises for such times. As believers, we have our anchor deeply rooted in His truth. Once we forsake all for God's kingdom, we must continue in that mind by not companying with workers of iniquity or following after unrighteousness. By faith we accepted Jesus, by faith we also obey His ordinances. Living for His will must take priority over any other thing in our lives.

> Forasmuch then as Christ hath suffered for us in the flesh, arm yourselves likewise with the same mind: for he that hath suffered in the flesh hath ceased from sin; That he no longer should live the rest of his time in the flesh to the lusts of men, but to the will of God. For the time past of our life may suffice us to have wrought the will of the Gentiles, when we walked in lasciviousness, lusts, excess of wine, revellings, banquetings, and abominable idolatries (1 Peter 4:1-3).

God's promise to never leave us nor forsake us (Hebrews 13:5) is a promise of preservation from all evil. The Bible says, "the Lord preserveth the faithful" (Psalm 31:23), but we have to be faithful to Him before we can be preserved. In everything let's hold on to Him and He, who has given us the grace, will also give the glory if we faint not (Psalm 84:11). And may the God of peace sanctify you completely; and may your whole spirit, soul, and body be preserved blameless at the coming of our Lord Jesus Christ.

Let's now consider the second aspect, which is the effect of our faith in the lives of others. A preacher came to my church some years ago and preached on the importance of salt. The sermon lasted only five minutes. But up till today I remember it as fresh as when I first heard it. That was because his sermon on salt brought sweetness into my life and for the first time, it dawned on me how little salt we put in our food and yet, how tasteless our food will be without that little addition.

Children of God are the salt of the earth (Matthew 5:13). Salt brings sweetness to what could have otherwise been tasteless or bitter. How then can we use our faith to bring salt, thus sweetness to the bitterness in other people? There are many people going around with bitterness in their souls. They're confused and fed up with life. Some are even mad with God. Let's not be judgmental. Instead let's bring sweetness to their bitter hearts by telling them about the love of Jesus.

We all at one time or the other in our individual lives, have gone and are going through hard times: hard times of separation from loved ones, of divorce, of wayward children, and of ill health. It's our faith in God that has taken us thus far. When in the midst of sorrow, faith tells us that God is in control and all shall be well. We hear the gentle whispering voice of assurance from the Holy Spirit telling us not to be discouraged; but to hold on, for the battle is almost over. That's the sweetening salt of faith in action.

There were practical instances in the Bible when God used men and women of faith to bring sweetness to other people's lives. Following their release from Egypt, the children of Israel got to the Wilderness of Shur. They were thirsty and needed water to drink. Unfortunately they wondered in the wilderness for three days and found no water. Finally they came to Marah, thinking it was over. But alas, the waters were bitter. When Moses cried to the Lord, He showed him a tree. Moses, because he had faith in God, cast the tree into the waters and it became sweet and drinkable (Exodus 15:22-25).

Another incident.

The prophet Elisha was at Jericho. The men of the city came and

Faith Is Salt

told him of their grievances: one, their water was bitter; two, their land was barren. Theirs was a combination of bitterness and barrenness. But God brought an end to these predicaments by the hand of His faithful servant.

> And the men of the city said unto Elisha, Behold, I pray thee, the situation of this city is pleasant, as my lord seeth: but the water is naught, and the ground barren. And he said, Bring me a new cruse, and put salt therein. And they brought it to him. And he went forth unto the spring of the waters, and cast the salt in there, and said, Thus saith the LORD, I have healed these waters; there shall not be from thence any more death or barren land. So the waters were healed unto this day, according to the saying of Elisha which he spake (2 Kings 2:19-22).

In these two instances, the bitterness and barrenness of these people became sweetness and fruitfulness because men of faith appeared on the scene. Of what relevance was the tree to the bitter waters of Marah, and of what relevance was the salt in a bowl to the waters of Jericho or the vastness of their land? It may appear not relevant to you and I. But God does not see the way we see. The restoration that came to the water and the land was not in the salt, but in the faith of God's men.

When Ruth lost her husband, she had every reason to be bitter. But because of her faith in God, she remained with her mother-in-law Naomi, who lost both her husband and her two sons, Mahlon and Chilion. Through Ruth, God restored sweetness to Naomi's life. She, who because of her bitter experience changed her name from Naomi to Marah–bitter–rejoiced in nursing a child (Ruth 1-4). When your family members or your in-laws are having bitter experiences, do you partake or forsake? Do you make them feel it's their sin that is causing their problems? Remember one of these days, it may be your turn.

When you notice bitterness in the spiritual waters of those around you, what do you do? Your neighbor has been eager to have a child. Finally after five years of marriage, she gives birth. But alas, the baby comes out brain damaged. That's the bitter water experience after a long period of thirst. She finally got it but it's not good for drinking. Don't shut your eyes. Like the Israelites, some of them have no idea what to do. The best they can do is grumble and complain against God. But you can make a difference.

The Word of God in your mouth is salt. Jesus said, "Ye are the salt of the earth: but if the salt have lost his savour, wherewith shall it be salted? it is thenceforth good for nothing, but to be cast out, and to be trodden under foot of men" (Matthew 5:1). When I need to sprinkle salt on my food, I don't pick an empty salt container. I pick one with salt inside. That's because I won't get anything out of an empty vessel. A faithless person is of no use to a faithless hurting soul. If we don't have faith, we cannot bring sweetness to other people's bitterness. You can only give what you have. But on the other hand, if we have faith but fail to use it to bring sweetness to others, it becomes ineffective. It has no flavor and that amounts to a negation of our profession.

When faith ceases to bring joy to people's lives, it's no longer serving the purpose for which it has been given to us. "For unto whomsoever much is given, of him shall be much required" (Luke 12:48). To whom much salt is given, much sweetness is expected. You either use it or you loose it.

Anywhere we are, our presence must make a difference, not only in our preaching, but also in speaking. Our speech must be seasoned with salt (Colossians 4:6) to bring healing to hurting souls, life to the dead in spirit, hope to the hopeless at heart and peace to the disturbed in mind.

A believer without salt is a believer without sweetness. He will bring nothing but bitterness to the burdened and doom to the depressed. We can't profess Christ while we bring curse on people. We can't profess sweetness when all we produce is bitterness. May the Lord who has called us make us a spring of salt water indeed, from which the bitter will drink and be sweetened.

67
FAITH SEEKS GOD

Seeking God is not only for unbelievers. I'm a believer and I seek God everyday. I seek the things of His kingdom. The day I got converted was just the beginning of my seeking. That's not to say the seeking will stop, for the day that happens, I know I'm no longer in His will. I seek because I want to know Him more and understand His precepts better. There's no end to learning. We will continue to learn until the Lord comes.

What are the things believers seek in God? The first and most important is His kingdom. The Bible says, "But seek ye first the kingdom of God, and his righteousness; and all these things shall be added unto you" (Matthew 6:33). God's kingdom comes before anything and it's inexhaustible in knowing. We can never know everything about His kingdom while we're still here on earth. We have to continue everyday to learn new things about it.

I have a problem and I don't know if you experience the same thing. Several times I open to a passage that I've read only God knows how many times and it's like I'm reading it for the very first time. John 3:16 is a familiar verse that almost any believer can quote. I've known that verse for so many years. I read it this year and I was touched in a brand new way. In fact, I was weeping. That leaves me wondering what happened the other times I read it? What on earth is wrong with my memory? Does it happen to you? It does? (Oh thank God, I feel relieved already.) But you know what? Each time that happens, the Holy Spirit tells me I shall continue to have that experience for as long as I open the Bible to read, for His words are new every day.

I know there are men and women of God who can recite thousands of verses off head. But I don't believe there's a single man or minister of God who knows the Word of God in its entirety. No matter how much you know, there's something somebody knows that you don't know. There's something you're missing out and something new that God wants you to know. Believers who no longer seek God through His Word are believers who are no longer saved. There's no way you can claim to have faith in God and not love to seek His kingdom and its righteousness everyday.

Seeking Him must be to a Christian what prey is to a lion. A lion will go out of its way to seek a prey; to consume it and digest it. Once it gets its hand on that prey, nothing can get it out. And that happens on daily basis. It's never tired of seeking and searching for something to eat.

That's how we are to seek God's kingdom. We seek it with our soul, our zeal and might. We seek it like water to quench our thirst and food to satisfy our hunger. As long as we are in this mortal body, hunger and thirst will always pay us visits. And we never stop entertaining them. We must never stop to entertain our hunger and thirst for the things of God. "Blessed are they which do hunger and thirst after righteousness: for they shall be filled" (Matthew 5:6). We must continue to seek and search His mind like never before. And once we get it, we determine that nothing will snatch it out of our minds.

Getting tired is not an option when it comes to the things of the kingdom. If we get tired, there's the devil that never gets tired of seeking whom he may devour. The Bible calls him our adversary (1 Peter 5:8). If the devil were not tired of seeking us to devour, why should we get tired of seeking our God, the only One who can save us from being devoured by him? Don't make a mistake to think that the devil is seeking those who are lost. They already belong to him. He has no problem with them. He's seeking you and I.

He wants to snatch us back from the heavenly road. We have to resist him. But if we don't know the word, what else have we to resist him? And if we don't daily seek to know Him, how do we know the word?

The Bible commands us to diligently seek Him (Hebrews 11:6). Diligent seeking is seeking without giving up. The psalmist David said, "One thing have I desired of the LORD, that will I seek after; that I may dwell in the house of the LORD all the days of my life, to behold the beauty of the LORD, and to enquire in his temple" (27:4). He knew the right thing to do at the right time. He knew the best time to seek God is while you're still living. A dead person is no longer qualified to seek the Lord. He's done with his journey. He has no other chance. The only time we can seek Him and find Him is while we're still living. No one seeks God in the grave.

We also seek His face. His face means His counsel and His will in whatever we do. "When thou saidst, Seek ye my face; my heart said unto thee, Thy face, LORD, will I seek" (Psalm 27:8). We must purpose to put Him prior to any decision we make. When we seek His face in every endeavor, He has promised to order our steps. We shall not miss the way.

This may sound awkward to you. But I seem to act crazy at times when it comes to seeking God's face in everything I do. Believe it or not, when I go to the store, as I go through the aisle, I communicate with Him in the Spirit to order my spending. I don't have enough to buy everything I need. So I have to spend wisely. There's always that temptation to pick the unnecessary and forget the essential. So I seek His face to take my eyes off the things that I don't need right away. And guess what? It works. I leave the store happy. I ask Him to direct me to an open parking space when the whole place is full. Instead of going round the lot, He leads me to where I need to go. I've done it several times and not once has He failed.

Brethren, let's not stop at accepting Jesus as Lord. Instead, let's continuously seek to know Him more by striving to know more about the imperishable things above, instead of the 'peril-shambles' here below.

When the angels announced the birth of Jesus to the shepherds in the field, they did not stop at hearing. They hastily went in search of Him who is the Savior of the world, in spite of the cold night weather. The searching brought more reality to them than hearing. They saw and knew more than they would have known had they stopped at hearing.

We too must not stop at hearing about the kingdom. Let's seek that kingdom and not relax until we see it with our eyes, for then and only would we know Him best and understand Him most.

68
FAITH SOWS TO GOD'S KINGDOM

When we sow, are we doing what the farmer does on the field? In many ways, yes. There are many things we sow to God's kingdom and there are different ways we reap. But one thing is sure; our reaping is commensurate to our sowing. Just like the farmer, you can never reap what or where you do not sow. Sowing begets reaping. (Read the parable of the sower in Matthew 13:1-9, 18-23.)

The greatest seed a believer sows in faith is the Word of God. That's not saying we reap pages off the Bible and throw them on the open field or bury them in dug holes. But by sharing the word with those who don't know Him, we're sowing kingdom seeds.

When the sower in the parable went out to sow, he sowed on different soils. He never intended that any of his seeds fall on hard ground, thorny soil, or wayside where the birds would come and devour them. He wished that his seeds fell on good grounds. That unfortunately was not the case.

There are those who want to hear the word but have no one to tell them. There are those who hear but don't respond. There are those who hear and love it, but for reasons that they don't know, find it difficult to obey. When we sow the words of the kingdom, not all will come to repentance. Of course we always pray all do. But let's not be disappointed when we see some of the people whom we tell about Christ heading straight to hell. Yes, we're to feel sorry and concerned, but we don't have to grow weary in sowing. The work of conversion is not ours to do. We have no control over the soul of a man. Only the Holy Spirit can convict and convert a sinner. You wonder how I know. Ask me about me. It has taken the Holy Spirit to bring me thus far. Not my sister, my mother or even my pastor; no one but God. The life I now live in this body, I live by faith in God's Son Jesus Christ, my Lord and my Savior. And to Him I give all the glory.

Noah preached to the generation of his days prior to the flood. The people did not believe Noah's words. They were drinking, making merry, marrying and giving in marriage. He didn't get wearied. He preached until God asked him and his family to enter the ark. They who failed to listen perished by the flood. Only Noah and his household, eight people in total were saved out of a whole generation. Yet the Bible calls him a preacher of righteousness.

On the other hand, some of those we tell about the kingdom may not respond right away. Some may not come to the realization of the truth we have sown until long after we have departed this earth. But when we get there, we shall see them and be glad we have not labored in vain after all. One thing remains constant. The Word of God is sent and sown for a purpose. If does not convert, it will convict or do both.

We also sow our gift, which can be our money or anything we give as faith offering. When a farmer goes to the field to sow, he has to ignore the winds if he means business because "He that observeth the wind," the Bible says, "shall not sow; and he that regardeth the clouds shall not reap" (Ecclesiastes 11:4). When we're ready to sow to the kingdom, winds and clouds are going to show up. These are the unexpected expenses that come at the least expected time. Things we never envisage will happen and bring discouragements to our willing hearts. But if we mean business with God, determination has to override disappointments. When we wish to give to the work of His kingdom and terminal illness shows up in the life of a loved one, a choice has to be made. Do we continue to invest in a sickness that will eventually bring death; or do we invest in the kingdom of a Savior that can save from sickness and give life? This is not an easy choice to make. It takes dedication and determination to the Almighty God.

When my second child was about three years, he had a form of bone disease, more like polio. One of his legs bent towards the other. He could not run without falling. We scheduled him for a bone correction surgery. Though it was going to cost a lot, but that was nothing compared to our love for this precious soul. His daddy was here in the States. I was with him and his brother in Nigeria.

A day to the operation, the Word of God came through our pastor that no razor should touch him. I was completely confused. I called my husband and told him that his little boy would not be having the operation. He consented. But what was I to do? I didn't want my son walking crippled. Suddenly I remembered we were having a church building project. It occurred to me that I should invest the money for the surgery into the church building program. I went on my knees and pledged every penny to that project. I made the desire of my heart known to Him. I was realistic in my plea. My boy had polio and I wanted his leg corrected. Since I had the money in hand, I paid my vow right away. A few months later, I looked at my boy and could not remember which leg was the bent one. I had no idea what happened to that leg; but one thing I know, God healed my son. It was a difficult choice for me to make. But it paid off for me more than the surgery.

We need to sow to His kingdom. It may be difficult. It may even be in tears. I won't deceive you, I sowed that money in tears. I was burdened for my child. But the Bible says, "They that sow in tears shall reap in joy. He that goeth forth and weepeth, bearing precious seed, shall doubtless come again with rejoicing, bringing his sheaves with him" (Psalm 126:5, 6). I sowed in tears and reaped in joy. Today, the boy who couldn't run without falling is a vibrant football player. God formed the bones and He worked on them without the help of any doctor.

His ways are past finding. The more we try to understand Him, the more confused we become. Only let's not be weary in sowing to His work. We don't know when the harvest will come. "In the morning sow thy seed, and in the evening withhold not thine hand: for thou knowest not whether shall prosper, either this or that, or whether they both shall be alike good" (Ecclesiastes 11:6). Let's sow in faith to His kingdom. If we don't get the reward here, we shall get it there.

Be not deceived; God is not mocked: for whatsoever a man soweth, that shall he also reap. For he that soweth to his flesh shall of the flesh reap corruption; but he that soweth to the Spirit shall of the Spirit reap life everlasting (Galatians 6:7-8).

Which would you rather reap, corruption or everlasting life? Choose the good one, choose everlasting life.

69
FAITH SPEAKS GOD'S WORD

When I was in College, I learnt about the Silent Trade. It was a form of trading used in those ancient times. The seller put his good outside where passers-by could see it. The buyer saw it and made a bid by putting a certain amount of money on it. He withdrew to a hiding place. The seller came back. If he were pleased with the amount, he took the money and left the item. The buyer came back and picked it. If the seller were not pleased, he just left the money and the good. The buyer then came and added more money. This would continue until the seller took the money and the buyer took the good. Oh boy! Don't I wish I could get the video recording? I can imagine how boring this would have been for them. Or let me say how boring it would be for somebody like me.

Well that was good for goods, but not good for gospel. How can we share our faith without speaking? It's not possible. Even Jesus didn't practice silent preaching. "And seeing the multitudes, he went up into a mountain: and when he was set, his disciples came unto him: __And he opened his mouth__, and taught them, saying, …" (Matthew 5:1-2).

The day I first read this passage, it was funny to me. He opened His mouth and taught. How else could He have taught? If He had to speak to a crowd that large, I guess the only wise thing to do was to open His mouth. But as I grew up in the faith, it made more sense to me. To open the mouth is necessary when we need to make our spiritual stand known, preach the gospel or command evil spirits out of a body.

Jesus taught His disciples about the coming persecutions. He strengthened them and bade them not to be afraid. But one thing they must

Faith Speaks God's Word

do: they must speak the word (Matthew 10:16-20, 27). They would suffer for gospel sake and be scourged for Christ's sake. But whatever betide, they had to speak the word.

There's no way we can preach without speaking. He who must preach must speak. People need to hear before they can believe. And they cannot hear unless we speak. "How then shall they call on him in whom they have not believed? and how shall they believe in him of whom they have not heard? and how shall they hear without a preacher? So then faith cometh by hearing, and hearing by the word of God" (Romans 10:14, 17). And I ask, how shall they preach without opening their mouths to speak?

The words we know are not meant for us to keep inside. We're to dish them out to those who have not heard. The apostles spoke the words incessantly, permitted or not permitted. They seized every opportunity they had to speak the word and preach the message, from the healing of the lame man by Peter at the temple gate to the healing of the lame man by Paul in Lystra. They were not overcome by fear for their lives. They knew their lives were in danger and they realized what speaking the word could do to them. But that didn't stop them from speaking the word. To them, not speaking the word signified the end of their existence.

Peter and John were arrested for speaking to the people after the healing of the lame man at the temple entrance. They were ordered not to speak the word. But the men of God defied that order.

> But Peter and John answered and said unto them, Whether it be right in the sight of God to hearken unto you more than unto God, judge ye. <u>For we cannot but speak</u> the things which we have seen and heard. ... And when they heard that, they lifted up their voice to God with one accord, and said, ... And now, Lord, behold their threatenings: and

grant unto thy servants, <u>that with all boldness they may speak thy word,</u> … And when they had prayed, the place was shaken where they were assembled together; and they were all filled with the Holy Ghost, <u>and they spake the word of God with boldness</u> (Acts 4:19-20, 23-31).

Of what effect was the command on them? None. They spoke the word irrespective of the order not to do so. When God says do, who is man to tell you don't?

Even the problems in our lives need to hear us speak before they obey. Jesus said if we say to a mountain to move, it shall be so. How do you say without speaking? I've never heard of a sign language that even the mountains understand. I know with God all things are possible. If a dumb man speaks to the mountain of affliction in his life using the sign language, I believe with all my heart God will honor his prayer. But for somebody who can open his mouth and speak audibly, I think it's dumb trying to use the sign language to command the mountain.

A pastor doesn't go to church on Sunday and remain silent while preaching, making himself believe the Holy Spirit already knows his mind and He will interpret everything. I don't think that's the kind of job the Holy Spirit does. Pastor, you have to speak the word for your congregation to hear. Faith comes by hearing. But hearing comes by the speaking of the word.

Though there may be occasions when the fear to speak the word grips our minds. The Bible says for us not to be afraid, but speak, and hold our peace (Acts 18: 9-10). If God says we should not be afraid to speak the word, then let's ride on speaking. He will be with us and give us audience.

70
FAITH is STEADFAST

To be steadfast is to refuse to be moved by just anything. One who is steadfast in decision usually finds it difficult to change his mind. He's not easily malleable. He holds strictly to his conviction. I don't believe in this principle when it applies to day-to-day activities, for no one knows it all and no one can be perfectly right. But when it comes to faith, it is a solid principle that we must long to have.

Many distractions will come our way. Parents will discourage us, relatives will threaten us. Instead of getting more friends, we gain more enemies. Not to talk of days of unanswered prayers, weeks of unwanted illnesses, months of incessant agonies in the spirit and years of unspeakable heartaches. All these put together will suck the kingdom out of any believer whose faith is not well rooted in God. But the scripture tells us not to be moved by our afflictions because we are appointed unto them (1 Thes. 3:3). Most of the time we forget that the kingdom of God is not bread and wine, but believing and waiting.

Satan, the tempter will make you believe your problem is unique to you and no one else is going through the same thing. That's a lie. It's just his trick to lure you away from the truth. You're to resist him <u>steadfast</u> in the faith (1 Peter 5:9).

How about false doctrines? In any place where people call on the name of the Almighty God, there will be false doctrines, just as it was in the days of the apostles. Apostle Paul, in his letter to the Colossians wrote, "And this I say, lest any man should beguile you with enticing words. For though I be absent in the flesh, yet am I with you in the spirit, joying and beholding your order, **and the stedfastness of your faith in Christ. As ye have therefore received Christ Jesus the Lord, so walk ye in him: Rooted and built up in him, and stablished in the faith**, as ye have been taught, abounding therein with thanksgiving" (Col. 2:4-7).

I've never had any cause to want to move a deep-rooted tree, but I can imagine how hard it will be to attempt it. I doubt the possibility except in prayers. Once a tree is well rooted, even when cut, it'll spring up again. That's how it should be with our faith. No amount of external force can destroy the root. It abides forever.

As long as we remain steadfast in His will, He will deliver us out of temptations. And according to the words of the apostle Paul, "Stand fast therefore in the liberty wherewith Christ hath made us free, and be not entangled again with the yoke of bondage" (Galatians 5:1).

71
FAITH SURRENDERS TO GOD'S WILL

To surrender is to give up and accept one's inability to continue or press forward. It could also mean to accept one's inadequacy in recognition of a higher supremacy. When soldiers go to war, there is always the opposing force. Both of them cannot win and both of them cannot loose. The side that surrenders is considered to have come to the end of their military tactics and ability, thus the looser.

This does not apply to us as children of God because we're not wrestling or fighting with Him. If we're warring, it's against our flesh. But when it comes to our faith, we must always surrender our will to God's will. Jesus is our perfect example. When the disciples came and asked Him to teach them how to pray, He said, "When ye pray, say, Our Father which art in heaven, Hallowed be thy name. Thy kingdom come. Thy will be done, as in heaven, so in earth" (Luke 11:2).

We're to ask to do His will each time we communicate with Him in prayer. If it were not necessary, Jesus would not teach it. And not only did He teach it, He demonstrated it. Three times He prayed in the garden of Gethsemane, not for His will but the Father's will to be done concerning His crucifixion (Mat. 26:36-44). Nothing aside from the Father's will was acceptable. This ought to be our attitude in prayer. Each time we go before Daddy, we're to pray for His will in everything we request. It wasn't easy for our fathers of old. But they obediently did the Father's will.

When God called Noah to build the ark, there's no record of him ever arguing with God. He obeyed the will of God and it was accounted unto him for righteousness.

Even greater was Abraham. God called him out of his father's land to a country he didn't know. Naturally the flesh will want to ask for certainty of direction. But not a faith that has learnt to surrender to the sovereign will of Jehovah and to trust Him for direction in life.

How about the time he was asked to go and sacrifice his only son? I mean talk of a difficult time to surrender to God's will...

a time when the voice of the devil will sound louder than that of God,

a time when one will be tempted to discard the instruction as coming from the deceiver himself,

a time when the story cannot and must not be told to anyone else, for one will be considered insane,

a time when one would wish it turns out to be a dream after all,

a time when there will be no more tears left in the eyes, for everything has turned into sweat drops,

a time when death would taste better than life,

... yet, Abraham surrendered to the will of God. His identity with God was worth much more to him than his Isaac from God. If He decided to have him back, so what? His will be done.

God delights in people who will do His will and follow His ordinances. When we try to do it our own way, we fail because we have not enough strength to fight the battle except given by God. The disciples went through a lot of trials and tribulations. But they never sought their own will above that of God.

Brethren, until we get to that stage in our faith when we can surrender our total will to the will of God, when doing what pleases Him gives us more joy than our earthly possessions, when we just love loving Him no matter what He takes us through, we have not yet accomplished His divine purpose.

Nay but, O man, who art thou that repliest against God? Shall the thing formed say to him that formed it, Why hast thou made me thus? (Romans 9:20).

He's the potter, we're the clay. No man can question what He does with us. Abraham didn't earn the title 'father of faith' by words; he earned it by works. He surrendered his will to that of God. Are you willing to do the same?

T

72. FAITH is TEMPERATE	291
73. FAITH TESTIFIES	294
74. FAITH is THANKFUL	297
75. FAITH TOLERATES	301
76. FAITH TRUSTS IN GOD	304

72
FAITH is TEMPERATE

To be temperate is to have self-control, not just for food, but in any situation that requires the ability to restraint from the urge to do it. It could be in drinking, fornication or anything that profanes God's holy name. It's appalling the way Satan is making great men and women fall these days for lack of self-control. Temptation is not something we pray not to come our way. The grace not to yield to it is what we need to ask for.

When Satan tempted Jesus, remember he chose a time when our Lord just finished forty days and forty nights of fasting. There can be no better time to tempt a man with food than when he's hungry. But we have a Savior who was tempted in all things but never yielded (Hebrews 4:15). He was temperate in nature.

Are we going to be faced with things that will almost make us sin? Yes.

Are we going to have an encounter with the flesh and feel like doing it the way other people in the world do it? Yes.

Are we supposed to do it? No! Others may, we cannot. We know what is right. We have a higher calling. What then are we supposed to do? We're to put on the Lord Jesus Christ, and make not provision for the flesh, to fulfil the lusts thereof (Rom. 13:14). We are to robe ourselves–by filling our minds–with the things of God; prayerfully and constantly bring the flesh into subjection, lest that by any means, when we have preached to others, we become castaway (1 Corinthians 9:24-27).

How hurtful it will be when you see those you won to the Lord going the golden road and you heading for hell, just because you lacked temperance when sister Delilah showed up at your door? Or how painful it will be when you see the people you brought to the Lord raptured and you're left behind because you have no self-control over gambling and pornography? Think of all the time you spend in the church, days of prayer and fasting, nights of vigil and intercession. Would you allow your labor to be in vain because of your inability to control your desires? Would you rather loose your place with God because you lack self-control?

Why do you think we say 'the God of Abraham, Isaac and Jacob', instead of 'the God of Abraham, Isaac and Esau?' For lack of self-control, because his temporary desire for a bowl of soup was more important to him than his permanent position in heaven, he lost it. He was replaced forever. He made every effort to get it back, but it was too late. He could no longer be counted worthy of a seat in heaven. He didn't realize the seriousness of what he did until after it was done. How pathetic?

Imagine how sweet the world would be and how close we would have been to God if Adam and Eve had exercised some self-control and stood their ground against the serpent. There wouldn't have been any cause for all the evils we're now going through. The fruit they enjoyed for a moment took from them and us what we would have enjoyed for eternity. How painful and absurd?

David was a man of faith, no doubt about it. But when he saw Bathsheba, he lost his temperance. For one split second of lustful looking, his faith eluded him for his flesh. Momentary gratification made his spiritual resume short of perfection.

How awful and sad to hear of bishops and pastors who engage in immoral practices because they lack self-control? Instead of subjecting their flesh, they subject their faith. They're controlled by their lustful desires. Most of the time, they did not start out that way. But somewhere along the line, something other than the Spirit of God took over and instead of launching a spiritual attack against it, they welcomed it with open hearts. One of the qualities of a good bishop is temperance (Titus 1:8). It takes the holy to correct the unholy. An intemperate preacher is not qualified to correct an intemperate member.

In every thing you do, strive to be temperate. There are times it will cost you your dignity to say no. But people need to know you for what you are and what you are not when they talk of your faith. Be it in your place of work, at home, in your neighborhood, at school or most importantly in the gathering of God's people, be temperate. Before you do, ask: If Jesus were to be present, would I do what I'm about to do? If the answer is not a resounding yes, please don't.

And I have a word for you Bathshebas and Delilahs who have no job other than making great vessels of God fall. You either repent or the Lord will demand their blood from you if you cause their downfall. You need to pray for God to bestow the Spirit of temperance on you. If you must stay in the body, don't bring destruction to that body. If you find it hard to exercise temperance, get out and let's enjoy our men of God. We need them and don't want you to take them away from us. Go somewhere else where you can fit in with your evil desires.

And to all of us in the faith, let's hold fast to our belief and not give place to the devil. And having done all, may it be said of us that in everything we were temperate.

73
FAITH TESTIFIES

I'm very familiar with this because we do it a lot in my country. To testify is to tell others what God has done for you. It can be used as a means of witnessing to others about your faith. People testify concerning deliverance from accident. Others testify about their salvation, how they met with Jesus as Lord and Savior. The list goes on and on.

Testimony is very scriptural and it gladdens the heart of God when we do it because it tells Him how much we appreciate what He has done. It also tells others about our God and some have come to believe through the testimony of other people.

Of all the patriarchs in the Bible, none testified like David. Most of his Psalms are testimonies of the Lord's goodness in his life. They tell of what the Lord did for him in times of trouble, how he called on God and He answered.

There were people in the Bible, who after receiving their healing testified to the goodness of God. When Jesus was at Gadarene, a man with an unclean spirit met Him. After rebuking the unclean spirit out of him, the man begged that he might remain with Jesus. But Jesus said to him, "Go home to thy friends, and tell them how great things the Lord hath done for thee, and hath had compassion on thee" (Mark 5:1-20). In short, go and testify. Verse 20 says, "And he departed, and began to publish in Decapolis how great things Jesus had done for him: and all men did marvel." This man didn't know Jesus before his healing. But after coming to his senses, he testified of the Lord's goodness.

How about the man born blind? After receiving his sight, the Pharisees summoned him for questioning because he was healed on the Sabbath. To them, healing on the Sabbath was anti-God and therefore sinful. Did that stop the man from testifying of the power of the One that healed him? No! In fact, he made the Pharisees feel religiously ignorant.

How about Paul, former Saul of Tarsus? He was an anti-Christ disciple. But one day on the road to Damascus, the powerful and irresistible hand of the Almighty gripped him while on one of his hate-inspired journeys to go and bring Christians bound to Jerusalem. After his conversion, Paul testified of his faith in Jerusalem, after which the Lord appeared to him and asked him to also testify in Rome. (Read Acts 22:1-22 and Acts 23:11.)

When we testify, people will be convicted and pricked in the heart. They may pretend they don't care. But deep down, they're touched. Sooner or later, they will come to repentance.

Not all the time do testimonies go without persecution. There are people who have been slain for their testimonies: "And when he had opened the fifth seal, I saw under the altar the souls of them that were slain for the word of God, and for the testimony which they held" (Revelation 6:9). That's why we need to ask the Lord to give us the boldness to witness of His power to others.

There are some parts of my country where you can't talk openly about your faith. (Ask the foreign Evangelists who have been to Kano, a Muslim dominated state in Nigeria.) In such places, we need wisdom and discretion. On the long run, it shall be for a testimony. Jesus said to His disciples, "But before all these, they shall lay their hands on you, and persecute you, delivering you up to the synagogues, and into prisons, being brought before kings and rulers for my name's sake. <u>And it shall turn to you for a testimony</u>" (Luke 21:12, 13).

When we suffer for the sake of the gospel, it's going to turn out for a testimony. We shall be threatened, punched and tortured for Christ's sake. The truth is, no spiritual crown is void of the cross. But at last, it shall be worth it all. Just know that the testimony you give today may be the only reason someone will come to Christ tomorrow. Do you have a testimony? Then do what the Samaritan woman did. Go home running and come back bringing others to the water that is not from the well. Testify.

74
FAITH is THANKFUL

    To be thankful is to appreciate something and be grateful for it. I don't consider myself the rigid type when it comes to principle. But I appreciate it when my children thank us for what we do for them. When they come home from school and find food ready on the table, I expect some appreciation. I won't crucify them if they don't, but I will cherish it if they do. The Bible tells us to offer unto God thanksgiving (Psalm 50:14).

    Thanksgiving should be the delight of anyone who has faith in God. If it were not important, Jesus would not do it. On several occasions, He gave thanks.

> And Jesus took the loaves; <u>and when he had given thanks</u>, he distributed to the disciples, and the disciples to them that were set down; and likewise of the fishes as much as they would (John 6:11). And he asked them, How many loaves have ye? And they said, Seven. … and he took the seven loaves, <u>and gave thanks</u>, and brake, and gave to his disciples to set before them; and they did set them before the people (Mark 8:5, 6).
> And as they were eating, Jesus took bread, and blessed it, and brake it, and gave it to the disciples, and said, Take, eat; this is my body. And he took the cup, <u>and gave thanks,</u> and gave it to them, saying, Drink ye all of it (Matthew 26:26-27).

    You may be thinking these were thanksgivings before food. And I know you do that too. But wait.

> Jesus therefore again groaning in himself cometh to the grave. It was a cave, and a stone lay upon it. Jesus said, Take ye away the stone.

...Then they took away the stone from the place where the dead was laid. And Jesus lifted up his eyes, and said, Father, <u>I thank thee that thou hast heard me</u>. And I knew that thou hearest me always: but because of the people which stand by I said it, that they may believe that thou hast sent me (John 11:38-44).

This was not for food. This was at the least expected place. Of all places to give thanks, Jesus gave thanks at the tomb of a dead and stinking body. He knew Abba Father would honor His prayer to raise Lazarus from the dead. And as appreciation in advance, He gave thanks. Not because he was ignorant of what happened. Of course He knew that Lazarus was dead. But He Himself is Lord over death and His presence means the absence of death.

Giving thanks should be to us what eating is to our bodies. We do it everyday without necessarily thinking about it. We do it all the time. We do it because we love to do it. Apostle Paul said for us to abound in thanksgiving (Colossians 2:6-7). To abound means to be full to overflowing. Except for any other reason, a vehicle full of gas will not stop for lack of gas. Once full of thanksgiving, we never stop giving thanks. We're to give thanks in every thing: for this is the will of God in Christ Jesus concerning us (1 Thes. 5:18).

Does it mean I should thank God when something bad happens to me? No! It means even when I'm in a bad situation, I should thank God for His promises of victory that will never fail. I thank Him because I know He's in control. The 'will of God' there is not referring to the bad event. It's not the will of my Father that any child of His should be in any Satan-glorifying situation. But it is His will that I give thanks for having Him as a Father that can be trusted to deliver out of that situation. Jesus didn't thank God for the death of Lazarus, but for the glory that his death would bring to God, which indeed was the case.

Faith Is Thankful

My little girl has a way of getting stuff from me. The moment she requests something and I assure her I will get it, she hugs me and says thank you mom. This puts an obligation on me to fulfill my promise because I hate to disappoint her. If I can do that with my child, imagine what is going through the mind of God when I thank Him for something He has not done. It puts an obligation on Him. He doesn't want me to doubt His faithfulness concerning His promises. And because I know He will never put His name to shame, I can rest easy.

Be careful for nothing; <u>but in every thing by prayer and supplication with thanksgiving let your requests be made known unto God</u>. And the peace of God, which passeth all understanding, shall keep your hearts and minds through Christ Jesus (Philippians 4:6-7).

Thanksgiving to God goes both ways, before and after. As we thank Him for what He will do, we also thank Him for what He's doing and has done. When we remember, "It is of the LORD's mercies that we're not consumed, because his compassions fail not. They are new every morning" (Lam. 3:22-23), that in itself is worth waking up every morning and thanking Him for. To think that were it not for the Lord's never failing protection over me, I should have been forgotten by now. I'm not in any way better than those who have gone on the journey of no return. It's because He still has a purpose for my life that I'm alive.

When I sleep, I have no idea what goes on around me. Yet, He faithfully keeps watch over me. I drive and come back home safely –not because I know how to drive–but because He has promised to go before me and be my rereward* (Isaiah 52:12). When I take a walk (or even when inside the house), many planes fly over me. Do I ever remember to say thank you Lord for not allowing them to crash over me? No! Why? Because I've taken

His protection for granted.

When Jesus went to Jerusalem, He passed through Galilee and Samaria. Ten lepers met Him and begged for mercy (Lk. 17:11-19). Consider the reaction of Jesus to the grateful cleansed leper. He asked him where the ungrateful nine were. After all, they too were cleansed. But it didn't matter any more to them. They were too happy and forgot being grateful. Giving thanks to God has nothing to do with race, culture or age. <u>ALL</u> should give thanks. We need to cultivate an attitude of gratitude so we can win the heart of God.

I say thank you Jesus just for fun. I say it in the bathroom, in the car, in the bedroom, and even in the store. I say it when He provides a parking space for me. My children say it on Fridays because they don't have to think of school for two days. At times I don't even know why I say it. But I say it anyway.

Don't wait till Thanksgiving Day to give thanks. Doing that implies that God should be thanked only one day in a year. Give thanks in the morning, give thanks at night. Do it at noonday and do it anywhere. It does not matter where we are or what we are doing, thanksgiving should be to us a way of life. And in case you can't think of anything to thank Him for, here's a suggestion. Thank Him for not creating you a turkey to be stuffed, roasted and eaten on Thanksgiving Day.

*Rear guard

75
FAITH TOLERATES

What! Faith tolerates? That's an act of compromise. No it's not. You're getting the words mixed up. It's one thing to compromise; it's a different thing altogether to tolerate. To tolerate is to bear with others without compromising your stand for truth.

Jesus tolerated a lot of things but He never compromised the truth. He taught His disciples to tolerate others who didn't belong to them but were not against them either.

> And John answered him, saying, Master, we saw one casting out devils in thy name, and he followeth not us: and we forbad him, because he followeth not us. But Jesus said, Forbid him not: for there is no man which shall do a miracle in my name, that can lightly speak evil of me. For he that is not against us is on our part (Mark 9:38-40).

I know of a particular denomination in my country that would never tolerate believers from other denominations. A male member can marry from another church and bring the woman into their church, so she can be purified from her past filth; but a female member cannot marry from outside the denomination. That will be a defilement of her spiritual purity.

And it does not matter for how long you have been a believer; you're not a citizen of heaven until you become a member of their church. Their members must not attend any crusade organized by other body of believers. "Be ye separate," they say. Well, if Jesus had separated Himself from us, I only wonder if any of us alive today would qualify to be called a believer.

A faith that preaches peace must be tolerant of others who are not of the same conviction or belief. That's not saying we join the ungodly wagon all in the name of tolerance. But if all we do is separate, how do we win them? The Bible says, "Him that is weak in the faith receive ye" (Romans 14:1). The only way we can win those who are weaker than us in the faith is to lovingly tolerate them. We don't have the same spiritual strength. We differ in faith as we do in shape. We must therefore tolerate one another for proper edification, no matter what entails.

> Let every one of us please his neighbour for his good to edification. For even Christ pleased not himself... (Romans 15:2-3).

I'm married to a man from a Muslim family. My husband is a convert of many years. His people are Muslims up till this day. The marriage is eighteen years and I can tell you, tolerating them has not been any problem at all. We tolerate them and they tolerate us, no fights, no fuss. They're the nicest family anybody can marry into. They love us and we love them. Does that mean we have compromised our faith? Not at all. They know where we stand when it comes to Jesus and our belief. We would never do anything to relegate their belief and they would never say anything to relegate our faith either. And even if they do, does that change anything about our Jesus? No!

I don't care what anybody says about my Lord, it cannot alter a single truth about Him. Call Him a liar or lunatic; I will tolerate you because that doesn't make Him less the Lord. Call Him Satan; it's not enough reason for me to kill you. Why? Because it doesn't make Him less the Savior. Calling Him a black sheep is the last thing that would get me mad at you. Not because I don't love Him but because that doesn't make Him less the White Lamb, seated on the throne of His Father. Or try and do the impossible. Burn all the Bibles in the world. It's not enough to take a single word out of it or alter the truth about it. And that's the difference between the Christian faith and other religions. What other people say about our faith cannot change our conviction to forgive them and still love them. Any religion that propagates and encourages the slaying of souls doesn't sound like a peaceful one to me.

The Bible says love bears all things. We're people of faith, therefore people of love. And if people of love, then we have to bear with others in the same Spirit of love and put on as the elect of God, holy and beloved, bowels of mercies, kindness, humbleness of mind, meekness, longsuffering; <u>Forbearing one another</u>, and forgiving one another, if any man have a quarrel against any: even as Christ forgave us, so also we do (Colossians 3:12-13).

Whether of the same faith or another faith, let's tolerate others in love. For then and only then can we win them to the cross.

76
<u>FAITH TRUSTS IN GOD</u>

August 2002, we received a sad news that left my husband and I completely devastated and for the first time in my life, I was angry with God. I've heard people say it but I never experienced it. But on that particular day in that month, I was furious with God. I felt like seeing Him so we could have a face-to-face dialogue, because I really wanted to know what else He wanted us to do as people of faith that we had not done.

To tell you how angry I was, it was our Bible study day and I made up my mind I would not go to church, so He would know I was really angry. By the time my husband left for work, I sat on the couch in front of the television, got the remote control and as I flipped from one channel to another, the Holy Spirit spoke to me: "Daughter, remember you don't solve a problem by running away from me, the problem solver. I know what you are going through. Just trust me. I'm in control." I got up immediately, dressed up and straight to church I went, still not completely happy. During the Bible study, the Lord used the lesson teacher to meet my need. He said something that met me right at the point of hurt. I went home rejoicing that the devil did not win the battle. (And by the way, the outcome of the incident was glorious.)

To trust God is to esteem Him concerning His promises for us His children. It is to see our situation the way God sees it, not the way we perceive it. When the flesh tends to make us believe we're about to sink into the water of life, we see ourselves walking on the troubled water just as Jesus sees it. We depend on Him even when it appears He's no longer interested in us. This is not as easy as it sounds. When the flesh wars against the Spirit, there's a tendency to wonder if God really cares. But as people of faith, we need to

Faith Trusts In God

trust Him for and in everything. Please don't get me wrong. I also have my moments of fears and doubts. The incident I just talked about is a proof. But it was still not a cogent reason for me to get mad at God. Indeed no reason is ever cogent to get mad at God.

People of faith are to put their trust in the LORD (Psalm 4:5). When we put our trust in the Lord, we accept our insufficiency without Him. It's an indirect way of saying apart from Him we can do nothing. I feel flattered when my baby feels unsafe without me. When she needs to use the bathroom, she asks me to watch her. Once I ask her to go, she never thinks otherwise. She believes I'm doing exactly as she desires. (Though that's not so. Aren't you glad I'm not God?) That's the way God wants us to function. Once we commit our ways into His hand, we need not worry anymore. He directs every step we take and trying to understand how He does it is of use. We can never understand because His judgments, the Bible says, are unsearchable "and His ways past finding out!" (Romans 11:33).

God was asking me just yesterday, "If your child can trust you this much, how much do you think you should trust me, the God that never fails? When I say I'm watching you, I'm watching you." That really touched my heart. Putting our trust in Him compels Him to be a refuge to us in times of trouble (Psalm 46:1). Refuge is something or someone you can depend on to save you from the hands of a greater force, a force more powerful than you are. The disciples of old went through a lot of perils and persecutions, but they trusted God in them all.

The Bible compares those who put their trust in the Lord to Mount Zion (Psalm 125:1). I have not the slightest idea what in the world Mount Zion looks like, but I can at least picture it from the perspective of the other mountains I've seen. The psalmist is saying that those who trust in the Lord are so strong in faith that no trial or tribulation can move, shake, discourage or intimidate them. Not the kind of moving that applies to moving from one position to another. But that they will remain strong and undaunted in the Lord when everything around them appears to be falling and failing.

The reason the Bible describes Abraham as a man not weak in faith (Romans 4:19) was because he trusted God even in the most difficult situation of having to sacrifice his own cherished son. He had rest when he was supposed to be troubled. A faith that trusts is a faith that triumphs.

> Blessed is the man that trusteth in the LORD, and whose hope the LORD is. For he shall be as a tree planted by the waters, and that spreadeth out her roots by the river, and shall not see when heat cometh, but her leaf shall be green; and shall not be careful in the year of drought, neither shall cease from yielding fruit (Jer. 17:7-8).

Many trees shed their leaves and turn brown in fall season. But there are some trees that remain green throughout the year. The season is never a reason for them to turn pale. When other trees become terminally brown, they remain forever green. So it is with you when you trust in the Lord. When others around you are getting sick and tired, you remain strong and tough. The heat of affliction and adversity will not affect you. Not because you're hard of feelings; not because you're insensitive to the hardships in other people's lives; not even because you're proud as some may consider your attitude. But because you're hard of doubt. You have learnt to trust that the source of your strength never runs and never will run out of supply. He is the **LORD ALMIGHTY**.

And do you know what happens to him who does not trust in the Lord?

> Thus saith the LORD; Cursed be the man that trusteth in man, and

maketh flesh his arm, and whose heart departeth from the LORD. For he shall be like the heath in the desert, and shall not see when good cometh; but shall inhabit the parched places in the wilderness, in a salt land and not inhabited (Jeremiah 17:5-6).

I don't want this to be my portion and I don't want it for you either. If trusting in the Lord is bad, ain't no point trying to be good. In any case, I don't trust Him to impress any man. I trust Him because it's the wisest thing for me to do. Solomon said, "whoso trusteth in the LORD, happy is he" (Proverbs 16:20). I have faith in God and I'll trust Him all the days of my life, because I love to be happy.

U

77. FAITH UNITES   309

78. FAITH is UPRIGHT   313

77
FAITH UNITES

How does unity apply to our faith? What has it got to do with us as children of God? Does it mean each person forgets his or her identity and instead claims to belong nowhere? No. That's not it.

It's true we're different people with different origins, from different races, and brought up in different cultures. I have my own identity and culture. I'm from Nigeria, from the Yoruba culture. Those who have traveled there will be familiar with what I'm saying. We live in America, different race, different culture, and <u>an entire different way of life</u>. When it comes to our faith in Jesus Christ, should this be a factor? NO! NO! NO! In as much we confess the same Jesus, we also share the same faith. There's no difference in the body of Christ.

I know that Jesus died for me. But when He gave His life on the cross, it wasn't because He hailed from my tribe. My tribe didn't even exist then. There was nothing like Nigeria and definitely no place like America or Britain existed. He did it, not because of my skin, but because of my sins.

Should it really matter what the colors of your eyes or the color of your hair when you talk about your faith in Jesus? I want to ask you a question. What is the color of your faith? If you can't answer that question, then should you ever care who is black or white in the faith? We base our faith on the Bible, not our body. And the Bible clearly states that brethren should dwell together in unity.

Behold, how good and how pleasant it is for brethren to dwell together in unity! (Psalm 133:1-3).

Just picture this description of unity and see how important it must be to God to see all His children as one. We cannot fathom how delightful and how pleasant it is to His heart when He beholds the unity in the midst of His children. That's like bringing heaven down to us. There will be no division in heaven. All will be one. And when we dwell together here in unity, we're already having a taste of how sweet it shall be over there.

As people of same faith, though from different denominations, we're to come together as one indivisible people under God and truly display to the world that we know what we believe. Christ cannot be divided and so is His faith. Discord has no place in the body of Christ because all it brings is harm and disharmony.

There was great unity in the church in those days. And the church today should not be any different, so long we confess the same Christ they confessed.

> And the multitude of them that believed were of one heart and of one soul: neither said any of them that ought of the things which he possessed was his own; but they had all things common (Acts 4:32).

This was true Christian unity. It's disheartening how different denominations try to prove they're the best. I know there are churches that put more emphasis on contributions than salvation, which in itself is horrible. But how about churches that preach the real truth? Should one prove it's better than the other when they profess to be serving the same God? I don't think so. And worse still, should there be divisions within the same congregation? I'm talking of brethren worshipping under the same roof. Is that what faith is all about? No! At least not the way I understand it. A sect within the same set is not of faith. It is condemned by the Word of God.

Now I beseech you, brethren, by the name of our Lord Jesus Christ, that <u>ye all speak the same thing, and that there be no divisions among</u>

you; but that ye be perfectly joined together in the same mind and in the same judgment** (1 Corinthians 1:10).

Apostle Paul sent this message to the Corinthian believers when he heard of their divisions; some claimed they belonged to Apollos, others to Cephas, and some holy enough claimed they belonged to Jesus. This is not what Jesus taught us. And we're to be His disciples not only in words but also in deeds.

When I meet a brother from another denomination or even another country, I'm supposed to make him feel at home and let him know that His Lord is my Lord. He has no reason whatsoever to feel different from me just because he's not from my country. <u>There is no culture in Christ, no race in redemption and no separation in salvation.</u> We are to be people of different cultures professing the same Christ. Christ is our focus and when Christ is the focus, culture has to vanish.

I therefore, the prisoner of the Lord, beseech you that ye walk worthy of the vocation wherewith ye are called, With all lowliness and meekness, with longsuffering, forbearing one another in love; Endeavouring to keep the unity of the Spirit in the bond of peace. There is one body, and one Spirit, …One God and Father of all, who is above all, and through all, and in you all (Ephesians 4:1-6).

If you know of a church that has two gods, that is not of the true God. He wants us to be one, no division or disunity. When husband and wife are united, they will move mountains. But when they're divided, they fall, for the Bible says, "And if a kingdom be divided against itself, that kingdom cannot stand. And if a house be divided against itself, that house cannot stand" (Mark 3:24, 25).

It's the will of God that brethren call upon Him. But He will not answer when there's disunity, division or discrimination of any sort amongst them. When we gather together to bind and loose in His name, it has to be done in unity.

> Again I say unto you, That <u>if two of you shall agree</u> on earth as touching any thing that they shall ask, it shall be done for them of my Father which is in heaven. For where two or three are gathered together in my name, there am I in the midst of them (Mat. 18:19-20).

Notice Jesus did not say, "If two shall assemble." Of course two enemies can assemble, they just won't agree. His Word says, "If two of you shall agree." Agreement is the principal thing that solidifies unity. It's in our unity that the Holy Spirit dwells. When the Holy Spirit came on the apostles, He met them united, with one accord.

> And when the day of Pentecost was fully come, <u>they were all with one accord</u> in one place. And they, continuing daily with one accord in the temple, and breaking bread from house to house, did eat their meat with gladness and singleness of heart (Acts 2:1, 46).

When we dwell together in the unity of the faith, we shall part the oceans and cast the mountains into the sea. The Bible says, "If there be therefore any consolation in Christ, if any comfort of love, if any fellowship of the Spirit, if any bowels and mercies, Fulfil ye my joy, that ye be likeminded, having the same love, being of one accord, of one mind" (Philippians 2:1-2). This is the real core of spiritual agreement. We're to be a multitude of different heights but one heart.

"Now the God of patience and consolation grant you (us) to be likeminded one toward another according to Christ Jesus: That ye (we) may with one mind and one mouth glorify God, even the Father of our Lord Jesus Christ" (Romans 15:5-6). Amen.

78
FAITH is UPRIGHT

To address this topic, I'll use the word 'upright' as two separate words: up and right. They're both positive terms. To be up is the exact opposite of being down. Which means faith is never a 'down' issue. Down syndrome has no place in faith. When we profess faith in the Lord, being down in any situation is not glorifying. I'm not talking about going down the stairs or being down in the Spirit. Once in a while, everyone gets the spiritual blues. At such times, the Holy Spirit helps our weaknesses; only we must remain sincere to the calling.

The kind of down I'm inferring is being found unjust in the things of life. How up are you when others are doing their stuff the way down? Do you stay with your head up or do you walk on your head and be counted with the sick in spirit and slack in soul?

Then comes the word right. It means not wrong. You can't be right and be wrong at the same time. Most of the time we find ourselves stuck with people who love to do things the wrong way. Getting money at all cost is more important to them than getting it the right way. Whichever way it takes to get the promotion, it makes no difference to them. The promotion means more to them than their dignity and integrity. As people of faith, when others are doing it the wrong way, we should maintain the right attitude.

There are times we may be the only odd one out of many. You know what? I think I'll be more comfortable being odd for right than being even for wrong. I don't believe in walking on my head. That everyone else around me is doing it doesn't mean it's right. So also I don't believe in joining the wrong majority to be noticed. I would rather be unnoticed for being right than noticed for being wrong. It's always better to be upright.

The Bible describes Job as an upright man. Even God testified to that when He said unto Satan, "Hast thou considered my servant Job, that there is none like him in the earth, a perfect and an <u>upright</u> man, one that feareth God, and escheweth evil?" (Job 1:8).

What made him blameless and upright? Because he loved God and hated evil. He loved God at all time and at all cost, and hated evil with the same magnitude. Until we do likewise, we're not complete. People may detest us. They may even attempt to harm us. But we need not fret but know that when they draw out their sword and bend their bow, to cast the poor and the needy, and to slay us for our upright conversation; their sword shall enter into their heart and their bows shall be broken (Psalm 37:14-15). We know that our defence is of God, which saveth the upright in heart (Psalm 7:10).

When you purpose to be upright in heart and refuse to bring shame to your faith, God will fight the battle you're supposed to be fighting. He knows you're doing enough work trying to be upright. He knows you will be weary if you also have to be fighting the battle of faith. So He takes it upon Himself and says, 'child, you need not bother your head about those people warring against you because you have chosen to do it my own way. You just ride on being upright. I have all it takes to deal with them and I shall deal with them'.

No matter what happens, God wants His children to stand head up in any given circumstance. When we stand for right, we need not bother what people think. We're above and they have to bow to us, now or later when the whole truth is revealed. They may throw us into the pit for being upright in the midst of corruption. But by the time the Lord is done taking us through the prison-school of forgiveness, He will elevate us to the palace and cause them to be in need of our help. Then they shall come and bow and there remember that we were right and they were wrong. Then they would appreciate our uprightness. And even when they depart our presence, conscience will catch up with them and they will accuse one another for their 'downwrong' actions.

Does uprightness have rewards? You bet.

Praise ye the LORD. Blessed is the man that feareth the LORD, that delighteth greatly in his commandments. His seed shall be mighty upon earth: the generation of the upright shall be blessed (Psalm 112:1-2).

When we live upright, we pass a legacy on to our children coming after us. How sweet to know that the uprightness I have now is actually been saved in the spiritual bank for my children and those coming after me? I have peace now and hereafter. Solomon said, "the tent of the upright will flourish" (Pro. 14:11). To flourish connotes abundance. I'll have abundance of peace and prosperity when I stand upright for my faith. If only for this reason, I think I vote for uprightness.

Another blessing that comes from being upright is strength. Not the kind of strength that comes from your loins, but from your Lord.

<u>**The way of the LORD is strength to the upright**</u>**: but destruction shall be to the workers of iniquity (Proverbs 10:29).**

There will be moments when weakness will set into the loins just for being upright. Times when others will forsake you for preaching uprightness in a work place that is full of corruption; in a worldly set up full of evil and immoral practices; in a family of unbelievers that will not tolerate your 'religious insanity'; in a congregation that places priority on contributions than Christ. Because you refuse to give up your faith rigidity for their fake religiosity, they see you as out of order and no longer in your correct senses. Trust me your loins will fail you for strength, but your Lord will never fail. His joy will be your strength to remain immovable.

Just hold on to your uprightness. The time is coming when it will be accounted unto you for righteousness. Their hatred for you is no cause for you to hate them. They hate you because they're ignorant of the truth. Pray for them. Jesus asks us to pray for our enemies. That includes those who hate us for loving the truth. And when we do that, God will save us and glorify His name.

V

79. FAITH VENTURES — 318

80. FAITH is VICTORIOUS — 321

81. FAITH has VISION — 328

79
FAITH VENTURES

To venture is to do something that one would ordinarily dare not do. But either because there's no other option; or due to a deep conviction, one is forced to take action. I'm not talking about daredevils, but children of God who did what they did, not to dare the devil but to damn his consequence based on their faith. It comes with an unbending determination to take a step.

Before venturing anything, there's an awareness of danger. It can lead to a defeat or death. But when faith is applied, it looses confidence in self and trusts God for a good outcome.

When queen Esther appeared before king Ahasuerus (her husband) on behalf of her Jewish people, to save them from Haman's plan to wipe them out of existence, she knew it was a dangerous mission. Her uninvited presence in the king's palace was against the law and it could lead to her death. But at the same time, she had to do something. She, because of her faith ventured the unthinkable and risked her life to save others.

Then Esther bade them return Mordecai this answer, Go, gather together all the Jews that are present in Shushan, and fast ye for me, and neither eat nor drink three days, night or day: I also and my maidens will fast likewise; <u>and so will I go in unto the king, which is not according to the law: and if I perish, I perish</u> (Esther 4:15-16).

Because of the nature of her venture, she made a divine preparation for divine intervention. She would approach the king, but not in the power of her flesh, for the flesh would fail. She soaked herself in the anointing that kings and princes cannot oppose and miracle followed. She met with the

Faith Ventures

king's favor and her people were saved. The enemy that planned the evil never lived to witness the deliverance of the people he wanted to destroy. But it took the venturing and determined faith of a woman who knew her God.

There are times like this when as God's children, we get to the end of the road. A time when Yochebed had to disobey the king's order to save her baby Moses. A time when Daniel had to enter the lion's den to prove his faithfulness to God. Those times when decisions will seem like mountains before Zerrubabbel. But a time to also know that such mountains will become plains, not by power, not by might, but by the Spirit of the Lord (Zechariah 4:7).

You may never have to stand before any king to put your faith to test. Yours could be as unthinkable as getting stuck on top of a burning building. Would you allow the fire to consume you or would you venture to take a jump of faith and trust that God will take care of the rest? Daring the difficult never goes without determination. You must determine and be ready for the outcome and that's where faith comes in. Human reasoning tells you the outcome may not be favorable, faith tells you all will be well.

A man gave a testimony sometime ago in my country. He met a lady on a bus and got to know from their little discussion that she was a Christian. The man was involved in some occults and for a long time, had been using his evil power to cause accidents and suck the blood of the victims. He was going to do the same thing on that fateful day but was hindered by the presence of that child of God. He then invited the lady to come and visit him. Of course she knew that was a dangerous mission but she went in the power of the Lord.

When she got there, the man wanted to rape her and possibly kill her. She wrestled all through and kept rebuking him in Jesus' name. Finally he gave up. As the lady was getting out of his door, she turned to him and made just one statement, "you will never have peace until you have Jesus." The man publicly confessed that from that very moment, he never had peace. He tried all his powers but to no avail. For years, after the sister had issued her 'no Jesus, no peace' decree, nothing worked for him. No peace, no happiness, nothing. Finally, he surrendered his life to the Prince of Peace.

Today, he's a great man of God, going about and declaring the goodness of God. But it took a determined and venturing faith of a dear sister, an Esther of our age. Imagine the number of souls that man would have sent to hell prior to their second chance if that sister had not ventured to go on the dangerous mission. More importantly, consider the number of souls that have come to Christ because of the man's testimony, and that because a sister dared to venture the impossible.

People who go on mission trips will relate more to this. Most of the time, they know they're taking trips to dangerous zones. But for the sake of the gospel and with God on their side, they go and return. Lives will be saved and God will take all the glory.

One of these days, you may find yourself in a situation that requires you venture to take a step towards your freedom and the freedom of others. If led by God to do so, don't hesitate. Just remember to put Him before you and He will guide you.

80
FAITH is VICTORIOUS

When people go to war, there's only one thing they strive to bring back home: victory. When two opponent sides compete, there's only one thing they wish: victory. Nobody talks about the beauty of the participants, nobody remembers how tall or how short. When victory is won, everything else becomes irrelevant. While everyone cheers for the victor, nobody remembers the victim. He who wins the race gets the praise. Does the same thing apply to our faith? A resounding Yes!

Keeping our faith is a battle and a spiritual warfare that is not fought with hands or sword: "For though we walk in the flesh, we do not war after the flesh: For the weapons of our warfare are not carnal, but mighty through God to the pulling down of strong holds" (2 Corinthians 10:3-5). Our battle of faith cannot be fought carnally. But when we apply spiritual power to spiritual battle, the result is victory.

You may be wondering, what are we fighting? There are a lot of things that war against us, visible and invisible.

Consider the children of Israel after they had left Egypt. Their ordeal at the Red Sea was both a visible and spiritual battle; visible because they saw their enemies with their eyes, chasing them from behind; and spiritual because they were no match for Pharaoh's army. There was no way they could have won Pharaoh's army in their own strength. Pharaoh had horsemen on horses, his army on chariots. What did the Israelites have? Their flocks and rods. No wonder they were sore afraid when they saw the Egyptians coming behind them (Exodus 14:10). But God does not go by horses and chariots to fight His battle.

> Some trust in chariots, and some in horses: but we will remember the name of the LORD our God. They are brought down and fallen: but we are risen, and stand upright (Psalm 20:7-8).

Moses remembered the name of the Lord. He knew it would take a complete faith in Him to overcome the men that pursued them on horses and chariots.

> And Moses said unto the people, Fear ye not, stand still, and see the salvation of the LORD, which he will shew to you to day: for the Egyptians whom ye have seen to day, ye shall see them again no more for ever. The LORD shall fight for you, and ye shall hold your peace (Exodus 14:13-14).

Was it the rod in his hand that made him so confident? No. What victory can a rod bring when you fight an army? None. But when the rod is injected with the power of God, it not only parts the Red Sea, it dulls the senses of the enemies. With their own feet they shall walk into the waters to be drowned forever and the children of God will sing the song of victory; the kind that eyes will see and mouths will open. That victory comes only in the power of God. When we have faith in Him, victory is sure. Our enemies will fall and drown.

When Daniel was to be thrown into the lion's den, he wasn't ignorant of the harm a lion could do to a man. He wasn't that young to be that stupid. He knew where he was going; he was going inside the den of ferocious lions. But he trusted the power of faith in his never failing God. He knew his God would be God whether in the lion's den or in the lunatic's dungeon. He went in valiant and came out victorious.

Go to 1 Kings 18:20. It says Elijah's Mount Carmel Victory, not Elijah's Mount Carmel fight. Once we have victory, people forget the fight.

Definitely one man's fight against four hundred is enough to make the news. But one man's victory against four hundred would sure make the headlines and appear in all bestseller magazines the following day, especially when it had to do with him and him alone in their midst. They had knives and lances, Elijah had nothing. But he had the greatest; he had God. Who won? You know the answer. Till this day, we're reading about the Mount Carmel Competition, not from the perspective of the loosing prophets of Baal, but from the perspective of the victorious Elijah.

When we apply our faith to the fight, the fighter of the battle, our very dear Father will gain the victory to Himself. The Bible says, "O sing unto the LORD a new song; for he hath done marvelous things: his right hand, and his holy arm, hath gotten him the victory" (Psalm 98:1).

Are there such things as invisible battles? Yes! These are battles we fight but can't be perceived with the naked eyes. They're battles in the Spirit. We wrestle against principalities and powers of darkness, of barrenness, of illness, of oppression, depression and obsession. The list is numerous. Anything that takes our peace is a spiritual battle and can only be fought by faith.

> Finally, my brethren, be strong in the Lord, and in the power of his might. Put on the whole armour of God, that ye may be able to stand against the wiles of the devil. For we wrestle not against flesh and blood, but against principalities, against powers, against the rulers of the darkness of this world, against spiritual wickedness in high places. Wherefore take unto you the whole armour of God, ... taking the shield of faith, wherewith ye shall be able to quench all the fiery darts of the wicked (Ephesians 6:10-16).

Principalities and powers are not new to this age. They have nothing to do with the advent of technology. As they are now, so they were then. Jesus had an encounter with the devil after forty days and forty nights of fasting. The Bible says Satan left Jesus for a more opportune time (Luke 4:13). Which means he didn't go finally. He left for sometime, to go and gather more momentum.

Conflicts in the Spirit are inward battles. The Bible lists the works of the flesh that war against our Spirit and our faith: "Adultery, fornication, uncleanness, lasciviousness, Idolatry, witchcraft, hatred, variance, emulations, wrath, strife, seditions, heresies, Envyings, murders, drunkenness, revellings, and such like" (Galatians 5:16-21).

Considering this list, how does one win the battle? Only a persistent faith in God, with prayer and fasting can earn us the victory. We have to constantly call on Him to deliver us from these spiritual perils. We have to meditate on His word day and night. Jesus didn't overcome Satan in the power of the flesh. He reminded and overcame him by the written Word. The Word of God that we store in our system will go a long way to help us when we face the enemies of our soul.

We shall all face these things one time or the other in life. But let's always remember that Jesus had given us the victory right from Gethsemane.

> These things I have spoken unto you, that in me ye might have peace. In the world ye shall have tribulation: but be of good cheer; I have overcome the world (John 16:33).

Once we overcome these fleshly battles, there's only one other battle we shall fight. And that is the battle against death. The battle against flesh is relative. What you fight may not be the same as mine. That's not the case with death. It's a contract we have all signed. It will come when it will come. And it doesn't matter to God what kind of death we die. I used to think that children of God could never die in an accident, in a plane crash or in such terrible ways. I don't pray it happens. But if it does as it has many times, does that make us less victorious? Not in the least, because "Precious in the sight of the LORD is the death of his saints" (Psalm 116:15).

Notice the verse doesn't say His saints who die normal death. If God were to go by normal or abnormal, He should not have sent His son to die on the cross. The issue is not what type of death we die. God doesn't care whichever route you take to get to Him. Just die and come to Him. But when you eventually go, would God see you as a victim or a victor? Jesus has conquered death on the cross and gotten us the victory. But that victory is reserved only for those who accept and profess Him as Lord and Savior. Sure He died for the whole world, but there's still a condition for the purpose to be realized in any life.

Anyone who denies that Jesus came in the flesh and gave His life as ransom for all cannot be part of the victory over death. When we talk of victory over death, it doesn't mean that those who love the Lord will not die. I already pointed that out. We shall all die. But as children of God and people of faith, we have victory over the second death. Second death? Yes! There's a second death.

> He that hath an ear, let him hear what the Spirit saith unto the churches; He that overcometh shall not be hurt of the <u>second death</u> (Revelation 2:11).
>
> Blessed and holy is he that hath part in the first resurrection: on such the second death hath no power, but they shall be priests of God and of Christ, and shall reign with him a thousand years. And death and hell were cast into the lake of fire. This is the <u>second death</u>. And

whosoever was not found written in the book of life was cast into the lake of fire (Rev. 20:6, 14-15).

But the fearful, and unbelieving, and the abominable, and murderers, and whoremongers, and sorcerers, and idolaters, and all liars, shall have their part in the lake which burneth with fire and brimstone: which is the <u>second death</u> (Rev. 21:8).

People of faith will not be part of this. So long we hold on to our faith in the Lord Jesus and never cease to believe that He died for our sins, we have the passport and the boarding pass. That's where our victory lies. That doesn't excuse us from the problems of this world. We live in the world. We shall have persecutions from every angle. People will hate us because we love Jesus. Friends will detest us because we care about the gospel. Enemies will attempt to get at us because we stand for truth. But we shall overcome at last.

When we die in this world, all we have done is shed our earthly bodies for a heavenly badge. Some of us may be lucky enough to still be alive by rapture. It won't make any difference when my sweet Savior shows up in the sky to take us.

But I would not have you to be ignorant, brethren, concerning them which are asleep, that ye sorrow not, even as others which have no hope. For if we believe that Jesus died and rose again, even so them also which sleep in Jesus will God bring with him. For this we say unto you by the word of the Lord, that we which are alive and remain unto the coming of the Lord shall not prevent them which are asleep. For the Lord himself shall descend from heaven with a shout, with the voice of the archangel, and with the trump of God: and the dead in Christ shall rise first: Then we which are alive and remain shall be caught up together with them in the clouds, to meet the Lord in the air: and so shall we ever be with the Lord (1 Thes. 4:13-17).

If I were dead, the grave will give me up. If alive, I shall be caught up together with the other saints. Whichever way it goes, I shall be victorious. Then I will look back and shun death to its face. When it sees me flying in my heavenly wings, guess what I will do. I will take a last look at it and ask, O Death, where is your sting? O Hades, where is your victory? But unfortunately, it will have no strength to answer because then, it would have been swallowed up in victory (1 Corinthians 15:54-58). Be comforted brethren. Victory is sure.

81
FAITH has VISION

When we talk of vision, most of the time we refer to our sight. I've been wearing glasses since 1979. I'm shortsighted, or near-sighted as Americans say it; same thing with my two boys. But my husband has a different vision. Give him a letter to read and you mess him up. But ask him to read the number on a vehicle that is parked a distance away, now you're talking. God created us with different visions, all good.

In the realm of faith, believers have different visions. The first aspect of vision I like to address is the type that comes as revelation either through dream or dialogue. This is scriptural but requires faith to carry it through.

When the angel Gabriel appeared to Mary to announce the birth of Jesus, she was wide-awake. She knew what was going on. She had a one-on-one dialogue with the angel. She even asked the angel a question and he answered. And I believe no other person around her would have seen or heard the angel because he was sent to Mary and Mary alone (Luke 1:26-38).

There are times God uses visions to correct, instruct or warn us of any spiritual fallacy we're about to commit. Such visions could be in form of dreams. A good example is Joseph, Mary's husband. The angel appeared to him four times, all in dreams: once before Jesus was born and thrice after His birth to warn him of impending dangers.

Then Joseph her husband, being a just man, and not willing to make her a public example, was minded to put her away privily. But while he thought on these things, behold, <u>the angel of the LORD appeared unto him in a dream</u>, saying, Joseph, thou son of David, fear not to take unto thee Mary thy wife: for that which is conceived in her is of the Holy Ghost (Matthew 1:19-20).

And when they were departed, behold, <u>the angel of the Lord appeareth to Joseph in a dream,</u> saying, Arise, and take the young child and his mother, and flee into Egypt, and be thou there until I bring thee word: for Herod will seek the young child to destroy him (Mat. 2:13).

But when Herod was dead, behold, <u>an angel of the Lord appeareth in a dream to Joseph</u> in Egypt, Saying, Arise, and take the young child and his mother, and go into the land of Israel: for they are dead which sought the young child's life (Mat. 2:19-20).

But when he heard that Archelaus did reign in Judaea in the room of his father Herod, he was afraid to go thither: notwithstanding, <u>being warned of God in a dream</u>, he turned aside into the parts of Galilee (Mat. 2:22).

These were visions that came in dreams. Joseph, the son of Jacob is another example. His dream of greatness started long before the palace. When he finally became the second in command to Pharaoh, it was the realization of a vision he had thirteen years earlier.

God communicates with us in different ways. I've never been in a trance. But God communicates with me in my dreams. That doesn't mean all dreams are from God. And that's where we need the discernment of the Holy Spirit. He interprets the mind of God to the children of God.

The other type of vision is the ability to see beyond the now, to see beyond the present situation through an eye of faith. We refuse to allow our present circumstances to dim out the vision of what we believe God can and will do concerning our situation. The Bible says, "faith is the substance of things hoped for, the evidence of things not seen" (Hebrews 11:1). It means that though we have not seen the victory as we expect, by faith we see it coming as we hope. A barren woman with a vision knows that though the child has not come as she wishes, but the child will come, as she desires. She does not hold any child in her hand yet, but she has a vision to prepare for that child that she will soon hold in her hands. She acts and functions like a real mother to a real child.

If you go back to the introduction, you'll notice I had a delay after my second child. But I always had the vision that I would still have at least one more. When the doctor told me to forget ever having another child, because I would never see my period again, sure he was right. But I refused to allow his verdict to rob me of my vision. I held on tenaciously to the promises of the Father while I continued to thank Him for the two boys we already have. Left to my husband, he didn't care. Whatever happened between Satan and me was my own business. And as far as he was concerned, two is good enough. Well, not for me. By the power in the name of the Lord who formed every organ in my system, the womb that was pronounced dead received life and come 1997, the Lord blessed me (I mean us) with a precious girl.

Eight years before she came, I already knew that whether boy or girl, the name would be Oluwatobi, meaning the Lord is great. (Sounds like a whole sentence, doesn't it? We call her 'Tobi.) That is the outcome of the vision I had long before her arrival.

When the Bible compares believers to the eagle (Isaiah 40:31), one of the things God expects of us is the ability to see beyond our problem or fuzzy situation. Eagles have an incredible vision that sees far ahead of their vicinity. Call it 10/10, that'll be perfect. They have quick, clear and powerful sight that can behold the sun when shinning.

People of faith must desire the grace to see like eagles, to be able to project into the mind of God, to know that though we walk through the valley of the shadow of death, the end of the road is not death but life. We must be able to see life beyond the grave, to know that though our Lazarus may be lying dead in the tomb, he will come out loose, living and laughing.

When Moses saw the Red Sea, he knew it was a sea. Remember he wasn't blind. He knew the difference between water and land. But he had a greater vision than the yelling battalion. He could see the way of God in the water of God. He knew that the One who said, "let the waters under the heavens be gathered together into one place, and let the dry land appear" was still the same. If He did it in Genesis, He would do it in Exodus. He knew that the Creator of the sea would take control over the sea. That was a great vision.

Remember the notable woman of Shunem in 2 Kings 4. She was already past childbearing age when she gave birth to her son. Then the worst happened. The son, her only child died. She ran to the man of God Elisha and even in her ordeal declared, all was well. Only a faith with a vision would declare all is well while a child lays dead at home. She knew her son was dead. But she saw beyond that. She saw a living child in a dead body. Though her child was dead, her vision was alive. She refused to kill her vision of a living son.

When the angel announced the birth of the Savior to the shepherds, it was in the night. It was dark. They were keeping watch over their flock. Under normal circumstances, one would expect them to hear the news, rejoice and keep on watching their flock, and may be in the morning go in search of the baby Jesus. But that's not how a faith with vision operates. No darkness is thick enough to stand in its way.

A faith with vision knows that though it is dark, God will give the light and lead the way. Those shepherds didn't consider the hassles of the journey.

The trip to them was worth the taking. The Bible says they came with haste to find the baby Jesus (Luke 2:16). Isn't it amazing that the first visitors to see the Good Shepherd were the good shepherds?

Faith with vision sees the end of the road, not the beginning. Most of the time, the beginning is never easy, never encouraging and never pleasant. But faith with vision will refuse to be dazed. I don't want to believe that the shepherds didn't have reasons to be discouraged. But that did not dim their vision of seeing the great Encourager Himself. They had a vision for their mission. They saw beyond the darkness, they saw beyond the field, they saw beyond the cold winter night, they saw baby Jesus waiting to be seen at the other end.

They had the vision that the innkeeper lacked. He had the greatest opportunity to see the Savior of the world come to the world. He could have been the man to relay the news to those who had not known. He could have at least pitied their condition. But alas, he missed it. To him, Mary and Joseph were nobodies, just a couple of ragged illiterates waiting to be counted in the census. They were a disturbance to him and giving them a room would deprive him of the money he would make that night. The Bible doesn't say there was no room in the inn. The Bible says there was <u>no room for them</u> in the inn. Which means others, more privileged than they were, could have arrived after them and checked into any of the rooms. But they could not because somebody had no vision. The sheep and the goats had a better vision. They were nice enough to share their manger and keep them company. They 'bleatfully' welcomed the arrival of the Great Shepherd.

If Esau had a vision, he would not have missed out the plan of God for his life. Unfortunately, his vision did not go beyond his stomach. All he wanted was the 'now'. If he knew that his profanity would take his eternity from him, he would have thought twice before talking once. He didn't look carefully, he didn't consider diligently. All he saw was the morsel, nothing but the morsel. No vision beyond the morsel. And that cost him his eternal dividend.

The same mistake took Adam and Eve out of the garden of God's love. They didn't have the eagles' sight. They could not see things ahead of them. They were bothered about the fruit they could not eat but were never grateful for all the other fruits they could partake of. What they lacked appealed more to their sight than what they had. They were spiritually short sighted. Their faith couldn't see beyond the fruit. They who were enjoying the presence of the Almighty became completely alienated from Him.

To have faith without vision is to have eyes without sight. It will be difficult and risky if a blind eye attempts to do what a sighted eye will do. The way a man with sight can cross a bridge is not the same way a blind person will cross the same bridge. The Bible says, "Where there is no vision, the people perish" (Proverbs 29:18). A body without eyes will fall into a ditch. So also a faith without vision is bound to suffer a spiritual crash. Vision keeps the believer's dream alive.

Abraham held on to his vision of the promised child. He saw beyond the deadness of his body and the barrenness of Sarah's womb. As Christians, God wants us to carry our faith to that level, the level that sees the stars in the sky and the sand by the shore, instead of the dead womb that can no longer produce.

There are times we envision a thing by faith and we begin to wonder what if it doesn't happen. Well, that's normal. There's no way we can sail through this journey bumps free, for that will mean we were either never in the faith or nurturing a dead one. But God is calling us to a height of clearer vision where we refuse to be moved by the prevailing circumstances. He's asking us to see pleasure in our pains; to see stars in our scars; to see the bright light of the morning gloriously shinning beyond the thick darkness of the night.

Whatever your situation is right now, I encourage you to see beyond that problem. See the hand of God in the things of God. See prosperity in your poverty; have a vision of good health in your time of sickness; see life in your dead situations. Do you have a vision? If no, pray for it. If yes, keep it alive.

W

82. FAITH WAITS — 336

83. FAITH WALKS WITH GOD — 340

84. FAITH is WATCHFUL — 343

85. FAITH is WISE — 346

86. FAITH WORSHIPS GOD — 350

82
FAITH WAITS

One of the reasons I hate to go to the emergency room is the time it takes to see a doctor. The nurse first attends to me and asks me to wait for the doctor. That waiting period is always aggravating. The least I've waited is one hour. And to think that the doctor, for whom I wait that long, comes and spends less than thirty minutes with me makes the whole picture unrealistic. But once he's done seeing me, there's a big relief because I know the waiting is over.

Every true Christian goes through a waiting period. If indeed you're in the faith and you have never had a waiting period, then there is one of three things wrong with you or your faith: one, you are not real with your faith; two, you're not what you profess to be; or three, you have spiritual pride. You want to make people believe you have attained the zenith of spiritual perfection and that only makes you a liar.

Even the dead in Christ have a waiting period. What do you think they're doing in the grave? Sleeping competition? Wrong. They're waiting to be called out and caught up with the Lord, to be with Him forever. Those who were slain are waiting to see God's judgment come upon their killers (Revelation 6:9-10).

If the dead have a waiting period, the living cannot escape it. At one time or the other, we shall all go through a waiting period and only our faith can see us through. God's Word says, "For we through the Spirit wait for the hope of righteousness by faith" (Galatians 5:5). A waiting period is not an experience anyone wants to have because most of the time, it's for something we desperately and eagerly desire, not something one can overlook if it doesn't come to pass.

Abraham and Sarah had a waiting period. For twenty-five years, they waited for the promised child. Twenty-five years is a long time to wait for a car, much more a child. It was even harder on Sarah for two reasons: one, the woman's body biologically dies to reproduction much earlier than that of the man; two, with the birth of Ishmael, it was obvious she was the one who had a problem and not Abraham. But God already said the promised child would come through her and they knew He would be faithful to His word. But could they be faithful to the waiting? It's easier for us to read and condemn Abraham for listening to Sarah to have Ishmael by Hagar. The waiting made the difference.

For a long time, Zacharias and Elizabeth trusted the Lord for a child. Not because they were not spiritually upright. The Bible describes them as "righteous before God, walking in all the commandments and ordinances of the Lord blameless" (Luke 1:5-7). And yet they had no child. But they both faithfully waited. And at God's own time, they became the proud parents of John the Baptist.

God's Word asks us to wait: "And the LORD answered me, and said, Write the vision, and make it plain upon tables, that he may run that readeth it. For the vision is yet for an appointed time, but at the end it shall speak, and not lie: though it tarry, <u>wait for it</u>; because it will surely come, it will not tarry" (Habakkuk 2:2-3).

The vision we see today may not come until years later. But we must not forget that "The LORD is good unto them that wait for him"(Lamentations 3: 25). Don't get me wrong. I'm as human as you are. I hate to wait and I always ask God to shorten my waiting period. But one thing I learnt over the years; it makes no difference to God how much I am in a hurry. He will do it only when

He will do it. But because He knows it's not an easy task for us, He renews our strength during the period.

> He giveth power to the faint; and to them that have no might he increaseth strength. Even the youths shall faint and be weary, and the young men shall utterly fall: But they that wait upon the LORD shall renew their strength; they shall mount up with wings as eagles; they shall run, and not be weary; and they shall walk, and not faint (Isaiah 40:29-31).

Why are waiting Christians compared to eagles? Eagles fly very high and for a long distance. But amazingly, they're never weary for flight. As Christians, God would have us wait on Him without getting weary and always remember that He will supply the needed strength as we go along. Such faith will not faint too soon.

However, this strength can only come by prayer. It is with the soul we wait (Psalm 62:5) and without prayer, the soul will get weary and faint for strength because when hope is deferred, it makes the heart sick (Proverbs 13: 12). If the waiting goes on for too long, it not only affects the heart, it affects the head and every artery in the system. And that's why we need prayers, possibly with fasting, especially if it's a waiting in adversity. Each passing day makes it seem longer and harder.

But just as my thirty minutes with the doctor makes me forget the period of waiting in the lobby, so shall it be with our waiting in the faith. Soon as Abraham got Isaac, it was no more than a 'once upon a time' story. Once our waiting period is over, we shall hardly remember what it felt like and the rest will be testimony.

This doesn't mean the end of waiting in life. As one waiting is over, another waiting comes. That's because our principal enemy the devil is never at rest. Whatever trials we go through are mere agents. We can conquer the agent, but not until we come to the end of our journey in this sinful world do we conquer the principal enemy. We shall continue to wrestle with him till the appearing of our Savior.

While we're still in this mortal body, we're subject to trials and tribulations. Our bodies will suffer and shred. We'll moan and groan and wonder if God still cares. But when Christ returns or if we die before the rapture, we shall no longer remember for how long we've waited for His return. Our joy will overshadow our memories of bad times and the suffering will be worth it all. But we have to persevere.

> For I reckon that the sufferings of this present time are not worthy to be compared with the glory which shall be revealed in us. For the earnest expectation of the creature waiteth for the manifestation of the sons of God. For the creature was made subject to vanity, not willingly, but by reason of him who hath subjected the same in hope, … For we are saved by hope: but hope that is seen is not hope: for what a man seeth, why doth he yet hope for? But if we hope for that we see not, then do we with patience wait for it (Romans 8:18-25).

No amount of worry can help. Be it for blessing, prosperity, salvation, or the return of our Lord, let's wait. Wait, I say on the Lord.

83
FAITH WALKS WITH GOD

Of the four seasons, summer is my best. The bright light gives me an opportunity to walk with my little girl. While my boys are out playing ball, my daughter wants to walk with mom. She holds my hands and feels secure that nothing can happen to her, that her weak and mortal mom cannot handle. As we walk, we talk and discuss about the things we see on the road. She tells me about her class activities and I use almost anything to tell her about God.

There are two reasons why we enjoy our time together: one, I love her; two, she loves me. That creates an agreement between us. The Bible asks, "Can two walk together, except they be agreed?" (Amos 3:3). The answer definitely is no. There can be no fellowship without friendship.

People of faith are called upon to walk with God. Though we cannot see Him face-to-face. But since by faith we believe that He is, by faith we have to also walk with Him.

For we walk by faith, not by sight (2 Corinthians 5:7).

Our walk with the Lord is not done on the street, but in the soul. We walk with Him in the light of His Word. What is the light? Jesus is the light of the world.

Then spake Jesus again unto them, saying, I am the light of the world: he that followeth me shall not walk in darkness, but shall have the light of life (John 8:12).

We must desire to please Him, for only then are we walking with Him. When others around us are walking in the ways of their powerless gods, we declare to walk **in the name of the LORD our God for ever and ever** (Micah 4:5).

I've walked in the way of the world before. When I look back on my past, I always wonder how I made it through that horrible period of safety fantasy. Now that I've come to know what it means to walk with the Lord, I feel safe. I picture Him standing beside me anywhere I am. I know He never leaves me nor forsakes me (Heb. 13:5).

Not only that. Because I'm conscious of His presence, I find it hard to do anything that will grieve Him. I think of my earthly parents. Because God says we should honor them, we reverence their presence. Some of us have almost made gods out of our parents. Well, nothing bad. But if we can do that with the ones who cannot give their lives for us, how much more should we reverence the ever-abiding presence of the God who loves us unspeakably?

When we walk in the flesh and fulfill its lusts, we grieve the Holy Spirit. But when we walk in the Spirit, we shall not fulfil the lust of the flesh (Galatians 5:16). Those who walk in the flesh have no goal because they have no calling. They don't care where they end up. All they do is walk, be it in the day or at night. They're spiritually aimless and blind. But we have a destination. We're going to heaven where we shall continue to walk with our Savior Jesus, on the streets of gold. The Jesus we walk with here we shall walk with there.

> Thou hast a few names even in Sardis which have not defiled their garments; and they shall walk with me in white: for they are worthy (Revelation 3:4).

The Bible records that "Enoch walked with God" (Gen. 5:22). Not because he held hand in hand with God as we do with our spouses, but because he loved and served God. Methuselah was Enoch's son. But what does the Bible say about him?

> And Methuselah lived an hundred eighty and seven years, and begat

> Lamech. ... And all the days of Methuselah were nine hundred sixty and nine years: and he died (Genesis 5:25-27).

Methuselah outlived his father by six hundred and sixty-nine years. What did he do in all those years? He lived and died. No record of his ever walking with God, as did his father before him. And how about Noah?

> These are the generations of Noah: Noah was a just man and perfect in his generations, <u>and Noah walked with God</u> (Genesis 6:9).

Remember these people lived during the dispensation of the law. We're living in the dispensation of grace through the blood of Jesus Christ. Theirs was a harder time to live. Yet, they walked with God. Their testimonies have nothing to do with how many Bible verses they knew. They didn't even have the Bible as we have it today. You may have the whole Bible in your head, verse by verse. If you don't apply it to your life, if the glory of God doesn't show forth in your life, you're nothing more than an empty vessel making the loudest noise. Walking with God does not consist of how many chapters of the Bible you know; but how much of the Bible can be seen in your life.

Let's walk with God. The walking we do today will leave a path for those coming after us tomorrow. The time is close by for our Savior to come and redeem His own and only those who are found walking worthy will be taken.

> And that, knowing the time, that now it is high time to awake out of sleep: for now is our salvation nearer than when we believed.... Let us walk honestly, as in the day; not in rioting and drunkenness, not in chambering and wantonness, not in strife and envying. But put ye on the Lord Jesus Christ, and make not provision for the flesh, to fulfil the lusts thereof (Romans 13:11-14).

I would rather walk with God than stroll with the devil. How about you?

84
FAITH is WATCHFUL

The vigilante program in my country is a program that allows men in the same neighborhood to keep watch over their area at night. Because of their awareness of an impending danger, they divide into groups and take turns to stand on guard so that harm does not come upon them unprepared.

As people of faith, we're to stand guard and keep watch over our soul so that no spiritual harm overtakes us unaware. Just as people sleep off in the flesh and thieves come and loot their homes at night, so do people sleep off in the Spirit and the thieves of their souls come and rid them of all they have spiritually worked for. Does that mean they will loose the possessions they have set up to decorate their homes? No. It's more than that. It's the loss of eternity with Jesus. He Himself said, "For what is a man profited, if he shall gain the whole world, and lose his own soul? or what shall a man give in exchange for his soul?" (Matthew 16:26).

Jesus told the parable of the ten virgins (Matthew 25:1-13) to teach us the importance of spiritual vigilance. The virgins awaited the arrival of the groom who would come at an unannounced hour of the night. Thus they had to be vigilant and alert. But five of the ten virgins were foolish not to take enough oil in their lamps. They went out in search of oil. By the time they returned, the groom had come and they were locked out. What they should have done first, they did last.

The groom is Jesus and the bride is the church. There are church members who will not be counted worthy to meet with the Lord. Not because they don't attend church regularly, not because they don't pay their tithes and contribute good offerings, not even because they don't obey the spiritual authorities that keep watch over their souls; but because they get complacent in their faith. They are not careful enough to be on guard. They are vigilantly unprepared. For a split second, they are spiritually careless.

They are Christians who place priorities on wrong things and leave the right things undone. Of course they attend every church service and take part in every church activity. They're the high-ranking officers of the church. But the lamp of their faith is no longer glowing. They have gotten carried away with church activities and forgotten Christ assignments. Their spiritual oil is running low and they don't know it. They care much about their now and leave their hereafter in jeopardy.

This should not be. We're to be ready at anytime to heed the call of our Lord and to remain watchful, for we know neither the day nor the hour wherein the Son of man cometh (Matthew 25:13). At a time we never expect, Christ will appear and the careless in Spirit will have no part in the rapture.

> But of the times and the seasons, brethren, ye have no need that I write unto you. For yourselves know perfectly that the day of the Lord so cometh as a thief in the night. …. Therefore let us not sleep, as do others; <u>but let us watch and be sober</u> (1 Thessalonians 5:1-6).

Remember the disciples Peter, James and John? While they were supposed to watch with the Lord, they slept (Mat. 26:36-45). Of course they were His disciples. They knew what faith was and they knew what it meant to watch. But when it came to the real deal, they were found wanting. They who had been with Christ for three years could not watch with Him for one hour. The enemies of their soul were alert, to come and steal the source of their strength from them. But alas, they were asleep. Three times He came and found them sleeping and three times He warned them. But their flesh was too weak to carry their faith. Sleep took over their watchfulness and shut their eyes off their Savior. Though so close to Him, yet so far away from Him. By the time they awoke from their slumber, the Lord had been taken. The source of their power had been snatched. The relationship had been severed. Though they attempted to save Him, but lo and behold, it was too late.

So shall it be for a Christian who fails to watch. Our enemy the devil, has no other job than going to and fro on the earth, walking back and forth on it, actively seeking whom he may devour. That's why we need to be sober and be vigilant (1 Peter 5:8). We have to be alert and awake, always ready to watchfully and prayerfully stand against him, lest at a time most unexpected, he comes and snatches our eternity with the Lord.

Watching is part of our spiritual calling. A guard on duty has to do what is expected of him. The time to be on guard is not the time to visit friends and neighbors, otherwise thieves will break in and he will not go free. So also in the spiritual realm. Faith is not something we put aside for sometime, to go and fornicate and run back. There's no sneaking out in the Spirit. You're either in the faith or you're out. You either get right with God or you get left by God. You cannot continue in your lustful desires and still make yourself believe you have faith in God. Fighting the good fight of faith includes remaining strong even when evil desires pop up. We all have our times of temptation, times we feel like doing what we know we should not do. But at such times, we're to watch, stand fast in the faith and be strong (1 Corinthians 16:13).

It's not an easy road we're traveling to heaven. Many are the thieves and robbers on the way and they will try to snatch our faith by distracting our spiritual attention. That's why it's imperative for us to keep the lamps of our faith filled with oil, so we never run out; so we never need to go and buy more oil and miss the return of Him for whom we have waited for so long. May the Lord grant unto us the grace to remain watchful till His appearing. Amen.

85
FAITH is WISE

The dictionary defines the word 'wise' as having or showing good judgment. I wasn't satisfied. So I decided to define it my own way especially as it applies to faith. To be wise is not to be foolish or stupid. (Good one, huh. Add it to your dictionary.)

When Jesus was born, the Bible confirms that He "grew, and waxed strong in spirit, filled with wisdom: and the grace of God was upon him" (Luke 2:40). But He didn't stop there. "And Jesus increased in wisdom and stature, and in favour with God and man" (v. 52). I know we serve a God who loves us unconditionally. But I'm sorry to say that there are believers who will miss the rapture because of their spiritual foolishness and stupidity.

Coming to the faith is the first step towards wisdom: "The fear of the Lord is the beginning of wisdom" (Psalm 111:10). But we're not to stop at the beginning. We're to increase in wisdom. Many believers start out wise but miss it along the way because of their foolishness. To the congregation, they're still great and Spirit filled. But to God, they're no more than a bunch of foolish virgins parading as wise.

Again let's see the parable of the ten virgins (Mat. 25:1-13). These were not people outside of the faith. They all started out well, they all knew the Lord and expected His return. But unfortunately, only five were wise. The other five were foolish. Not because they didn't have lamps, not because they didn't have oil in their lamps, but because they didn't have enough oil in their lamps. When it was almost time for the Lord's arrival, their lamps got dim. Their foolishness was stronger than their faith. When they came to watch out for the Lord's return, they didn't envisage He would take that long to arrive. They spent so much time expecting but made only a little preparation. That's not how a wise faith operates. No wonder the Lord said He never knew them.

The coming of the Lord cannot be made faster than the appointed time. The Lord will come when He will come. Ours is to live as if He will come today but wisely prepare as if He will not come in the next hundred years. While we expect Him tonight, we take enough oil for our spiritual lamps, enough to last for as long as we expect His return. That way our lamps will never run out of oil and never go dim.

I don't read this story blaming the foolish virgins. I feel sorry for them. They spent the entire night keeping watch for the Lord they would never see. They expected His return but missed it at the very last minute because they were not wisely prepared. They stayed awake for nothing. Why would they come expecting that somebody's oil would suffice for their lamps?

When we prepare for heaven, God will not overlook our foolishness based on the wisdom of those with whom we walk or talk. Every soul will be individually responsible for his or her heaven. Your father's wise walk with the Lord is not going to save you. You have to make your own preparation. There's no next of kin in the kingdom of God. Nobody is going to help you reap what you sow, whether good or bad. You do the sowing, you also do the reaping.

Enoch's wisdom could not save Methuselah's foolishness. Same thing applies to every candidate in the faith. It won't matter for how long you keep awake, your last moment will determine your final rapture. Your identical twin will not be able to reserve a space for you in the heavenly boat. It's your job to stay focused and wise.

We also need wisdom in our day-to-day dealings with others, especially in our relationship with unbelievers and even other believers. There are times it requires wisdom to know what to say and how to say it when sharing our faith with unrepentant souls. There are places where the preaching of the gospel is a no-no. It's not every time we can act blunt. Even Jesus did not act blunt: "After these things Jesus walked in Galilee: for he would not walk in Jewry, because the Jews sought to kill him" (John 7:1). This was a deliberate attempt to avoid death. He had the power to render them blind so they wouldn't see Him. But he would rather act wise to teach us a lesson. When we feel the strong urging of the Holy Spirit to be quiet, the wisest thing to do is to be quiet. The spirits of the prophets are subject to the prophets (1 Corinthians 14:32). And even when we need to speak, we need to ask for the leading of the Holy Spirit.

> Then said he unto them, Nation shall rise against nation, and kingdom against kingdom:... But before all these, they shall lay their hands on you, and persecute you, delivering you up to the synagogues, and into prisons, being brought before kings and rulers for my name's sake.... Settle it therefore in your hearts, not to meditate before what ye shall answer: <u>For I will give you a mouth and wisdom,</u> which all your adversaries shall not be able to gainsay nor resist (Luke 21:10-15).

It's always better to let the Holy Spirit fill us with words. On several occasions when I should have been completely dependent upon Him, I practiced what words to say. I felt the Holy Spirit needed some help, so I gave Him a helping 'mouth' and ended up miserable. That was wisdom from the head, which you will agree with me never works. Only the Holy Spirit can make wise. Let's be realistic, were it not for the grace of God, none of us can out smart the devil. He knows the Bible in its entirety and is ready to thwart it for you at any time. If he tried it with Jesus, he'll try it with anybody.

When we go into a world of the anti-Christs, Jesus wants us to "be wise as serpents, and harmless as doves" (Matthew 10:16) and "walk in wisdom toward them that are without" (Colossians 4:5-6). 'Those without' are those not of the faith. They don't function on the same level we do. They don't have the same understanding of God as we do. We operate on the realm of faith; they operate on the realm of flesh. That's why we need wisdom to deal with them accordingly, if we don't want to loose them forever. We have to prudently win them over to God.

We cannot be wise on our own. God's Word says for us not to be wise in our own conceits (Romans 12:16). Being wise in one's own conceits is an act of pride. Such hearts are unteachable. They cannot take correction, especially from someone younger in age. To them every correction is a challenge of their authority or wisdom. I believe they're wrong. Only God knows it all and only God gives true wisdom.

Let's ask for the wisdom that comes from above and He will give it to us.

86
FAITH WORSHIPS GOD

Worship is one of the activities I enjoy during church services. People lift their hands to worship Him who alone is worthy to be worshipped. But I always wonder what happens after we depart and go our different ways for the day and the week. Does the worship continue?

Worship is not something we're to do when we come to services only. It's an integral part of our faith. Though we can't see God with our eyes, but by faith we believe that He is. By faith we also ought to worship Him. It has nothing to do with venue. God can be worshipped anywhere. He's seeking those who can worship Him in Spirit and truth anytime and anywhere.

The woman saith unto him, Sir, I perceive that thou art a prophet. Our fathers worshipped in this mountain; and ye say, that in Jerusalem is the place where men ought to worship. Jesus saith unto her, … But the hour cometh, and now is, when the true worshippers shall worship the Father in spirit and in truth: for the Father seeketh such to worship him. God is a Spirit: and they that worship him must worship him in spirit and in truth (John 4:19-24).

This woman didn't understand the true meaning of worship. To her, worship meant sacrificing animals on some dirty rugged mountain. That's not the kind of worship God expects from us. He wants us to worship Him from the heart, not in flesh but in Spirit. They of old worshipped many gods. People of faith are to worship the only true God, the God who sent His only Son to die for our sins. We're to worship Him with undivided attention. One with spiritual prostitution cannot come to His presence.

No husband ever loves to see his wife having affairs with other men, and no woman ever loves to see her husband fornicating with other women. When we ascribe the greatness due Him to other gods, it is spiritual fornication. And our God is a jealous God and doesn't want His children to have fellowship with other gods. Once married to Him, forever married to Him.

> Thou shalt fear the LORD thy God, and serve him, and shalt swear by his name. Ye shall not go after other gods, of the gods of the people which are round about you; (For the LORD thy God is a jealous God among you) lest the anger of the LORD thy God be kindled against thee, and destroy thee from off the face of the earth (Deuteronomy 6:13-15).

We are to worship and serve Him only (Matthew 4:10).

There's only one group of people who don't need to worship God: those who won't die. As long as you'll never die, you're free. Otherwise, it is mandatory for you to worship Him, who alone has the power over your soul. He made you and formed you. So why won't you worship Him?

Consider the leaves on the trees, how they bow before Him. They dance to the tune of His music. They go left and right, and adore their sustainer. Go to the ocean and see the wonders of God through the movement of the waters. See the billows worshipping the Lord. Listen to the birds of the air and their melodious music. They have no harp, no flutes, no instruments of any type. Yet, they sing every morning to worship the One who gave them tones. Hear the crickets chirping every night at the back of your yard. They glorify the One who gave them their sweet voices. Look at the lilies and see how they glorify God with their beauty, such beauty that even Solomon's glory could not stand. They have neither read the Bible nor gone to church. No one has ever told them to worship God. But they know it's the right thing to do. Their beauty radiates their appreciation of their Creator.

Even the angels are commanded to worship Him (Hebrews 1:6). How much more should we that are made in His image "worship the LORD in the beauty of holiness" (Psalm 29:2)? Worship opens the throne to heaven. When we worship God, He hears us and grants the desires of our hearts (John 9:31). Our worship should not be limited by our feelings.

When Abraham was going to sacrifice his son, he definitely could not have been in a good mood. But for him, it was still going to be a time to worship God.

And Abraham said unto his young men, … <u>I and the lad will go yonder and worship</u>, and come again to you (Genesis 22:5).

Go and worship when the son would soon be placed on the altar of sacrifice? Exactly, that's what the passage says. And God saw his heart. He knew Abraham would have worshipped Him no matter what happened. And instead of worshipping with the death of his only son, he worshipped rejoicing in the victory over death.

Let us join the hosts of heaven in worshipping our God, for we know that our worship is not going to end here. We shall continue over there if we don't relent. The heavenly choir is waiting for us.

> After this I beheld, and, lo, a great multitude, which no man could number, of all nations, and kindreds, and people, and tongues, stood before the throne, and before the Lamb, clothed with white robes, and palms in their hands; And cried with a loud voice, saying, Salvation to our God which sitteth upon the throne, and unto the Lamb. And all the angels stood round about the throne, and about the elders and the four beasts, and fell before the throne on their faces, <u>and worshipped God,</u> Saying, Amen: Blessing, and glory, and wisdom, and

thanksgiving, and honour, and power, and might, be unto our God for ever and ever. Amen (Revelation 7:9-12).

As we wait to join the choir there, let's sing with the choir here. What we shall do when out of this body, let's do while still in this body. And may the Lord count each and every one of us worthy for the heavenly worship that shall never end.

Y

87. FAITH YEARNS FOR GOD 355

87
__FAITH YEARNS FOR GOD__

I was reading Psalm 63 and decided to take a trip with David to the wilderness of Judah, a dry and thirsty land where there's no water. I pictured myself stuck in a situation where I longed for water and found none. I imagined how much I would desire to have someone come to my aid; and how dear that person would be to me for the rest of my life. And then I wondered if I could be that yearning for God.

To yearn is to desperately desire something or somebody. As people of faith, God wants us to continuously yearn for His love and earnestly long for His presence.

Consider the human tummy. No matter how much food goes inside it today, that will never suffice for the next day. It's going to demand another ration tomorrow. The human body has a longing desire for satisfaction. We consciously or unconsciously offer the sacrifice of food everyday and yet, nothing close to satisfaction.

That's the way our soul should be when it comes to our faith in God. We must never be satisfied with the ration of today. We must have a longing to know Him more, love Him dearer and serve Him better.

David longed for God's power and glory the same way his dry throat would long for water in a dry land. That didn't mean he had no faith. It didn't mean God had departed from him. It just meant that he wanted more and more of God.

When my husband came to the United States, I was alone with our two boys back in Nigeria for eighteen months. We were both yearning to be reunited. We all couldn't wait to see one another. But soon as we saw, our attention diverted to something else. That is because we're human.

That's not how faith in God operates. We don't yearn for God today and yearn for money tomorrow, the next day, yearn for a luxurious car. Faith yearns for God today as if it never knew Him yesterday. David said, "My soul longeth, yea, even fainteth for the courts of the LORD: my heart and my flesh crieth out for the living God" (Psalm 84:2). When the body has been starved for a period of time, there will be no strength left. If that goes on for longer than normal, you begin to feel dizzy and that can lead to fainting. That was the situation with David. His soul longed for God to that extent he fainted in the Spirit. He felt completely void of the Spirit of God and longed for a reunion.

As each day breaks, the yearning for Him comes afresh. We forget about yesterday and start all over today. That way, we'll stay fresh in the faith. And as we do, He'll continue to satisfy us and fill our hungry soul with goodness (Psalm 107:9).

Z

88. FAITH has ZEAL FOR GOD   358

88
FAITH has ZEAL FOR GOD

    I know individuals who were naturally zealous towards their secular jobs. When they came to know the Lord, they carried that zeal into the gospel and now handle their faith with the same zeal they had towards their vocation. And there are people who were zealous for evil. But when they came to the faith, they turned it around for good.

    Before his conversion, Paul had a zeal for persecuting Christians. But soon as he came to Christ following his experience on the road to Damascus, he didn't allow that zeal to die. Instead, he turned it around for good and began to use it for the things of the kingdom. He handled his faith with all his heart and might.

    He was one of the apostles that suffered most for the course of the gospel. But the more he suffered, the more zealous he got. He was neither tired of suffering nor tired of being zealous. He loved the gospel with the same intensity that he hated it before his conversion. He suffered for it with the same suffering he inflicted on the believers he once persecuted. He saw his every affliction for the faith as a form of humility. He got to that stage in his life that infirmities became pleasant than painful. He would rather boast in them than be proud of his successes. That's the kind of zeal God expects of His children. Doing it gives us strength and not doing it gets us weak.

    David, because of his zeal for God, became an alien to his mother's children (Psalm 69:8-9). He was so zealous for the Lord that he forgot his people. While I don't say this should be the case, for God would hold us accountable if we fail to care for our family members who are less privileged than us. But on the other hand, Jesus said, "Think not that I am come to send peace on earth: I came not to send peace, but a sword. For I am come to set a man at variance against his father, and the daughter against her mother, and the daughter in law against her mother in law. And a man's foes shall be they of his own household. He that loveth father or mother more than me is not worthy of me: and he that loveth son or daughter more than me is not worthy of me" (Mat. 10:34-37).

Jesus wasn't saying we should hate our people when we accept Him as Lord. That would be a contradiction of the love He showed and preached. He's instead teaching us that the zeal for heaven will consume to that extent that nothing on earth will matter any more. The works of God and His kingdom will always take priority over any other thing. Our unbelieving family members will see us different and even consider us out of mind.

How zealous are we for the salvation of those around us? Their journey to hell should bother us and make us sympathetic towards them. We must be heart-broken for them and be ready to go any length to witness the Lord Jesus to them. Those who go on mission trips face a lot of danger. Some end up in prison. Some are maimed for life. Some even lose their lives for the sake of the gospel. But that must not discourage those who are coming behind. It's the grace of God that keeps the rough going smooth and strengthens the weak bones of our faith. When He sees the zeal, He supplies the strength.

And as I end this book with this topic, I urge you brethren to continue in a zealous Spirit for the Almighty God who has called us for His divine purpose; to be vessels unto honor, sanctified and made ready for the Master's use, prepared unto every good work (2 Timothy 2:21). May the unfailing grace of the unfailing God keep you unfailing in your faith, in Jesus' name I pray. Amen.

Attributes Of A Working Faith

"NOW UNTO HIM THAT IS ABLE TO KEEP YOU FROM FALLING, AND TO PRESENT YOU FAULTLESS BEFORE THE PRESENCE OF HIS GLORY WITH EXCEEDING JOY, TO THE ONLY WISE GOD OUR SAVIOUR, BE GLORY AND MAJESTY, DOMINION AND POWER, BOTH NOW AND EVER. AMEN" (JUDE 24, 25).

FAITH

FAITH, How Best Can I Describe You?

Like An Axe, You Cut Through My Fears,

Like Dynamite, You Shatter Them All.

You Are My Only Weapon Of Warfare,

To Give Me Victory Over Battles Of The Flesh.

You Lift Me Up When I Am Down,

And Strengthen Me When I'm Weak.

You Give Me Joy In Time Of Sadness,

And Give Me Comfort In Time Of Sorrow.

You Uphold Me When Falling,

And Carry Me When Frail.

You Keep Me Afloat The Waters,

Yes, The Turbulent Waters Of Life,

So I Shall Not Sink, But Stay Alive.

When I Get Stuck At The Red Sea Of Life,

And Flesh Tells Me I Shall Soon Drown,

You Assure Me That Is The Devil's Lie,

And Right Before My Eyes, Dry Land Appears.

You Impart Into Me The Boldness I Need,

To Command Mountains Of Trials To Move.

You Enable Me To Trust In Time Of Doubt,

And Give Me Peace In Time Of Turmoil.

You Give Light To My Path Of Darkness,

And Give Me Courage In Time Of Fear.

You Give Me Hope When I'm Hopeless,

And Encourage Me When Discouraged.

You're Water To My Thirsty Soul,
You're Food To My Hungry Spirit.
Like Salt, You Sweeten My Bitterness,
Like Balm You Soothe My Aching Spots.
When Things Are Looking Bad,
You Assure Me All Will Be Well.
You Make Light My Heavy Load Of Cares,
And Make Easy My Yoke Of Burdens.
You Give Me Patience In Tribulation,
So I Can Finish The Race Set Before Me.
You Give Me The Zeal To Press Forward,
And The Grace To Never Look Back.
I Wish I Have Better Words To Describe You,
But For Now, Faith, This Is All I Can Say.

Foye Adedokun. ©2004

Printed in the United States
22287LVS00003B/181-183